Beyond Abuse
in the Christian Home

Beyond Abuse
in the Christian Home

Raising Voices for Change

EDITORS:
CATHERINE CLARK KROEGER
NANCY NASON-CLARK
BARBARA FISHER-TOWNSEND

WIPF & STOCK · Eugene, Oregon

BEYOND ABUSE IN THE CHRISTIAN HOME
Raising Voices for Change

Wipf & Stock
A Division of Wipf and Stock Publishers
199 W. 8th Ave., Suite 3
Eugene, OR 97401

www.wipfandstock.com

ISBN 13: 978-1-55635-086-3

Manufactured in the U.S.A.

Contents

Tributes to
Dr. Catherine Clark Kroeger

*Unbeknownst to our beloved Dr. Catherine Clark Kroeger,
we (Nancy Nason-Clark and Barbara Fisher-Townsend)
have decided to offer in print a tribute to the life and work of Cathie.
We have asked those who have contributed to this volume to join us in
raising our voices in celebration of a life well lived!*

Cathie Kroeger is so many things—a true saint, a tireless trailblazer and one of the most unique, generous, compassionate human beings I have ever met. She is self-effacing despite her great genius, and her ground-breaking scholarly work on Biblical equality is fundamentally changing the way the scriptures are understood. She is a modern day prophetess, an uncompromised and courageous voice shouting in the wilderness. Cathie is my 'shero' and I am humbled and honored to call her my friend.

Julie Owens

Cathie is a brilliant, fierce, and wise woman who is the rarest of scholars—she actually believes the pursuit of the truth is meant to enter the dark corners of heartache with the hope of the gospel. It is an honor to be led by such a noble and generous woman into this fray.

Dan Allender

Aloha Cathie, Thank you for sharing your expertise and scholarship with me. Because of your encouragement, guidance and trust when we were working together on my first book more than a decade ago, I have been able to join Sisters and Brothers across the globe in efforts to prevent and end men's violence perpetrated against women and children. May God continue to bless your courage and faithfulness. In gratitude,

Al Miles

Tributes to Dr. Catherine Clark Kroeger

Cathie Kroeger has been a tremendous inspiration to us. She has coura-geously called Christians to reform our understanding of the equality of men and women, based on exemplary biblical scholarship and powerful storytelling. She works with tireless energy and speaks with a humble au-thority that continues to compel Christians to rethink their understanding of the equality of men and women. We thank God for all the gifts she has shared with us and the extraordinary example she has been to all of us!

Karen and Bruce McAndless-Davis

Dear Cathie, Thank you for your years of hard work and remarkable enthu-siasm for domestic violence prevention in general and PASCH in particu-lar. The PASCH conference in Southern California a few years back was a turning point for me both professionally and personally. May God Himself continue to richly bless you, your family, and the work of your hands.

Dan Schaefer

Cathie Kroeger's courageous diligence in biblical scholarship has opened doors of hope for men and women who want to be faithful believers, liv-ing in equality and safety.

Martha Thorson

You are the woman who made my story of being a woman on this planet make sense. I am indebted.

Nancy Murphy

I first met Cathie in February 2004 at the PASCH formation meeting in Eugene, Oregon. It seems like I have known her forever. She has welcomed me into her home, encouraged me as I worked on my dissertation research, praised me when I finished my Ph.D., provided wise advice on the world of academe, led by example, and served as a *force majeur* in the struggle to end abuse in families of faith. May I commend her on a life well-lived.

Barb Fisher-Townsend

Catherine Kroeger's unrelenting determination to eliminate domestic vio-lence in families of faith is an inspiration to each one of us. Not only does her kind and gentle spirit model true Christian compassion, her scholarship and dedication to PASCH are incredible examples of how research can be used to further the cause of social action. As my career progresses, her work will continue to serve as an example for me.

Lanette Ruff

Cathie, Your work importantly addresses the impact of abuse upon the spirit and the vital role that the spirit plays in healing. Your work has informed our work, and will continue to do so, as we strive to end domestic violence in communities of faith.

Irene Sevcik and Marlette Reed

Dr. Catherine Clark Kroeger is a tireless warrior of the gospel of Christ and its social justice message. Determined, selfless, astute, learned, generous, practical, wise, and full of integrity, her life exemplifies the image of woman expounded in Proverbs 31. In our many travels together, I enjoy most when she translates our Scriptural readings directly from the Greek during our morning devotions. Cathie is a reflection of Christ by word, scholarship, and action. Women and men around the globe have been enriched by her books, her stories, her hospitality and most of all—her warmth. She is a role model *par excellence*. When I grow up, I want to be a little bit more like her.

Nancy Nason-Clark

Catherine Kroeger is one of the foremost Christian evangelical feminist scholars and activists of our time. She expertly has provided a biblical framework for the promotion of biblical equality and opposition to violence against women. Gratefully, I am also able to call her my teacher, mentor, and friend.

Beth Gerhardt

For—Your heart for the hurting, your dedication to Biblical truth, your reflection of Jesus, your inspiration to become all God has planned—I join with thousands of survivors whose lives you've touched to say a most heart-felt thank you!

Joyce Holt

Contributors

Catherine Clark Kroeger, Ph.D., is an adjunct associate professor of classical and ministry studies at Gordon-Conwell Theological Seminary. She holds a Ph.D. in classical studies from the University of Minnesota. Catherine is founder and former president of CBE (Christians for Biblical Equality) as well as founder and current president of PASCH (Peace and Safety in the Christian Home). She has authored and edited numerous books, including *Women, Abuse and the Bible: How Scripture can be used to Hurt or to Heal* and *Healing the Hurting: Giving Hope and Help to Abused Women* (both with James R. Beck); *I Suffer Not a Woman: Rethinking 1 Timothy 2:11–15 in Light of Ancient Evidence* (with Richard Clark Kroeger); *No Place for Abuse: Biblical and Practical Resources to Counteract Domestic Violence* and *Refuge from Abuse: Healing and Hope for Abused Christian Women* (both with Nancy Nason-Clark).

Nancy Nason-Clark, Ph.D., is a professor of Sociology at the University of New Brunswick in Canada and Director of the Rave Project. Her books include: *The Battered Wife: How Christians Confront Family Violence; No Place for Abuse: Biblical and Practical Resources to Counteract Domestic Violence and Refuge from Abuse: Healing and Hope for Abused Religious Women* (both with Catherine Clark Kroeger), *Partnering for Change* (co-edited) and *Feminist Narratives and the Sociology of Religion* (with M.J. Neitz).

Barbara Fisher-Townsend, Ph.D., is a Postdoctoral Fellow on The RAVE (Religion and Violence E-Learning) Project at the University of New Brunswick. She also teaches family violence related courses in the Department of Sociology and for the Muriel McQueen Fergusson Centre for Family Violence Research certificate program in family violence at the University of New Brunswick. Her research focuses on the role of faith and hope in assisting men of faith who have acted abusively to move toward changed thinking and behavior.

Julie A. Owens, B.A., is a survivor of DV who has worked in the field of violence against women for almost 20 years. The daughter of a prominent pastor, her personal story of survival is featured in the documentaries, "Broken Vows: Religious Perspectives on Domestic Violence" and Day of Discovery's "When Love Hurts." She trains faith leaders for the FaithTrust Institute and Peace And Safety in the Christian Home (PASCH), and is a Site Coordinator for the Religion And Violence e-learning (RAVE) project.

Dan Allender, Ph.D., is President and Professor of Counseling Psychology at Mars Hill Graduate School in Seattle, Washington. He received his Master of Divinity from Westminster Theological Seminary and his Ph.D. in Counseling Psychology from Michigan State University. Dan is the author of *The Wounded Heart* and *The Healing Path* and has co-authored several books with Dr. Tremper Longman (*Intimate Allies, The Cry of the Soul, Bold Love and Bold Purpose*).

Rev. Al Miles, an ordained minister in the Church of God, works for Pacific Health Ministry as the coordinator of the Hospital Ministry Department at The Queen's Medical Center, in Honolulu, Hawaii. Rev. Miles is the author of *Domestic Violence: What Every Pastor Needs to Know; Violence in Families: What Every Christian Needs to Know; and Ending Violence in Teen Dating Relationships: A Resource Guide for Parents and Pastors.*

Karen McAndless-Davis, M.Div. and Bruce McAndless-Davis, M.Div., are ministers of the Presbyterian Church in Canada. Karen is co-author of *When Love Hurts.* Bruce is pastor of St. Aidan's Presbyterian Church in New Westminster, British Columbia.

Dan Schaefer, Ph.D., is a licensed psychologist who is director of Person to Person Resources Inc., a private group practice of mental health professionals located in Northwest Ohio. He has been running 2–3 domestic violence groups for men every week for about 7 years and presents regularly at national conferences on the topic. He also teaches counseling courses at Spring Arbor University.

Rev. Martha Thorson, D. Min., is a Pastoral Counselor and Spiritual Director living and working in Hemet, California.

Nancy Murphy, D. Min., is the Executive Director of Northwest Family Life in Seattle, Washington and a Licensed Mental Health Counselor. She has a Doctorate in Global Leadership from Bakke Graduate School and is the author of *God's Reconciling Love: A Pastor's Handbook on Domestic Violence.*

Lanette Ruff, Ph.D., is a Postdoctoral Fellow in the Department of Sociology at the University of New Brunswick, working on the Religion and Violence E-Learning (RAVE) project. She completed her PhD dissertation entitled "Religiosity, Resources and Regrets: Religious and Social Variations in Conservative Protestant Mothering" in the fall of 2006. Her research interests include the experiences of women and children in families of faith.

Marjorie Kroeger, M.A., is a Licensed Mental Health Counselor specializing in sexual addictions, practising in Northborough, Massachusetts.

Elizabeth Gerhardt, Th.D., is a Professor of Theology and Social Ethics at Northeastern Seminary in Rochester, New York.

Joyce Holt is the founder of Hagar's Sisters, a support group for Christian women survivors of domestic violence located in the Boston, MA area.

Irene Sevcik, Ph.D., is the Director of FaithLink, a Calgary-based organization focused on raising awareness of family violence and increasing capacity of spiritual/religious communities to respond to disclosures of abuse, as well as building collaborative working relationships between spiritual/religious communities and secularly-based service providers.

Marlette Reed, B.Ed., M.A., is a chaplain in the city of Calgary, working in community and hospice settings. She also works with FaithLink as a part time resource coordinator in the Christian community. She is a licensed minister.

Introduction

Catherine Clark Kroeger
Nancy Nason-Clark

IN JANUARY 2004 a newly founded evangelical organization, called PASCH, was formed. While the word denotes the Passover or time of new beginnings, PASCH also stands for *Peace and Safety in the Christian Home*. During February of 2005, PASCH held its first international conference in Newport Beach, California. Attended by 250 men and women, the conference sought to sound out a call to bring those interested in creating peace and safety in Christian homes across North America to one place at one time. Through a series of plenary addresses, and dozens of workshops, the conference theme rang out: The Christian community must wake up to the prevalence and severity of abuse in its midst and offer both practical and spiritual resources to assist victims and their families and to call abusers to accountability, justice and changed behavior. Back by popular demand, a further conference was held in the Spring of 2006, at Gordon-Conwell Seminary, just outside of Boston, Massachusetts.

Very early on in the planning of these conferences, it was the dream of Catherine Clark Kroeger that an edited book might emerge from the papers, presentations and discussions. For some time, we let that idea percolate. Nancy Nason-Clark put together what she saw as a possible outline for an edited collection and Barbara Fisher-Townsend was invited to help with the editorial work that such an initiative would involve. Cathie's dream, which we endorsed, was a collection that would call the Christian community to action. We needed the prophetic voice, the priestly voice, voices of the therapeutic community and voices of researchers. We needed both data and strategies for pushing forward the call to churches and the faithful they represent.

So we invited a distinguished group of scholars, survivors, advocates, pastors, and therapists to join together with us in providing a collection of essays to inform and motivate the Christian community on issues of abuse.

In essence, PASCH was born out of the cries, confusion, and frustration of the people of God. As we encountered many horrifying situations of domestic abuse in Christian homes, those of us who seek to address various aspects of the issue concluded that we needed a fellowship of concerted study, prayer and action. Honest investigation disclosed that the rate of abuse among Christians was no less than that in the general population—even though it was often cleverly concealed. The insidious evil lurked in all denominational and non-denominational groups, in all ethnic and racial groups, in all socio-economic and political groups; and yet its very presence was so often denied, minimized, or ignored by the church of Jesus Christ.

In many instances this was not because of indifference but because of ignorance as to how even to think about the problem. Conservative Protestants hold the Bible to be their only infallible rule of faith and practice—and how could the faithful confront the ugly issue when the Scriptures spoke of the permanence of marriage, of Christ's love for his bride the church, of the strength of the family? Our theology of the family, sometimes based upon the dictates of self-styled gurus rather than upon the actual biblical precepts, raised a multitude of questions. How could a bruised and battered wife be likened to the bride of Christ? What would happen to the reputation of the church if news got out of violence within a member's family? How could an endangered victim be placed in a safe location if that meant separating a married couple? Without violating the mandates of Scripture, could a survivor be provided with food, shelter, monetary assistance or prayer support?

This in turn required answers to other questions: was it right to turn our back on those within our own faith communities when their need was greatest? Could we really refuse to acknowledge the stark reality and the desperate need? Had we really understood what the Scriptures taught about how to bring the love of Christ to such circumstances? Did we have any preparation to respond appropriately when dire situations arose? How could we make sense out of shattered dreams, the disillusionment of victims, the bewilderment of ambulance drivers, shelter workers, therapists, law enforcement personnel, and health care professionals who must cope with the harsh reality. Why had this happened? Where was God? Where was the church? Wasn't reading the Bible making matters worse?

We concluded that we needed to work together: that each of us possessed one piece of the puzzle and that by God's grace we could collectively begin to put the pieces together. The topic of abuse is ugly, which is why so many Christians shy away from discussing it. But in this volume we have tried to present an accurate, faith-based analysis of abuse in the Christian family context. We hope that various chapters stimulate discussion—sometimes debate—and in so doing prompt pastor and people to action.

We call on you the reader to consider the various ideas and perspectives offered throughout the book. Hopefully each chapter will prompt you to consider afresh how you conceptualize violence amongst families of faith. Like you, the reader, the contributors to our collection come from various faith traditions, work in different contexts, and see the issue in part based on their own narrative and training. Yet, despite our differences—and our ongoing debates—we are unanimous that violence has no place in the home. Every home should be a safe place; every home a shelter. When abuse occurs in families of faith, it is the responsibility of the church to offer compassion and support to victims and to call those who act abusively to accountability and justice.

The book is divided into three sections. In part 1, *Raising Our Voices: Looking Back*, we offer a number of chapters where authors look back on their own personal experiences—of survivorship or offering help to those impacted by abuse. Julie Owens, whose ex-husband is serving a life sentence for attempted murder on her life and the life of her father, discusses insights and information she wishes her pastor had known when she turned to him for help in the midst of her own despair and pain. Dan Allender uses the lens of Scripture and his own experience as a therapist, educator, father, and husband to speak from the heart about the impact of the Fall on men's and women's lives in relationship with each other. Al Miles reflects on his own experience as a pastor and resource person frequently called upon by denominational leaders to assist when violence impacts clergy families. Rev. Miles considers both the difficulties and the opportunities of speaking out against violence in the Christian family. Karen and Bruce McAndless-Davis offer one couple's story of the long journey towards accountability and dramatic change.

In part 2, Raising Our Voices: Assessing the Contemporary Scene, there are a number of chapters where authors consider current Christian patterns of looking for, or offering, assistance to individuals and families impacted by domestic violence. Psychologist Dan Schaefer offers a batterers' intervention group as part of his clinical practice. In his article, he focuses on strategies and resources used to assist violent men to accept responsibility for their past abusive behaviour. Martha Thorson, a spiritual director, knows the difficult and delicate nature of forgiveness in contemporary Christianity. Her chapter highlights the role of forgiveness in the life of the church and in the life of an abused woman who wants to move on from the pain of the past. In their co-authored article based on extensive file analysis of over one thousand men who attended a batterer intervention program, Barbara Fisher-Townsend, Nancy Nason-Clark, Lanette Ruff and Nancy Murphy consider how abusive men think about their behaviour and contrast this with what police reports document. Highlighted also is the important role of helping men develop empathy with victims and responsibility for change. A further research article written by Barbara Fisher-Townsend discusses the journey from a state of hopelessness (which pervades those impacted by abuse) to hope, a concept rather elusive in the literature on batterers. Lanette Ruff reflects on her dissertation research on conservative Protestant mothers. In her chapter she outlines both the role of perfection amongst mothers and the regret they later experience. Marjorie Kroeger, a therapist in the Boston area, offers insights into the nature of sexual addictions by focusing on a specific case in her private practice. Based upon their work in Calgary, Alberta, Irene Sevcik and Marlette Reed discuss the role of FaithLink, a multi-disciplinary collaborative model of professionals responding to both victims and abusers in the aftermath of domestic violence. Their chapter reveals the advantages of working together for change.

Finally in part 3, Raising Our Voices: The Prophetic Call for Future Action, we offer a number of chapters where authors look to the future and consider how the prophetic call for action can impact assistance offered to individuals and families experiencing domestic violence. Nancy Nason-Clark argues that the healing journey requires both the language of contemporary culture and the language of the spirit. In her article, she explores the unique and specific experiences of Christian victims of domestic violence, as well as the role of faith communities in bringing abusers to accountability, justice, and change. Using the framework of

Martin Luther's theology of the cross, Elizabeth Gerhardt defines abuse as both a human rights issue and sin. Rather than accepting the notion that suffering builds character, she advocates that the task of both the individual Christian and the church is to proclaim and serve those who have been disadvantaged. Joyce Holt reflects on her experience of establishing Hagar's Sisters, a support group for abused Christian women. She considers how churches and their leaders might take seriously the pain women have experienced and assist them in developing Christian resources and community to effect change. Finally, Catherine Clark Kroeger calls the Christian community to speak out against violence in its many and varied forms. She argues that Scripture is unequivocal in its condemnation of violence and offer of respite to those who suffer.

PART ONE

Raising Our Voices

Looking Back

1

A Survivor Looks Back

*What I Wish Pastors had Known
When I was Looking for Help*

Julie Owens

T HE HOME IN WHICH I grew up is a Christian one. My father is a well respected Presbyterian minister who, many years beyond retirement, still preaches every Sunday. My mother is a classically trained soloist and former church choir director who is so well known for her hospitality that a Christian women's shelter is named in her honor. I was one of five children who practically grew up in churches. It's no surprise that we are now involved in ministries as diverse as domestic violence, music therapy, inner-city community organizing and children's performing arts. We are a very close family and my parents are role models for a mutually respectful, affectionate, caring marriage partnership that is rooted in Biblical equality.

I neither knew nor understood anything about domestic violence while growing up. Even later, when I was in the midst of experiencing it myself, I had no name for the chaos and misery in my marriage. No one from whom I sought support—from the numerous ministers to professional marriage counselors, from mental health professionals to concerned church friends—ever actually named it as 'domestic violence,' so of course I never considered myself a battered woman. While my supporters were very kind and caring, they were untrained and fundamentally unacquainted with the issue of partner violence. The focus of their attention while intervening, therefore, was either on repairing my fractured mar-

3

riage or addressing my husband's personal problems. Neither the impact that his extreme behavior was having on me nor his potential for physical violence was ever discussed. As a result, I was completely unaware of the dynamics of domestic violence and the escalation of violence that typically occurs at the point of separation or divorce.

It was not until several months after a dramatic post-separation attack on my father and me that I called a secular community agency for help. I had been plagued by terrifying nightmares and other symptoms of posttraumatic stress. I asked them if I could come to their support group for abused women, saying somewhat apologetically, "Look, I know I'm not really a battered woman, but my husband stabbed me when I filed for divorce, so could I please come anyway?" Although our church had rallied around us and supported us every step of the way, it was in that secular domestic violence support group that my healing journey began in earnest. As a result, I have spent considerable time in the intervening years trying to prepare church leaders and communities of faith to help other families who find themselves in similar situations.

Often I am asked what I wish pastors had known when I was seeking help during my abusive marriage. I have had many years to consider that question. While the complete lack of knowledge of those who intervened probably increased the danger of my situation, I feel great compassion for them. They were sincere and they did try to help. Through no fault of their own they were simply unequipped for the job. The sad truth is that the places where they were educated did nothing to help the students understand or deal with abuse in Christian families. They were never taught what domestic violence is and isn't, the many myths and misconceptions surrounding it, what the scripture says about it, or how best to counsel those whose lives have been impacted by violence.

Thankfully, in the years since my experience, more and more seminaries and Christian schools have begun offering classes on family violence or incorporating curriculum addressing abuse issues into their counseling courses. Based on the stories I continue to hear on an almost daily basis, however, it is clear that there is still much more to be done. I hope that by sharing my experiences and the lessons I have learned, pastors and Christian counselors who are not yet trained about the issue of domestic violence will understand the importance and value of enhancing their knowledge base.

My story, like that of so many other survivors of abuse, started in a seemingly ordinary way. I was thirty-two when I married David, a man who adored me, who professed to love my God, and who appeared to have so many of the qualities I was looking for in a husband. He doted on me, laughed easily, got along well with my friends, and loved spending time together. There was no hint of abuse or controlling behavior during our courtship, just sweetness and sharing, fun and togetherness. My friends loved David and thought we made a wonderful couple. We were both ready to settle down and shared the dream of living a simple life in the Texas countryside. Since we were older and convinced that in each other we had found "the one," a prolonged engagement seemed unnecessary. We were eager to begin our life together. After discussing the many options, we decided to marry in a sweet, simple ceremony. We exchanged vows at sunset in a lovely little Presbyterian chapel on a river, surrounded by friends. At my request, a friend read aloud from my favorite chapter of the New Testament, First Corinthians 13 "Love is patient, love is kind, love isn't jealous or boastful or proud . . . ." We immediately started planning for a more traditional ceremony and honeymoon back home in Hawaii that would include my large family and my many friends. I could not wait to introduce David to my family and to the islands. I knew that he would love them both.

We were surprised but overjoyed when we learned very soon after our wedding that we were expecting our first baby. We immediately called our loved ones to share the wonderful news and then went to work shopping for baby items. We had spent many hours dreaming and talking of how wonderful it would be to have children together, and we were thrilled that our dream was coming true. I couldn't wait for a baby to snuggle and love, and David wanted nothing more than to raise a child in a close, loving family that would be different from the abusive home in which he had grown up.

I could not have been happier. But that was soon to change. It was not long before David seemed to begin to transform right before my eyes. Instead of being the playful and sweet man I had fallen in love with, he became more and more moody and critical everyday. Before we married he had seemed to love my independent, out-going personality. Now he made cruel, hurtful remarks about me and accused me of flirting if I innocently made eye contact with any other man. He wanted the two of us to be together at all times and seemed threatened by anyone else with whom I spent time, co-workers and friends alike.

David insisted on driving me each morning to the school where I worked, then picking me up each afternoon. He popped in to my classroom to bring me gifts, showed up to take me out to lunch, and called frequently during the day to check on me. Soon he was even volunteering part-time in my classroom, where the students and teachers loved him. He seemed unwilling to leave my side for fear I would betray him somehow. These things that seemed like acts of sweetness initially later were revealed as merely a means to monitor and control me.

At home when we were alone, periods of increasing darkness began to creep in and overtake the good times, eroding my newlywed happiness. At first I wrote it off as marriage adjustment issues that would take care of themselves as we spent more time together and adapted to life as a couple. I wanted nothing to spoil my happiness. Daily I would tell myself that I was married to a man I loved and I was having his baby. I had a job I loved and I was content with my life.

Before long, though, our relationship began to deteriorate to such a degree that I could no longer pretend it would somehow magically improve. I had to consider for the first time that perhaps the man I had married had hidden a great deal from me about his true nature. His affectionate ways and loving attentions had given way to ever-increasing displays of unfounded jealousy and insecurity. Although I was faithful and fully committed to David, for some reason that I could not fathom, he was not able to trust me. As a result, he insisted on knowing every single detail of my comings and goings, and became very agitated when he was not included in every minute of my daily plans. I could not comprehend why the man to whom I was so completely devoted would behave in such a way. He had begun to routinely berate me and call me names, swear at me and disrespect me in ways that were unthinkable. I was dejected and confused.

I was thrilled to be carrying the precious baby that we so wanted, but I began to fear that perhaps I had made some terrible mistake. While David's devoted attention had been wonderful before we married, it had become increasingly oppressive. Before long I was feeling like a prisoner, under siege in my own home. We lived far out in the country, away from other houses. This was in the days before cell phones, and the home phone soon was being ripped out of the wall and thrown across the room whenever I received or made calls. The car keys were even hidden from me in an effort to keep me home.

At one point David started to routinely wake me in the middle of the night to interrogate me or accuse me of crazy things. I was exhausted from the pregnancy and from working full time in a stressful position, but he would refuse to let me go to sleep or stay asleep. Instead, he would follow me from room to room harassing me, even insisting that the baby I was carrying was not his. Nothing I could say would calm or appease him. I would sob in frustration and beg him to let me sleep. My heart was breaking. When he started going through my many old boxes of mementos, tearing up photos he found of me with any other male, friends and relatives alike, I was dumbfounded. Even my favorite picture of my grandfather and me was ripped in half. When things were at their worst and I told him that I could not take it any longer, I would attempt to leave the house. But he would body-block or restrain me, refusing to let me out the door. Once he even took the spark plugs out of the car so that I could not leave the property. I tried to remain calm during these turbulent times, but I had never felt so helpless, dejected or alone.

When things were calmer, I would try to comprehend the downward spiral that my marriage had taken. It simply made no sense. I could only think that David must be sick. Since David was in recovery from a drinking problem and attended AA meetings, I called an addictions counselor. I was urged to attend an Al-Anon group. I did so, and the members were kind, but they did not seem to understand what I was experiencing any better than I did. They told me that when he acted irrationally, I should, "Just see the word *sick* flashing on his forehead." When I described the horrible things he called me, I was told to ignore it. "If he called you a chair, would that make you a chair?" someone asked. I was told to remember that addiction is a disease. I had pledged to love my husband "in sickness and in health" and now he did indeed seem to be sick. In fact, he seemed to have morphed into someone I no longer even knew.

I was exhausted. I tried to reason with David. I prayed for wisdom. I talked with doctors and with pastors. I wanted nothing more than to get away from the constant chaos, but I loved my husband and I wanted to help him. I thought I knew "the real David," and I wanted him back. When, in frustration, I asked him one day why he had never done any of this before the wedding, his chilling response was simply, "You never would have married me!" It stopped me cold. For the first time, I was forced to face the possibility that perhaps in our courtship David had purposely deceived me. I had to wonder if now he really knew what he was doing when he acted so terribly.

Still, he had never once hit or physically hurt me, and he seemed incredulous and pained when I told him that I feared that he might. He insisted that he would never ever hurt me, that he loved me more than life itself. But I was beginning to fear his anger and the threats that he had begun to make during the explosive episodes.

By the end of my first trimester of pregnancy, I was exhausted, miserable and having stress-related pregnancy problems. Although my Ob/Gyn didn't ask what was causing my stress, she insisted that I do whatever it took to reduce it and protect my unborn baby.

I finally left David after a particularly terrifying event during which he woke me during the night and threatened to commit suicide with a loaded gun. The evening before, I had tried again to gently approach the subject of a temporary separation. I managed to take the gun from him and spent another long harrowing, sleepless night listening to him rant and rave. In the morning after he left for work, I called my school and told them I needed an emergency leave of absence. Some dear friends helped me pack up my belongings and I left town.

I cried all the way home as I fled to my sister's home on the west coast and then on to my parent's home in Hawaii. I was devastated and confused. For three months, I stayed with my parents and sought support and answers from anyone who would listen. I attended counseling sessions and sought spiritual advice. I was treated with compassion and counseled to try harder, to pray harder, and not to give up on my marriage. After a lengthy separation, during which David received intensive counseling, he joined me at my parent's home for a trial reconciliation.

Living with my family seemed wiser than moving away and becoming isolated with David, just in case he returned to his old ways. David had agreed in advance to this arrangement and also to attending three AA meetings each week and other conditions. Together we saw a licensed psychologist for marriage counseling once or twice a week. Still, no one named what had happened in our marriage as 'abuse' or 'domestic violence', and so I was never warned that David's old behaviors would most likely resume and probably even escalate. We attended church regularly and talked to pastors. My church friends commented on how much he obviously adored me and how we seemed like a great couple.

At first things were better and David was on his best behavior, but after a month or so, his jealousy and erratic, unpredictable behaviors began to return. He usually hid them from everyone but me. We continued the weekly marriage counseling.

When two months later our baby was born, we immediately fell madly in love with him. David had chosen his name, Joshua, after vividly dreaming that God had chosen that name for our son. Despite our joy over the baby, David's verbal and emotional abuses did not abate. He was apparently threatened by my close family, who stood by me and intervened whenever they witnessed him being rude to me. He began staying out until late at night and would never tell me where he had been. Once when I tearfully suggested another separation, he told me that if I ever left him again, he would take the baby and I would never see him again. This was something new and terrifying.

David adored and admired my father, who treated him like a son, and doted on my mother, who was always kind and nurturing. Nevertheless, he clearly resented the fact that he could not dominate me while we all lived under the same roof. I did not want to expose my parents to any unpleasantness, but I also knew instinctively that things would be much worse if we moved elsewhere. I worried that the baby might pick up on our stress and that his development might be adversely effected, so I tried to be cheerful despite the misery in my marriage and was happy that Josh had his grandparents to distract him and play with him when things were tense.

Over and over, I prayed for insight. I wanted to be a good wife, but I wanted peace and I knew I could not live like a prisoner indefinitely. I was becoming depressed. In my head I would sing the same scriptural song over and over. I had learned it in church and it always brought me peace. While David would rant at me, or drive recklessly with us over the mountains, I would calm myself by silently singing, "You are my hiding place. You always fill my heart with songs of deliverance. Whenever I am afraid, I will trust in You. I will trust in You. Let the weak say 'I am strong in the strength of the Lord.' I will trust in You." This became my daily mantra.

Despite all I was doing to try to hold my marriage together, it continued to unravel. One horrible night David came home around two o'clock in the morning, and grabbed me up out of my sleep, holding a carpet knife to me as if he were preparing to slice me. This was the first ever physical assault on me, although I was not injured. David began interrogating me nonstop, demanding to know who I been on the phone with when he had called and gotten a busy signal earlier in the evening. This hostage situation went on for hours and was terrifying. He held the knife to me the entire time, although I pleaded with him to let me go. Even when I had to go to the restroom, he held tightly onto my arm and kept the knife close to my face, murmuring and threatening me under his breath. He promised to hurt my father if I made any noise and woke him up, and so I cried silently all night.

Near morning David finally fell asleep and I took the knife and hid it. I sat and waited for sunrise, trying to figure out how I could get away from David without jeopardizing my family. The next morning, when he awoke and realized that I had hidden the knife, he demanded to know where I had put it. When I refused to tell him, he looked me right in the eyes and coldly stated, "I should have killed you last night when I had the chance."

I made an emergency call to our marriage counselor who suggested that I go to a shelter. I considered it briefly, but told her I was afraid that if I left him, he might hurt my family. I was also afraid that if I stayed, he would hurt one of us. There seemed to be no good solution. I felt completely trapped. I knew that my God did not expect or want me to live and raise my baby in such destructive chaos, and yet I did not know what to do. I just knew that I had to do something.

My dreams were totally shattered. It was clear that I could not stay married to David. I knew now that he could really hurt me. The next day I visited a Christian attorney from our church for advice. I told him everything. I said I was terrified for my family and myself. When I asked if I should get a restraining, he said "No. We can get one later if you need one. There are laws against assault." He agreed to help me with a divorce, but he offered no other support or information. When I got home and told David I had filed for divorce, he punched me in the face. I almost dropped the baby. This was first time he had hit me.

Two weeks after this, David reluctantly moved out. Several months later in my first support group, I learned about Dr. Lenore Walker's 'cycle of violence theory.' I could easily relate to this. The three distinct phases she described were clearly evident in David's pattern of behavior, although in many relationships I am told this is not the case.

The 'tension-building' phase is the first and the longest. It is dominated by tensions that build and build, much like a pressure cooker. The 'explosion phase' follows, after which there may be a temporary reduction in tension. Walker dubbed this the 'honeymoon phase.' I never liked this term, since true honeymoons do not follow violence. It has also been referred to as the 'hearts and flowers phase' or the 'period of loving contrition.' My support group leader, Luana Nery, called it the "manipulative kindness" phase. That is a perfect description, since the "kindnesses" that follow violent episodes are anything but random. This phase is especially evident in the early stages of an abusive relationship. After acting abusively, the batterer usually begs and pleads for forgiveness, cries and perhaps plies his victim with gifts. Because she loves and pities him, and often because she really believes that she has "the *real* him back again," this works for a while. Eventually, though, the tension starts to build again, and the cycle repeats. Usually the 'honeymoon' period will disappear altogether eventually. The irony is that neither the victim nor the abuser can see this pattern at the time.

For the first few days after moving out, David was cooperative and pleasant, trying to win me back any way he could. Against my wishes he dropped in whenever he wanted, but it was always to bring me money or gifts or to make promises of change (manipulative kindness). But when I was resolute about getting a divorce, he became spiteful and cruel, and started to leave hate-filled messages and accusatory notes for me (tension building). Just five days after he moved out, the explosion occurred with all its fury. Of course I never saw it coming.

My mother was out of town and dad and I had accepted an invitation to join some church friends for a dinner picnic on their sailboat. It was a beautiful and peaceful evening, the first I had enjoyed in a very long time. Afterward, I picked up the baby from the sitter's and arrived home about forty-five minutes before Dad. As Josh slept peacefully in his car seat, I got out of my car and was ambushed by my estranged husband. I instinctively screamed as he grabbed me and threw me up against a wall in the darkened hallway just inside the house. He closed the outer door, and pressed a knife against my throat, threatening to kill me if I did not shut up. He was wild. He swore and screamed and savagely beat me over and over and over in the face. He stuck the knife into the flesh of my neck so I could no longer speak or scream.

After being subdued, I was forced at knifepoint into a chair in our bedroom. I sat stunned as rivers of blood poured from my face. My mouth throbbed inside and out and my cheekbones felt like they had been shattered. David told me that he had come to kill my father, and that he intended to "cut his eyes out" and "drip every drop of blood from his body." I was horrified and could not believe that this was happening. It seemed as if everything was occurring in slow motion. I was disoriented and in shock.

David told me that he had already cut the phone lines and that there was no use trying to get help. Try as I might, I could think of no way to stop the horror that was unfolding before my eyes. I was paralyzed with fear and disbelief. I tried to think of how to stop him. I knew I could never overpower him. He was agitated and seemed possessed, demonic. He opened and closed his fists repeatedly as he berated and mocked me. I pleaded with him to leave us alone, to spare my father. I told him that dad loved him, that my family and I loved him. I reminded him that God loved him. This made him even more furious. He snarled and stuck the knife deeper into my neck, screaming obscenities and repeating what he had planned for dad.

All this time, David watched the window. When he finally saw the lights of my father's car arriving, he listened for the door to open and then suddenly released me. He raced out in to the hallway with the knife over his head, screaming wildly as he ran. I yelled a warning as dad opened the door and I lunged after David, attempting to hold him back. In a flash of fury, he turned and stabbed me deeply in the abdomen to get me off of him. I had no idea that I had been hurt. I could only think of trying to save my dad. David immediately began slashing at dad. The knife cut through his eyebrows and across his face. Later more than 40 stitches were required to repair his largest wound. Miraculously, dad's eyes were untouched, although we did not know this until later. As a matter of fact, I nearly lost an eye as well when David tried to wrench it from the socket after he wounded my father and I tried to restrain him.

The events of that night are the stuff of which nightmares are made. Dad and I were taken to the hospital where our wounds were explored and tended. I was hospitalized for three days. David was located and arrested the night of the attack. He was eventually charged with attempted murder and kidnapping, among a host of other felonies. He later pled no contest to attempted manslaughter and was given a twenty year maximum sentence and a ten year minimum.

In the aftermath, as stated earlier, our stunned church stood solidly with us. Over time, our wounds healed. God remained faithful and blessed my family abundantly. Until that time of healing, though, there were many new and different struggles ahead of me.

When, several months after the assault, Luana, the leader of my victim support group, told me about Rev. Marie Fortune's book, *Keeping the Faith: Questions and Answers for Abused Christian Women,* I immediately obtained a copy. In it, I found information, spiritual encouragement, and comfort. Rev. Fortune explained that by seeking a divorce from an abusive husband, a Christian wife has not failed her marriage. Instead, she wrote, husbands who abuse their wives have already broken the sacred covenant of marriage. By abusing their wives, they abandon them emotionally. The wife's declaration of divorce merely makes public what has already been done by the abuser. I think I breathed an audible sigh of relief. I went on to read and understand so much more about what the scriptures had to say, not only about abuse in marriage and divorce, but about mutual submission, forgiveness, and suffering. That little book became my constant companion, and I shared it with many, many others.

Meanwhile, my husband was in prison awaiting trial. At first I received numerous apology letters from him. He claimed to be sorry for what he had done, but he never really seemed to take responsibility for it. He seemed sorrier about being in jail than for doing what he did to dad and me. I felt great pity for him, but as I learned more about domestic violence, I began to realize that these insincere 'apologies' were his way of trying to manipulate his victims and make us feel guilty. He was more angry than sorry, especially because we were cooperating with the state in his prosecution, although we really had no choice in the matter. I received several credible tips about death threats he was making about me from prison; he even sent me his copy of the restraining order that he was served, as if to say "You think a piece of paper can stop *me*?"

When I read the words of Psalm 55, it seemed to speak directly to me. "The words of his mouth were smoother than butter, but war was in his heart. His words were softer than oil, yet they were drawn swords."

I struggled to understand what had happened, to forgive David and to find God's will for my future. I wrestled with the command of Jesus to "forgive seventy times seven." I wanted to forgive, but I was not sure what that meant. Seeking advice, I made an appointment with the same Christian lawyer that I had seen before the attack. When I asked if he could help me with my legal concerns, he insisted that I take the baby to the prison right away, because, as he put it, "a bad father is better than no father at all." Despite my fear of David, I was tempted many times to do just that. I wanted him to get help. I often thought about the words of

Jesus, "I was in prison and you did not visit me." I put myself in David's shoes and wondered how it would feel to be imprisoned and separated from my baby. I did not think I could survive that, and my heart hurt for him. If there was any possibility that he could learn and really change, I reasoned, maybe at least Josh could still have a father again. After all, we serve a God of miracles! I knew that no one was beyond the reach of Jesus' healing touch, and I prayed for a miracle.

Fortunately, however, Christian friends who had a sophisticated understanding of the complexities of domestic violence and the danger of contacting David advised me not to intervene with him directly. One dear Christian sister, JoAnn, who was also a survivor, saw my struggles. She explained gently that if I injected myself into David's recovery process, I would simply "become an occasion for abuse." He was obsessed with me, she reminded me. By distracting him from his own necessary inner work, she said, I would actually be a stumbling block to him! I felt immediate peace and confirmation that she was speaking the truth. I felt great sorrow but also great relief to know that I was not responsible for tending to David's spiritual needs. I would have to trust God to send others to do that.

In my survivor support group, I also learned that it is possible to love someone and to consciously choose not to have him in my life. I was reminded to focus on my long-term best interests and urged to accept that I could not be the person to help my husband, although I secretly sent others to minister to him. I focused on caring for my baby and on keeping us safe. I was still heartsick, but I told myself that my job was to stay strong for my son and create a future for us. It was not easy, but my family, friends and church supported me. I went back to college and graduated with honors. I never worked in special education again, but instead focused my efforts on domestic violence prevention and intervention.

Seven years after David's incarceration, I was shocked to learn that he was about to be released from prison, three years before the end of his 'minimum sentence.' When that same week the phone company mistakenly published my unlisted phone number and address, he called me from prison to say that he was being released and that he knew exactly where I lived. He read my address to me. Terrified, I immediately moved and quit the job that I had loved which was managing a Christian transitional abuse shelter in which my son and I also lived.

Because of the dangers he presented to me and my family, when David was released from prison, he was transported directly to the airport and sent to the U.S. mainland to serve out his parole. One of many parole conditions was a ban on returning to Hawaii. I felt somewhat safer knowing this, but I have never since had a published address or phone number.

This turned out to be a good decision, because according to several sources, David has apparently never quit looking for me. Although he was out of prison for several years, he was eventually re-incarcerated, this time for threatening one of his family members with a knife. Through this criminal case, I learned that while David had been free on parole, he had illegally purchased a gun and bragged that he was planning to kill me. Today he is serving a life sentence. I have been told that he cannot be considered for parole until the year 2025.

With the benefit of years of hindsight, I never pass up an opportunity to share with caring Christians the information I have learned the hard way about domestic violence. Had the ministers and helpers from whom I sought support been educated on this topic, perhaps my story would have turned out differently. We will never know. But for the sake of all the Christian victims who today find themselves equally trapped and endangered, I pray you will take the following information to heart and pass it on every chance you get.

Based on my personal experience, here is what I wish Pastors knew when I needed help:

- what domestic violence IS;
- what domestic violence IS NOT;
- how to identify the signs of domestic violence;
- to assume that a victim is usually telling the truth when she shares what has happened in her relationship;
- to NAME the abuse and to call it domestic violence;
- not to assume that just because there has been no physical abuse, domestic violence is not occurring;
- to avoid marriage counseling when violence or abuse is occurring;
- to always maintain *safety* as the highest priority;
- the importance of maintaining a domestic violence victim's confidentiality;
- the importance of validating a victim's feelings, respecting her wishes and supporting her decisions.

I wish pastors had known how to identify what domestic violence IS

In terms of *knowing what domestic violence IS*, I needed pastors to under-stand what I was experiencing. Domestic violence is a pattern of coercive, controlling behavior, exercised by one intimate partner over the other. It is a belief in the right to absolute power and control over the partner. It is not just physical abuse. In fact it never starts with that. It can be verbal abuse, sexual abuse, destruction of property; abuse of pets, emotional abuse (isolation, financial control, blaming the victim, minimizing or denying the abuse, using and/or abusing the children, making threats, threatening suicide, 'manipulative kindness,' etc.). Anyone can be a victim. Typically, women are the victims, but men can be victims too. I have met with and counseled several abused men. It is much more likely, though, that when a man comes to you and claims to be an abused husband, he is actually an abuser who is hoping to convince you that his wife is the one with the problem. True victims tend to be reluctant to disclose. But bad-mouthing the partner is typical abuser behavior. Abusers want you to believe them and do only one thing–nothing! They will often try to reach the police or your office before the victim and attempt to manipulate those in authority into siding with them. They tend to be very slick and believable, and often a victim finds herself trying to "prove" that her partner is abusive, while he tries to convince you that she is a liar or "crazy." Often I recommend the paperback book *When Love Goes Wrong: What to Do When You Can't Do Anything Right*, by Ann Jones & Susan Schechter, to those who wish to understand domestic violence. In addition to other helpful information, it contains an exhaustive checklist of abusive behaviors, many of which are very subtle.

I wish pastors had known how to identify what domestic violence IS NOT.

In identifying *what domestic violence IS NOT*, I needed pastors to have the knowledge to be able to dispel the numerous common societal myths and stereotypes that I held about domestic violence. In my mind a 'battered woman' was someone who was weak and was always getting beaten up. That was not my reality.

There are a number of things I have learned over the years that help bring the reality that was mine to light:

(a) *Domestic violence is not a relationship in which the couple frequently "fights."*

It is a relationship in which one partner is being routinely subjugated and abused by the other. Although both individuals may get hurt, it is the victim who is hurt the worst and the most often. Only the victim lives in fear.

(b) *Domestic violence is not a "marriage problem" or a "communication problem."*

It is a *violence* problem that stems from a *belief system* problem. Anyone who believes that he or she has the right (especially the God-given right or responsibility!) to "keep another person in line" is a potential abuser. Working with either a victim or an abuser (or both) on communication skills or marriage issues will *not* be helpful if violence has occurred. The violence will continue, and it will escalate.

(c) *Domestic violence is not an anger problem.*

Everyone gets angry. Anger is a feeling. Anger never hurt anyone. Domestic violence is not an anger problem. Therefore the commonly prescribed 'anger management' classes for the abuser will not help. In fact, longitudinal research shows that abusers can be just as violent (or even more violent!) when they are calm. (For more information on this, see the fascinating research described in the book *When Men Batter Women* by Neil Jacobsen, Ph.D. and John Gottman, Ph.D.) Abusers, like all of us, can and do get angry at other people. They may become upset with a boss, a co-worker, or even the police and judges who hold them accountable. Yet rarely do they act violently towards them. Why? They know they would suffer an immediate negative consequence. Thus domestic abuse is better understood as a behavior, a choice—not as a *feeling*.

(d) *Domestic violence is not the result of stress.*

Certainly stress may be a factor. We all get stressed from time to time, however we do not all get violent when stressed, although many of us have extremely stressful lives and/or jobs. Additionally, abusers often at-tack their victims at times that are completely non-stressful, such as while attending or after a party or when things are quiet and calm.

(e) *Domestic violence is not caused by using alcohol and drugs.*

The fact is that most batterers or abusers are not alcoholics or addicts and most of those who abuse substances are not batterers. While studies have shown that there is a correlation with increased severity of injuries when alcohol is involved, it does not 'cause' the violence. Batterers who do get drunk or high often do so with their friends. However, they rarely, if ever, beat up their friends when they are impaired. Moreover, sometimes the most violent abusers strictly abstain from drinking or drugs. This is important to understand, because as I now often remind addiction professionals, when you sober up a wife beater, guess what you get? A sober wife-beater!

(f) *Domestic violence is not the result of a 'sickness' or mental illness.*

Abusers are not sick. Even those with a genuine mental health diagnosis cannot attribute their abusive behavior solely to their illness. Most mental health patients are never violent, and those who are can usually be medicated. If domestic violence was the result of a true illness, the sick person would be unable to control when and where he displayed it's 'symptoms.' He would not be able to abuse *only* his spouse or partner and *only* behind closed doors. The Jekyll and Hyde behavior that victims describe is manifested at will by the abuser who is attempting to manipulate someone to "get his way."

Formerly violent abusers who are genuinely working to change tell us this quite openly. Did you know that abuse is often directed only at parts of the victim's body that are covered by hair or clothing? Domestic violence is not about the loss of control—far from it! It is rather about the use of power and control to get one's way. Nevertheless, victims are often told by untrained helpers (as I was by my fellow Al-Anon members and others), "Your husband is sick. He can't help himself." When victims hear this, their struggle is exacerbated because they have promised to remain married 'in sickness and in health.'

All of these are commonly misunderstood myths about domestic violence. Even highly trained counselors, professional social workers, licensed psychologists and psychiatrists typically do not understand these issues very well. For anyone who is interested in better understanding batterers, I highly recommend the excellent book, *Why Does He Do That? Inside The Minds Of Angry And Controlling Men,* by Lundy Bancroft.

I wish pastors had known how to identify the signs of domestic violence

I needed the pastors I approached to 'read between the lines' and be observant about signs of abuse. Routine assessment for abuse should be incorporated into pre-marital counseling, marriage counseling and family counseling. In all interactions with couples, especially those who are seeking relationship advice or those who are clearly struggling, pastors should always be on the look-out for signs of power and control issues. Some of the possible warning signs that domestic violence may be occurring include:

- There have been separations in the past;
- You know he was abusive in a former relationship;
- You know his father abused his mother;
- He has an explosive temper;
- He won't let her talk in counseling sessions;
- He tries to control where she goes, who she talks with and what she does;
- He accuses her of having affairs;
- She says things like, "He's a Jekyll and Hyde" or "I walk on eggshells" or "He's mean when he drinks" or "No one believes me when I tell them the way he treats me;"
- He seems to always want to be with her (or conversely, he leaves her alone for days);
- He controls the money. The property is in his name only;
- She may be forced to cancel their counseling appointments if he can't come with her;
- He may not 'let' her work or 'let' her drive;
- He may insist that she stay at home (often this includes an insistence that she home school the children);
- He may badmouth her or her family to you, or try to convince you she is the only one with a problem;
- He may try to convince you that she is 'crazy' or is 'a terrible mother;'
- He may try to get her arrested, or get a restraining against her. If so, he uses this as evidence to convince you that he is 'the real victim;'

- She may say he has threatened to take the children from her;
- He may have moved her far away from her family or support system;
- The police may have been called to their house;
- She may have bruises or unexplained injuries, or wear long sleeves in hot weather;
- She may seem depressed or afraid to talk;
- She may be using drugs or alcohol to self-medicate or cope;
- She may make excuses for him or minimize any abuse that you know has occurred.

I wish pastors had known to assume that a victim is usually telling the truth when she shares what has happened in her relationship.

I needed pastors to believe me. Victims are typically too embarrassed or afraid to talk about abuse at all. Despite common misconceptions, there is little value in lying about abuse. When a victim does work up the courage to disclose the truth, she is often not believed at all or is herself blamed for provoking the abuse. The truth is that victims are much more likely to minimize their abuse, not exaggerate it.

Abusers can be very charming in public and many can easily 'con' a pastor or Christian counselor in the same way they con police and judges. I have heard many stories from victims whose abusers have convinced their pastor that his wife was lying or exaggerating. Many women have left their churches because the church sided with her abusive husband.

I wish pastors had known to NAME the abuse and to call it domestic violence.

I needed to be educated about what was happening to me. I needed to know that I was experiencing domestic violence and that God did not want me to be abused. Without being taught the dynamics of power and control and the typical escalation pattern of domestic violence, I could not have possibly anticipated the dangerous potential of my abuse situation. Since no one named the problem, I was not referred to domestic violence agencies that could have helped me carefully plan for my separation and divorce. When I was finally presented with domestic violence information in my first support group, I remember vividly that it was as if a light bulb went on over my head and suddenly everything made sense.

I wish pastors had known not to assume that just because there has been no physical abuse, domestic violence was not occurring.

Everyone I approached for help minimized the lethal potential of my marital situation. Since I had not been hurt physically, it was assumed that violence was not a concern. Anyone who had been trained in domestic violence intervention could have easily identified the escalating continuum of abuse and warned me that the worst violence (and nearly all intimate murders) occur during or after a separation.

I wish pastors had known to avoid marriage counseling when violence or abuse is occurring.

Marriage counseling assumes equality between the partners. Equality allows the give and take necessary for compromise. But it is impossible to compromise with an abuser. Furthermore, a partnership mentality is imperative to ensure truth-telling and safety in the couples' counseling setting. Domestic violence victims are frequently beaten for telling the truth in such a session.

Marriage counseling assumes that the relationship is one of mutuality and trust. Nothing could be farther from the truth when domestic violence is occurring. A 'relationship problem' or 'marital distress' can often be helped by both persons working on it, but domestic violence cannot. Only the abuser has the power to stop the abuse. Unfortunately, few abusers ever take full responsibility for their abusive behavior. They are much more likely to blame the victim, minimize their abuse and/or deny the abuse altogether. Marriage counseling often keeps the couple stuck in the tension-building phase of the 'cycle of violence' for longer, but it will not prevent the next episode of abuse. It may even endanger the victim.

Typically couples counseling is never recommended until the abuser has been violence and abuse free for at least a year. This may be difficult for the couple that approaches you for help to understand, but it is the responsibility of the pastor or counselor to explain that safety must be the priority.

I wish pastors had known to always maintain safety as the highest priority.

Safety did not appear to be a priority for any of the pastors I approached. Certain statements should have been made loudly and clearly, such as "What you are describing is abuse," "It is not your fault," and "Domestic violence is a crime." Pastors also need to say, "I am concerned for your safety," "I will not discuss this with anyone, including your husband," "would you like to know your legal options?" and "would you like to call the local domestic violence agency? They can work out a personal safety plan with you."

A lethality (or dangerousness) assessment needs to be completed to help victims understand the many factors that indicate potential for physical violence. As well, a personalized safety plan and knowledge about all of the local resources and options for abuse victims is required. Had I been able to meet with other victims and survivors, I might also have been provided with additional support and ideas for staying safe.

I wish pastors had known the importance of maintaining a domestic violence victim's confidentiality

Women need to know that nothing they report in confidence will get back to their abuser without permission. It is important to understand that unless a physical assault is occurring, the decision to call the police about domestic violence should be the victim's if at all possible. Mandatory reporting requirements for abuse of an adult are very rare.

Without a victim's clear permission, it can be dangerous to confront the abuser. Even with her permission, it may result in further abuse. The victim may suddenly be blindsided by an abuser who becomes enraged by her perceived 'betrayal.' Many abuse victims have been beaten after just such an event.

I wish pastors had known the importance of validating a victim's feelings, respecting her wishes and supporting her decisions

Remember the adage "Do No Harm." Even if you do not agree with a victim's decisions, allowing her self-determination is crucial. She will likely come back to you later for help if you are not coercive or judgmental. Her decisions must be respected. She has had her power taken from her by the abuser and an important part of her recovery process is being empowered to make her own decisions. Sometimes this is hard for helpers, who may believe that they know what it is best for her. I try to avoid giving advice, and always remind myself that each victim is the expert on her own life.

Today, I can thank God for what has happened in my life, although I would not want to re-live it. I know that it was only through these dramatic experiences that I have been brought to the place where God wants me. I am grateful for all those compassionate pastors and Christian friends who tried to help me, even when they were ill-equipped. By sharing my experiences here, I pray that you too will find the courage to minister to suffering families in search of safety, support, justice, and peace.

2

Raping Eve

Facing the Unrelenting Fury of Adam

Dan Allender

I ONCE SPOKE WITH a pastor who had invited me to do a conference on
sexual abuse in his church. He was gracious and thanked me for coming and said, "I'm glad to help those who struggle in this area, though it
is not a conference I'd ever attend." I asked him to explain. "Well, it would
be similar if someone asked me to attend a conference on Vacation Bible
schools. I'm all for the work, but I don't have time to be part of all the good
things in the church."

There is an obvious logic to the limitations of his time. But I pressed
him by saying, "I appreciate your dilemma of making choices, but I'm cu-
rious as to what percentage you think sexual abuse or any other kind of
abuse exists in your congregation, whether it is past abuse experienced
or observed or current abuse they suffer?" He paused and said he had
never considered the question. He then answered, "Perhaps ten percent
have some history of abuse, past or present."

When I shared with him the research findings regarding sexual, physical, and emotional abuse he was stunned. He said, "I had no idea abuse or
violence of any kind was such a huge problem." I could have cried. The data
he heard from me was written clearly in our promotional materials and in
the private correspondence between our office and his associates.

My burden in this chapter is to address an obvious and difficult
question: How can we help the church face the extent of violence among

us? How can the issues of violence and abuse be addressed not as a matter of the suffering of a few but as a real concern in all relationships?

Any attempt to broaden awareness and not create an us/them view of abuse has a potential pitfall. The moment one places the issue of domestic violence or sexual abuse within the larger context of issues that are endemic in all relationships; it is possible to water down the focus on specific, criminal acts of abuse. Said differently, isn't it possible that if everyone struggles with violence in relationships, then we don't need to take seriously the more obvious, heinous kinds of abuse?

The issue is like sailing between the Scylla and Charybdis—there is danger on either side. If we broaden the issue we run the risk of diluting the focus on abuse; if we maintain the focus only on clearly definable domestic violence we create the impression that violence is not widespread. My attempt will be to sail between the dangers and invite the entire people of God not only to face the clear violations of dignity in domestic violence, but also to see the roots of violence in what could be considered normal moments of relational failure.

I have a deep desire to see domestic violence brought from the personal interaction happening within a clinical setting to the attention of the whole congregation. One of the difficulties is the fact that the topic itself is shameful. It makes most people uncomfortable even to hear the terms *domestic violence, battering, sexual abuse.* Any deep human suffering or struggle opens the heart to questions about the goodness of God. Difficult and often unanswerable questions often cause good-hearted people to choose to back away from even investigating or learning some of the basic details about issues of abuse. In addition, the questions often arise due to their own unaddressed past suffering that is similar in some form to the harm they are now asked to address in another. It is far easier to escape the conversation.

Let me illustrate how hard it is to engage others in the topic of violence. We live on a small island in Puget Sound and I have a thirty-five minute ferry trip from work to my home. On a recent trip I sat next to a friend. When I sat down with him, after greetings he asked, "What are you doing this weekend?" and I said, "I am going to a conference." He said, "What conference?" He asked, so I decided to tell, and I said, "I am going to a conference on domestic violence." Have you ever done that? Did you do that prior to coming? How did people respond? My friend said, "Oh." It was clear he did not intend to ask any more. I added that I was going to be a presenter on that topic. He said "well, oh really." And then he said to me this phrase, "I am so glad for people like you." Do you hear already the point of differentiation? "I am glad for people like you who are willing to help those who get caught in the web of that kind of harm."

He meant no harm, but in a brief turn of a phrase he marginalized helpers, and he separated himself from those who harm and those who have harmed. Let me state my premise. We must face the war that exists between men and women. It is a war that is spoken about in the core text of the Bible that delineates our condition as a result of what is called "the fall." Men and women are inherently caught in a conflict that is summarized by the phrase: "And though your desire will be for your husband, he will be your master." (Gen. 3:16b, NLT)

This passage comes in a pericope that delineates the consequences of Adam and Eve's rebellion against God. It tells us what suffering is ahead, yet not as a final inevitability because it is promised that the serpent, a symbol of evil, will be destroyed and the rest of the Bible is a working out of the promise of reconciliation.

Yet there are tensions between genders that must be acknowledged or we accurately can be accused of not facing reality. The focus of this article is not to look parsimoniously at the harm of men against women and the harm of women against men. It is a legitimate task to focus on one/the other/or both. What would be illegitimate is to imply that any social ill is entirely the province of one gender. The Bible makes it clear that the fall is not due to one and only one failure. My focus of this essay is to look exclusively at the male's part in the process of violence against women.

In every world, in every age, men hate what women bring to the reality of relationships. Men are terrified about what it is that a woman calls his heart to be and to become, to do, to give, and to receive. Domestic violence is different than the common struggle all men bear against women, yet it shares a common genetic heritage. To see the genetic heritage we can begin by saying that every man struggles with anger.

To even use the phrase "an angry man" is a redundancy. There are some men who clearly know they are angry. Based on a myriad of conversations with men I would say that, on the basis of anecdotal data, most men do not see themselves as struggling with anger.

What I want to talk about primarily is—what is the consequence of the fall for a woman? What is the consequence of the fall for man? And because my topic is not primarily about the unique struggles and failures of women I will not spend much time on her fall, but only enough to set the context of man's failure of violence.

The curse for women is twofold: 1. She will have pain in childbearing; 2. She will desire her husband and he will rule over her. Notice how concrete the language of consequences is for both men and women. For men, it will be thorns and thistles, and for women pain in childbirth. It would be a violation of the passage, however, to think that in either case, the concrete limits the extent of the consequences. For example, does a woman who shuts down menses through medication escape the curse? Or does a man who chooses not to work the land and bleed and sweat in harvesting crops escape the curse? Of course not; yet, we often think of a woman's curse as if it were truly limited to menses and birth labor. That is foolish, and simply not an adequate reading of the biblical text.

What is the nature of the curse for a woman? The passage seems to assume that one of the distinct capacities of a woman is to give birth, nurture, and to grow relationships. A woman has a unique eye for relationships. The work of Carol Gilligan, *In a Different Voice*, points to research data that indicates men and women look at the world and relationships in distinct manners. She further argues that the differences are not related to mere social construction or conditioned social norms.

To believe that God created male and female is not to assume that social conditioning or social construction plays no factor in our understanding of what it means to be a man or a woman. It does, and it is powerful, yet it is also arguable that God has made men and women to reflect or reveal different aspects of God's character. I believe that a woman has been created uniquely to reveal something about God's mercy and tenderness. That belief makes no assumption then about what a woman or man is best suited to do related to career, calling, or interest. A woman can do anything she desires—from being an astronaut to a zoo director. But she will do whatever she does with a degree of mercy and tenderness that is not foreign to a man, yet different.

Mercy is neither male nor female, yet something about the way a woman tends and cares for others will give sensual, tacit experience to the word. Often we find in scripture the notion of compassion or tenderness related to God as our mother (Zeph. 3:16, Isa. 42:14; Isa. 49:14–18; Isa. 66:11–13). It is easy to set up a false binary—women are tender and men are not. It is simply not true. An individual man can be far more tender in comparison to one specific woman. But if there is any value in thematic summaries, then it is possible to say that women tend to be more nurturing, tender, and merciful as the first course of response, in comparison to men.

Mercy reflects the truest heart of the gospel. If the gospel is to be spoken of in any meaningful way it is as the story of reconciliation. It is the story of God receiving us back home after we have fled from it, and the story of him pursuing us in the back field as we labor for him in self-righteous fury. God is our host who invites us to a banquet that is beyond our wildest hope or desire.

A woman's curse is that her desire to invite others to the banquet will be foiled by a man's fear of failure and she will feel lonely. He will add to that loneliness by blaming her as Adam did when he was confronted by God. This agony includes literal child birth but also involves all birthing and growing of relationships, male and female, child, or friend.

The second part of the curse for a woman is the relationship between desire and mastery. There will be hunger in her for her husband, and the man's response will be to rule or be her master. The presence of a hunger met with the reality of loneliness and disappointment is connected to the phrase 'and he will rule over her.' The word rule or master in Hebrew does not directly imply someone or something abusive. Nor does the word desire indicate something that is clearly wrong. It is only the context of those words that implies that both desire and mastery are not to be seen as 'happy' words.

The next time the word 'desire' is used, it refers to God's question to Cain about his plan to kill his brother. God asks, "But if you don't do what is right, sin is crouching at the door; it desires to have you, but you must master it." (Gen. 4:7, NIV) The word 'desire' from this context seems to imply desperation. Man's response is to rule against or over it. His response is not implied as engagement or honor, but of control and dominance. What will be the result of the fall in relationship between a man and a woman? There will be conflict and that conflict will be one that leads to greater loneliness, greater powerlessness on the part of the woman. And, in turn, a greater sense of urgency in a man to avoid failure.

Please, before you misread another sentence, this is not an effort to normalize conflict between the genders that takes away responsibility from either gender or assumes one gender is more at fault than the other. Let me consider the consequence of the fall for men.

The first is that whatever he does he will face thorns and thistles in all his endeavors. He will sweat and bleed and nothing on this earth will be easy for a man. There will be nothing easy in providing food for his family. Nothing will be done without severe obstacles; the earth will be dry and the thorns will be sharp and the result will be a man will live with a constant sense of futility.

If there is a common theme I hear as I work with women, particularly describing relationships with a man, it is the sentiment, "I feel like I'm too much. I have too much emotion, desire, anger, therefore if I want to keep my relationship with a man, then I must turn the rheostat down to where he is comfortable. I have to figure out if he can handle me so that if I am too smart, or emotional, or gifted, how I can hide. If he finds out that I make more than him, forget it, indeed if I am more mature, if I have something about the way I live, where I as a woman think better, live better, or am a better mountain climber, then the relationship will at some point not work."

A woman basically has to hide her glory; she has to hide what a beautiful being she is because a man may not know how to submit to her glory and delight with awe and gratitude in how God has made her, especially if her glory exposes what he fears is the absence of his own.

What is the war for a man? As a result of the fall every man struggles with some degree of fear about failure and futility. The second aspect of man's consequence is that you are from dust and to dust you will return and everything you do will crumble as well. Another way of saying that is everything a man does, he will face failure. Nothing will last, so if we take those two core words, futility—why bother because nothing will work and then, failure—nothing I do will provide final satisfaction, then it should be clearer why many men are angry.

What is the core issue for a man? It is the sense that I am never enough. I am not enough, I am not big enough, I am not smart enough, I have not got enough to be able to handle the world.

If we look then at the reality of a man's war with futility and failure, it becomes clearer why he wants someone to blame or someone to suffer for feeling that he is not capable of making his world work. In my work with men I hear language that indicates that they have to be in control, they need power, and if they don't get power and control, then the response is to intimidate and to shame until they do. And if that doesn't work then the response is either to flee or to intensify the fight.

What I am asking you to do is to connect the two worlds—a woman fears the exposure of loneliness and often hides. A man fears the exposure of his failure and often controls. Do men hide? Do women control? Obviously! Sin is not unique to one gender, nor are the paths for individualizing sin differentiated exclusively by gender. Nonetheless, as a general theme, more women than men hide their glory and turn down their inner world to keep from being lonely, and more men than women use intimidation, including flight, as punishment for exposure, than women.

Women more often silence their voice to keep peace rather than to speak from their heart to invite a man tenderly and boldly to mercy. It is natural to flee. It is what both Adam and Eve did after they heard God walking in the garden and they knew they were naked.

But what did Adam do as he was addressed first by God? It is the most audacious and inconceivable engagement recorded in the Bible. God approaches Adam and Eve and asks, "Who told you that you were naked? Have you eaten from the tree that I commanded you not to eat from? The man said, "The woman you put here with me—she gave me some fruit from the tree, and I ate it." (Gen. 2:11–12, NIV) The question God asks requires a simple yes or no. Adam instead launches into a brilliant statement of three facts: 1) you created the woman who, 2) gave me the fruit that, 3) I ate. There is nothing untrue about his words, yet it is obvious it is an assault against God and Eve with a slight acknowledgement to eating but not to his rebellion. He assigns first guilt to God. If you had not made her, we would not be in this mess. Second he blames Eve for giving him the fruit, even though the passage prior places Adam at the scene of the deception with him remaining silent. His confession is so conditioned by blame that it is ludicrous, yet that hides the real offense. His assault against God and Eve reflects a violence that refuses to submit before the glory of God. Adam will not fall on his knees and repent.

If we were to try to name a man's thematic failure it is a refusal to bend the knee to a glory he doesn't own or create. What is man's response to God's glory calling him to name his own failure? It is the violence of blame, the scrambling for control and mastery. He throws contempt in the face of God.

Man before beauty, which is any glory that reflects the creator, will either attempt to absorb it and if he cannot possess it will eventually try and kill it. He will stand against a beauty he cannot own, and envy and eventually attempt to destroy it if it cannot be gained. Do you see the stance of a man as he begins to name the reality of where he is before the living God? I will blame you God for what you created in my world. I hold you accountable for the parents you gave me; I hold you accountable for the fact that my father was an alcoholic; I hold you accountable for the fact that you put me in this particular eon; you are responsible, and I am not. And then, secondly, I will blame another so that I am not implicated.

What is the core rage of a man? He does not want to name the fundamental reality of what would restore him, not only with God but with others, particularly with his own wife. What is it that a woman really wants from a man at that point of failure? It is not an apology, or at least not merely an apology; it is ownership, and ownership of what? To me one of the most glorious phrases, and the one that I would ask if you are interacting with leaders in the believing community, if you are interacting with pastors, interacting with seminary presidents, you are interacting with others who have any authority in the context of their service to the kingdom of God, one of the fundamental questions I would ask you to ask—do you see yourself to be the chief of sinners in your church? Do you see yourself to be, in your organization, the chief of sinners minus one?

There is a glorious phrase in 1 Timothy chapter one. If you read that section, and I invite you to do so at your own leisure, you will find in verses 1–11, a list of sins that is more severe than those found in any of the apostle Paul's other letters. There he includes among those whom the law of God comes to expose as mother and father killers. In the ancient era matricide or patricide was as severe a sin as could be conceived. In this list he is saying there is no group of sinners that are more dark and wicked.

Then in verse 15 of the first chapter of Timothy, Paul says, "Here is a trustworthy saying that deserves full acceptance: Christ Jesus came into the world to save sinners—of whom I am the worst." I want you to notice the tense of the verb—it is not *I was*. He is very particular about the tense he uses and he says I *am* the chief of sinners. He says I am the worst of all, I am far worse than any pervert, father killer, mother killer, or slave trader. I am your apostle. I am the one in many ways who shaped the core convictions as the New Testament is being written, and I want you to know my stance before you, that is there is no one on this earth who will ever be equal to the heart I know I possess. It is not an issue of comparing sins to get to the final assessment; it is merely the call to know one's own heart and what each of us is capable of doing, not merely what we have done or not done.

From the age of twelve through the age of twenty I was involved in illicit pharmaceutical sales—that phrase, if it dawns on you eventually, will probably be translated and you will hear it again as I was a drug dealer. Was I as bad as others who did more harm? Why compare—you want to bring your sin to me and you want to tell me that you were ten years involved in drug abuse, that you have had three affairs with different pastors, that you have been involved in legions of sin? Do you want a litany to litany comparison of sin? How will we ever determine who is the chief of sinners? Paul claimed it for himself canonically. The only question between you and me ought to be this, who is number two? Let me tell you what this becomes an antidote to as we deal with the last few thoughts on the topic of domestic violence.

As we work with perpetrators we will always have a tendency to see them more darkly than ourselves. If you are a woman who has been deeply harmed by men, I understand only a small amount of the heartache you have suffered. I have spent my life since at least 1986 working with men and women who have been sexually abused, and when somebody says you are an expert on sexual abuse I can say only that each person is an expert on their own experience.

We are all similar in that we are all made in the image of God. But we must enter the experience of others aware that we cannot make our story normative for another. My history may help me understand better the suffering of another, but only if I am first open to knowing and naming my own unique ways that I fail in relationship with others. I have to address that I am always the first and biggest sinner before I can enter your heartache with any hope of truly hearing you well. We need to be engaged in a different kind of dialogue between genders—one that acknowledges we see much the same, yet we see with a different set of eyes and speak with a different voice.

As a man that requires I take seriously my propensity to intimidation, to flight when I feel out of control, and my shame in exposure. If I will follow Paul and allow for my failure to be the basis of being able to say, this is trustworthy statement: Christ Jesus has come into the world to save sinners–of whom I am the worst, then I can more readily see how my sin silences you. I cannot keep you from being afraid and it is not my responsibility to get you to speak. And as you speak and your voice is full of fury or false accusation, I do not have to agree to stay in the dialogue. I simply need to know that whatever point of failure of the other, I am always the chief of sinners—minus one.

The new dialogue between genders based on an ownership of our need for grace requires that women speak with boldness. Violence and intimidation cannot be excused, though it is to be forgiven. Hiding glory is not to be endured, though it is to be forgiven. The dialogue means we must have more women who are Old and New Testament scholars, church historians, and rocket scientists. We desperately need, in evangelical circles, more women to be teaching in our schools because their hermeneutical way of seeing the Scriptures will be different. It will compel us to talk about the role of culture and social construction in reading any text, especially the Bible.

I need the voices of those who are not like me. If I am not to be blind, and I am one blind man, and if I am not to be deaf and biased by the parameters of my own self protection, then I desperately need you to be involved with me. But we need dialogue and the dialogue can never occur without trust. But when we are in relationship, you already know that I am a man who struggles with lust and anger. It will not be easy. We will each want to flee and to hurt each other. And so the reality is, we are both adulterers and murderers in a conversation that will likely not go far unless we have a heart to be broken by sin and even more so overwhelmed by the goodness of grace.

Do you see why men rape Eve? Because you call us to relationship, you call us to mercy, because you call us to a context not of authority and power and monologue but to dialogue; you call me to name the reality of my own sin and anyone who does that I sadly say, and I do not say this boastfully, you are in for a fight. Because even if I claim I am open to you, wait until you face my defensiveness; wait until you begin to bump up against the fact that I am a privileged white male and I do not want to give it up.

Do you understand why diversity is God's plan? Not just male-female but age, race, eon, even geography, begins to re-shape how we start to ask and answer some of the core questions. If we are not in relationship with people who kindly and warmly unnerve us we will not grow to become what our gender is to reveal.

What are we left to consider? Let me offer two last thoughts. May we have a dialogue about the issues of abuse that begins with an awareness that every human being struggles with anger that Jesus calls murder. It is not mere hyperbole. It is truth. Every man is capable of harming his wife at levels that are horrific, illegal, and utterly contrary to the heart of God.

He is not only capable, but even without clearly exercised domestic violence every man hurts his wife in ways she will experience as a murdering of her heart. The dialogue cannot begin between genders until man first answers God without contempt and blame.

Second, may we invite the larger community of God to a discussion of domestic violence that does not focus only on the most heartbreaking and horrific stories. There are untold numbers of stories about profound heartbreak and harm that also must be told. May those stories be told and told often; perhaps they ought to be the majority of stories told both from the standpoint of victim and perpetrator. May the stories be honored with our grief and respect when they are told. We know that is not true that domestic violence only happens in certain kinds of homes and families. We need to give voice to the more common, tacit, unnamed violence among us that we have so often come to see as inevitable and not worthy of note. It is when that violence is called abusive, and when hiding it is seen as collusive, that we can begin to invite the larger congregation to reflect on their own experience as both victim and perpetrator.

Oddly, it is when we are each indicted by Jesus' claim that we are adulterers and murderers that we can pause and take in the wonder of this trustworthy statement:

Christ Jesus came into the world to save sinners—of whom I am the worst.

3

Calling the Pastor

Al Miles

THE ONE-WORD HEADER ON the email I received in my office that late Monday afternoon was both alarming and straightforward: *Help*!!! The message had been sent by the national director for clergy ethics and morality at one of the largest evangelical Christian denominations in the United States. The director, Frank, who himself is an ordained evangelical Christian minister, explained in the body of his text that the senior pastor of a very thriving parish, Pastor Joe, had earlier in the day "confessed his sins to both me and several brethren in leadership at his church." I phoned Frank immediately to obtain more details on this situation and to find out how he thought I could help.

Pastor Joe, I soon learned, has been married to his wife, Margaret, for twenty-nine years. Highly respected throughout their community for modeling both Christian servanthood and social justice, the couple has received numerous humanitarian awards. They have three adult children, all of whom are also actively involved in church and civic activities in their communities. Amidst the countless awards and endless accolades lie two dark secrets Pastor Joe had not previously shared: during his entire marriage he has been emotionally, physically, psychologically, and sexually abusive to Margaret. He has also had extramarital sexual affairs with a dozen women worshipping in his parish.

"The brethren and I need you to fly to our city tonight," pleaded Frank as we spoke on the phone. "The future well-being of our entire denomination could depend upon you and me resolving this messy situation as soon as possible." Pressed by me to provide specific details on how he envisioned my presence aiding and abetting this particular church in its time of need, Frank laid out a six-day plan of action.

Tuesday afternoon, the brethren, Pastor Joe and I will meet with you so that Pastor can, once again, confess his sins. In moments of weakness, he now realizes how Satan took hold of him. On Wednesday, you'll meet with both Pastor Joe and Sister Margaret to give Pastor the opportunity to apologize to sister for wronging her. On Thursday, ten of the twelve women Pastor Joe confessed to having extramarital sexual relations with have agreed to meet with you, and Pastor Joe and Sister Margaret. The women want to apologize to Sister Margaret for having affairs with her husband; apologize to God for their sinful behavior; and want to apologize to Pastor for seducing him. On Friday, all the other men in leadership roles in the church will meet with Pastor Joe and you. This will provide yet another opportunity for Pastor to cleanse himself of all unrighteousness. On Saturday, evangelical pastors from across the state will gather in our sanctuary with you to meet with and pray for Pastor Joe. Our spiritual leader will humbly seek their approval to continue in the ministry God has called him to serve. Finally, on Sunday, we want you to hear Pastor Joe preach a sermon on the importance of Christian forgiveness. You'll witness, firsthand, the tremendous blessing this wonderful man of God is to his wife, family, congregation, and to our entire community.

The responses from Frank and other male church leaders to the abuse, betrayal, and violence perpetrated by Pastor Joe against his wife and other women in his congregation is all too common. Complicated and messy, these situations often evoke compassion, excuses, justifications, and sympathy for Christian male offenders; whether or not they admit to committing the sinful acts in question. In stark contrast, the same situations evoke a strong negative reaction toward violated Christian women, often blaming them for their own victimization and doubting the veracity of their stories.

It's important to acknowledge the awkward and difficult position the entire Christian church is placed in when violence impacts clergy families or other couples worshipping within the congregation. Leaders and laity alike are most often ill-prepared to deal with such a complex and repulsive issue as domestic violence. Further complicating matters are the cultural and religious teachings adhered to in most Western societies on the responsibilities and roles of females and males. Of special note—these precepts are not usually based on one's character or integrity, but on one's gender.

For example, within the walls of many Christian churches it is taught, sometimes subtly and at other times blatantly, that males possess certain God-ordained privileges and rights which, for some reason, are not granted to females. This divine entitlement gives males authority over women, children, animals and plants, and over the entire universe. Scriptural interpretation and translation bolster the widely embraced doctrinal teaching.

In addition, many Christian churches teach females to assume a subservient position to the alleged God-ordained authority of males. This is especially the case in regards to a husband's "headship" over his wife. Once again, Scripture is interpreted and translated in such a way to strengthen this widely-held doctrinal teaching.

Returning to Pastor Joe and the response from male evangelical Christian leaders to his confessed sinful behavior—after learning over the phone the plan of action Frank and other men wanted to fly me to their city to help implement—I respectfully declined their invitation. I explained to Frank that attempting to resolve in six days all the hurt Pastor Joe had caused to his wife and other women in his parish for nearly thirty years was both unrealistic and inappropriate. I then offered Frank an alternative series of four action steps which, over a long period of time, would help the entire congregation, including Pastor Joe, return to health and wholeness.

First, in accordance with the Christian Scripture, Pastor Joe needed to be immediately taken out of his current, or any other, position of leadership in the church. In Titus 1:7–9, the apostle Paul writes about the early Christian church and its leadership. He clearly describes the qualities that "bishops," or "overseers" need to possess:

> For a bishop, as God's steward, must be blameless; he must not be arrogant or quick-tempered or addicted to wine or violent or greedy for gain; but he must be hospitable, a lover of goodness, prudent, upright, devout, and self-controlled. He must have a firm grasp of the word that is trustworthy in accordance with the teaching, so that he may be able both to preach with sound doctrine and to refute those who contradict it.

The confessed acts of emotional, psychological, physical, sexual and spiritual abuse and violence Pastor Joe perpetrated against his wife and several other women in his congregation disqualify him from continuing, at least at the present time, to serve in any leadership capacity within the church.

Second, Frank, all the other leaders in the congregation, and their particular evangelical Christian denomination, need to hold Pastor Joe fully and solely responsible for his abusive actions and behavior. Satan is blamed for the twenty-nine years the spiritual leader abused his wife, Margaret, and sexually betrayed twelve additional women in the congregation. Recall the words of Frank in describing Joe's behavior: "In moments of weakness, he now realizes how Satan took hold of him." Note also how the sexually abused women somehow came to assume the blame for Pastor Joe's sins against them. Once again, the words of Frank during our phone conversation are very revealing: "The women want to apologize to Sister for having affairs with her husband; apologize to God for their sinful behavior; and want to apologize to Pastor for seducing him." The best chance for this particular Christian congregation and denomination to regain health and wholeness is for Pastor Joe to be held accountable, exclusively, for the sins he chose to perpetrate against his wife and other women whose trust he betrayed. Joe must also totally shoulder the responsibility for the hurt he caused other congregation members with his lies and manipulation.

Third, a structure must be created by church and denomination leaders whereby Sister Margaret, the other twelve violated women, and the entire congregation can seek emotional, psychological, and spiritual care to help them overcome the damage caused by Pastor Joe. The individual and group counseling and support gatherings must be offered free-of-charge and have no time limit in regards to the number of sessions one can attend. The person facilitating these meetings must not be a member of Pastor Joe's church. She or he needs also to possess specific expertise in dealing with situations of domestic and sexual abuse involving clergy or other Christian leaders serving within a local congregation or in a national position within a Christian denomination.

Fourth, Pastor Joe needs to be encouraged to seek offender-specific treatment. While congregation and denomination leaders and laity need to pray continuously for their fallen minister and his family, Joe needs additional help that most Christian clergy and parishioners are not qualified to give. Batterers' intervention specialists and counselors trained specifically to work with perpetrators of domestic and sexual violence offer the best hope for Pastor Joe to cease the behavior that caused others so much hurt. These intervention strategies also afford Joe the best opportunity to return to a life of emotional, psychological and spiritual wholeness.

It is essential that Frank and the other congregation and denomination leaders do not promise Pastor Joe that he will be restored to a position of Christian leadership on a local, state, regional, or national level.

The long-term, four-step action plan I presented over the phone to Frank in response to his proposed six-day plan of action, left him awestruck. After several moments of silence, he said, "Ours is a reconciling denomination. We promote compassionate care and Christian healing instead of punitive actions." Attempts to ensure Frank that my action plan offered compassion and the best hope for healing and reconciliation to everyone involved in this tragic situation went for naught. This particular national director for clergy ethics and morality at one of the largest evangelical Christian denominations in the United States ended our conversation with a rather chilling phrase: "The brethren and I will use all our God-given authority and wisdom to make sure Pastor Joe stays on the straight and narrow," Frank concluded. "We'll watch him very carefully so that, in weak moments, he'll be able to resist Satan's deceptive powers." To date, Joe remains the senior pastor at the church where he abused his wife, Margaret, twelve other women, and deceived the entire congregation.

In order for Christian pastors and other denominational leaders to most effectively address situations of domestic violence occurring in their midst, they must first gain knowledge on this complicated global problem. Domestic violence involves a pattern of abusive behavior in which a person uses coercion, deception, harassment, humiliation, manipulation and/or force, in order to establish and maintain power and control over that person's intimate partner or former intimate partner. Perpetrators use economic, emotional, psychological, physical, sexual, spiritual, and/or verbal tactics to get their way.[1] While a small percentage of men are also violated, primarily by other men in same-sex intimate partnerships, the American Medical Association estimates that two million women in this country are assaulted by an intimate partner every year. The actual numbers are probably much higher because victims often do not report attacks, fearing both the stigma associated with abuse and the threat of reprisal from perpetrators. In addition, a report published in July 2000 by the Justice Department's National Institute of Justice and the Department of Health and Human Services' Centers for Disease Control and Prevention states that nearly twenty-five percent of surveyed women say they have

---

1. Miles, *Violence in Families: What Every Christian Needs to Know*, 2002, 27.

been raped and/or physically assaulted by a current or former spouse or partner in their lives. These alarming statistics do not include many of the emotional, psychological, and spiritual tactics male perpetrators use to abuse their female victims.[2]

Christian women and men are as likely as all other couples to face situations of domestic violence. There are women serving and worshipping in our churches and denominational headquarters who suffer a secret, hell-on-earth type of existence, perpetrated by men who claim to love them. There are men who sit in the pews, and stand in the pulpits of every Christian denomination, who proclaim the joys and wonders of a Christ-centered life. At the same time, these self-proclaimed "men of God" beat, cuss, rape, and violate their wives and girlfriends in many other evil ways.

Listed below are some practical steps Christian pastors and other leaders within congregations and denominations need to follow in order to deal most effectively with situations of domestic violence occurring within their communities.

- *Make the safety of a victim-survivor and her children top priority.*

This is a vital first step. Often clergy and congregations express the desire to "save a marriage" and "keep a family together at all costs." These laudable goals can only be considered after a perpetrator has gone through offender-specific treatment, after there is reasonable certainty that his abusive behavior has completely stopped, and only if the victim-survivor wishes to continue in the relationship. Forcing or pressuring a victim-survivor into remaining with, or returning to, an abusive partner is both dangerous and inappropriate.

- *Hold the abuser accountable.*

Accountability involves several critical steps: showing remorse to the individuals we harm with our actions; taking full responsibility for the hurt we cause; seeking ongoing help to change our destructive and sinful ways; and demonstrating a willingness to pay restitution to the individuals we violate. A perpetrator will often manipulate pastors and other Christians into believing he has "repented of all unrighteousness." True repentance, however, involves a one hundred and eighty degree turn away from actions and behavior that caused others harm. This radical change takes lots of

2. All figures cited in *Violence in Families*, 27.

hard work on the part of the violator and plenty of time. A perpetrator of domestic violence rarely takes responsibility for the destruction he causes. Instead he blames alcohol, children, drugs, job stresses, mood swings, race, Satan, upbringing and, especially, the very woman he is violating. Bear in mind, none of these is the real cause of the abuse. The acts of destruction stem solely from the conscious decision on the part of the offending man to use abuse and violence. It is a choice he has made.

Additional challenges are faced by congregations and denominations when, as was the case with Pastor Joe and his wife, Margaret, a male Christian leader violates his female intimate partner. Often, church and denomination members, both leaders and laity alike, are coerced and tricked by the abusive male's power into offering excuses for his inappropriate behavior. At the same time, he manipulates the congregation and denomination into blaming the violated woman for her own victimization. Clergy and other congregation leaders must therefore be careful not to get taken in by an abuser's deceptive and slick ways. We must also resist accepting the notion that no self-professed "man of God" would use violence and other abuse tactics to control his wife or girlfriend. A perpetrator's often nearly immediate proclamation that he is a "man changed by God" is also a tactic for which Christian leaders and laity must watch. A final caution: male Christian batterers, especially those in leadership positions, are extremely adept at misusing sacred texts to escape accountability. A prime example: had I accepted Frank's offer to assist him and other male leaders in their six-day plan to keep Pastor Joe comfortably in his leadership position, I would have been treated to a sermon entitled "The Importance of Christian Forgiveness." Rest assured this particular homily was not chosen randomly. I am certain Pastor Joe told the congregation that God inspired him to preach on forgiveness. However, this "divine" providence had a more self-serving purpose. It prevented any member of the congregation and entire evangelical denomination from questioning Pastor Joe's right to remain in such a high profile and prestigious position after admitting to violating Margaret and twelve other women who trusted him as God's servant. Christian leaders must take extra care not to let perpetrators like Pastor Joe misuse the sacred virtue of forgiveness as a type of free pass to escape accountability and justice.

- *Listen to and believe a victim's story.*

Always thank a victim-survivor for the courage and trust she demonstrates by sharing her story with you. Tell her that there is no excuse or justification for domestic violence. Refrain from asking for more details about the abuse than what a victim-survivor volunteers (especially if you are a male and there has been any act of sexual violence). Also, never ask a victim-survivor what took her so long to disclose the abuse or why she stays with her abuser. These questions could seem to the victim-survivor like she is being blamed for her own victimization.

- *Do not recommend or participate in couples' or marriage counseling.*

It is a common, but dangerous, mistake to suggest that a battered woman and her partner or husband seek couples' or marriage counseling. Domestic violence is *not* about men and women struggling as a couple. It is about the conscious decision of one partner, usually the male, to use abusive and violent tactics to maintain power and control over his female intimate partner. Couples' or marriage counseling is inappropriate and risky in these situations, and could lead to further abuse or even the death of a victimized woman.

- *Maintain healthy boundaries.*

No single person, not even those who have worked against domestic violence for decades, has the knowledge and training to deal alone with all the complexities associated with this pervasive problem. Clergy and congregations must not go beyond their level of training. Otherwise, we will end up causing more harm than good and might even further endanger the life of a victim-survivor, her children, and even our own lives. To be most effective, clergy and congregations need to partner with and make referrals to community service providers: advocates, batterers' intervention specialists, child protective services providers, crisis intervention counselors, law enforcement officers, legal professionals, shelter workers, and victim and witness assistance personnel, to name just a few. In addition, clergy and congregations must take added precautions so as not to foster an emotionally dependant or sexual relationship with a victimized woman. Bear in mind, a victim-survivor is very vulnerable.

- *Help a victim-survivor to establish a safety plan.*

Clergy and congregations can assist a victim-survivor by helping her establish a safety plan that can be implemented quickly should her husband's or boyfriend's abuse continue or escalate. Include in this plan a safety kit, kept in a place where the perpetrator will not discover it, that contains items such as cash, a change of clothing, toiletries, an extra photo identification card, a copy of her children's birth certificates and childhood immunization records, and a list of phone numbers of counselors, friends, pastors, physicians, and shelters. It bears repeating: although clergy and congregations can offer vital assistance to a victim-survivor in the area of safety planning, remember that we must work with a team of community service providers to offer a victim-survivor the best possible opportunities for safety.

- *Seek education and training.*

If clergy and congregations are to take a vital role in helping a victim-survivor and a perpetrator of domestic violence, then it is essential that we seek proper and ongoing education and training. We must keep updated on the articles, books, videos, and workshops that can help us become effective team members. Remember, even with this training, never try to care for a victim-survivor or batterer alone.

- *Focus on the equal value and worth of all humankind.*

Far too often Christian pastors and other church and denomination leaders, especially those who are men, have interpreted and translated the Hebrew Bible and Christian Scripture in a male-centered manner. This patriarchal construct has, since the dawn of time, provided men with power and privileges over women and children that were never intended by God and Jesus Christ. The overall message from both divine beings centers on the dignity, love, respect, value and worth of all humankind. When pastors and parishioners model and teach an egalitarian way of living, it reduces greatly the opportunity for male batterers, both those who are and are not Christians, to use divine beings, sacred texts, and church doctrine and teachings to justify acts of abuse and violence. Preaching and teaching the equal value and worth of all humankind will also help empower female victims and survivors of domestic violence to seek refuge and safety for themselves and their children, realizing that no one deserves to be abused or abusive.

- *Preach and teach the love, respect, value and worth of all humankind and condemnation of violence espoused by Christian Scripture, God, and Jesus Christ.*

Here are several passages from Christian Scripture that serve as a reminder to pastors and other leaders of God's and Jesus Christ's love, respect, value, and worth for all creation and their condemnation of violence:

o *Be subject to one another out of reverence for Christ.* (Eph. 5:21, NRSV);

o *For you were called to freedom, brothers and sisters, only do not use your freedom as an opportunity for self-indulgence, but through love become slaves to one another.* (Gal. 5:13, NRSV)

o *The husband should fulfill his marital duty to his wife, and likewise the wife to her husband. The wife's body does not belong to her alone but also to her husband. In the same way, the husband's body does not belong to him alone but also his wife.* (1 Cor. 7:3–4, NIV)

o *Do nothing out of selfish ambition or vain conceit, but in humility consider others better than yourselves.* (Phil. 2:3, NIV)

o *You have heard that it was said to those of ancient times, "You shall not murder"; and "whoever murders shall be liable to judgment." But I say to you that if you are angry with a brother or sister, you will be liable to judgment; and if you insult a brother or sister, you will be liable to the council; and if you say, "You fool," you will be liable to the hell of fire.* (Matt. 5:21–23, NRSV)

o *And the tongue is a fire. The tongue is placed among our members as a world of iniquity; it stains the whole body, sets on fire the cycle of nature, and is itself set on fire by hell…With it we bless [God], and with it we curse those who are made in the likeness of God. From the same mouth come blessings and cursing. My brothers and sisters, this ought not be so.* (James 3:6, 9–10)[5]

o *For a bishop, as God's steward, must be blameless; he must not be arrogant or quick-tempered or addicted to wine or violent or greedy for gain; but he must be hospitable, a lover of goodness, prudent, upright, devout, and self-controlled. He must have a firm grasp of the word that is trustworthy in accordance with the teaching, so that he may be able both to preach with sound doctrine and to refute those who contradict it.* (Tit. 1:7–9, NRSV)

o *Wives, be subject to your husbands, as is fitting to the Lord. Husbands, love your wives and never treat them harshly.* (Col. 3:18–19, NRSV)

- *Frequently engage in self-examination.*

Male clergy and other male Christian leaders must be willing to engage frequently in examining their own attitudes about and behavior toward females. Consider the following questions: Do I treat females with the same respect, value, and worth that I do males? Do I ever blame my female intimate partner for my actions and behavior? Does my female intimate partner have the freedom to be her own person? Can my female intimate partner dress as she pleases; style her hair in the way she wishes; choose her own friends and acquaintances; select her own career path; express her spirituality in all the ways she desires? Do I ever coerce or manipulate my female intimate partner into engaging in any activities, sexual or otherwise, in which she herself has stated she would rather not participate? Am I myself involved in pornography? Do I ever refer to my female intimate partner, or any other woman, in a derogatory or vulgar manner? Do I laugh or remain silent when other males make disrespectful comments about girls and women? Do I ever push, restrain, slap, strangle, or in any other way physically prevent my female intimate partner from doing what she desires? Do I ever attempt to silence my female intimate partner? Do I ever threaten my female intimate partner with violence? Do I ever tell my female intimate partner that I am going to commit violence against someone else, including myself? Do I seek Scripture or religious doctrine and traditions that help maintain the patriarchal system? Do I become defensive when I hear that God and Jesus Christ grant females the same exact privileges and rights as males; or, that no male ever has the right to abuse any female, emotionally, physically, psychologically, sexually, or spiritually? Men cannot be trusted allies in the struggle to prevent and end the violence male Christian leaders perpetrate against women and children if we ourselves are not modeling egalitarianism, love, and respect in our own lives. Referring to the role of "bishop," or "overseer" in First Timothy 3:5, the apostle Paul writes: *[F]or if someone does not know how to manage his own household, how can he take care of God's church?* Christian male leaders who aspire to work in partnership with females to address situations of domestic violence need to first strive toward being able to truthfully answer no to all the above questions.

CONCLUSION

Behind the beautiful smiles and warm hugs Christians offer one another each week lies a filthy secret: situations of domestic violence are as prevalent within, as they are outside, of the Body of Christ. There are men who praise God and preach Jesus who also beat, cuss, rape, and abuse their female intimate partners and children with impunity. There are Christian women who live not with the blessed assurance of a Christ who died for their sins, but in a real-life nightmare perpetrated by men who promised to love and respect them.

Christian pastors and lay leaders can provide both vital support to victimized women and children and the opportunity for abusive men to stop hurting the people they claim to love. In order to be effective and trusted allies, however, these leaders must frequently take account of their own attitudes and behavior toward females; seek ongoing training in how best to respond to situations of domestic violence occurring both in their congregation and community; know when and where to refer Christian women and men involved in this pervasive problem; and preach and teach the equal value and worth of all God's creation, female and male.

4

One Couple's Story
of Dramatic Change

Karen and Bruce McAndless-Davis

Tʜɪs ɪs ᴛʜᴇ sᴛᴏʀʏ of one couple whose lives have undergone dramatic change. Bruce and Karen McAndless-Davis are both ordained clergy. They live on the west coast of Canada and have been married for eighteen years. The text that follows was offered as a luncheon address at the 2006 PASCH Conference held at Gordon Conwell Seminary in Boston. Their story has not ended, although the abuse has. In an effort to contextualize their address, we held a telephone interview with Karen and Bruce to update and expand on their remarkable journey.

Bruce

I am a pastor. I come from a family of pastors—both of my parents are in ministry as well. I am a child of the manse. I've sung in the choirs, taught Sunday school, organized Alpha courses, done missionary work in Asia and Africa and I go Christmas caroling every year. So my credentials within the church of Jesus Christ are pretty good.

But, for the first ten years of my relationship with my wife Karen I was abusive. On April 21, 1993, I pushed Karen down on the bed and I wrapped my hands around her neck, and as I choked her, I asked her if she wanted to die. I was in a full-throttle rage. I stopped choking her but, as she tried to flee, I punched her in the abdomen and broke one of her ribs. As Karen collapsed in pain and fought to get her breath, I stood over her and ridiculed her for "being so dramatic."

Karen

After Bruce's rampage, I ended up in the emergency room. It was there that the reality of my situation began to sink in. I was seeking medical attention for an injury that my husband had inflicted on me. How could this have happened? How could a husband who I thought of as loving and kind do such a hurtful thing to me? What was going on?

The shocking realization that Bruce was abusive took as long as it did because nothing in our society and no one in my circle of friends, colleagues, and relatives had ever helped me to see abuse for what it was. In fact, the world I lived in largely denied the existence of domestic violence. And when domestic violence was talked about, the stereotypes I was given for abusive men and "battered women" simply did not fit my personal experience.

Bruce and I were both committed Christians. We had grown up in good, loving Christian homes. Bruce and I had known each other as kids and started to date when we were in youth group together. We were middle class, from nice suburban homes. We're both university graduates. In a nutshell, we didn't fit the stereotype of a couple who might struggle with abuse.

Bruce

I thought I believed in equality and respect, not domination and violence. But clearly my behaviour betrayed some different attitudes and beliefs. I didn't lose my temper, I took control whenever I felt like my power in the relationship was threatened. My actions were intended to control Karen and I did this in a whole variety of ways. I would abuse her intellectually by arguing with her relentlessly and taking every opportunity to make myself look superior. I would embarrass her in public. And in private, I would carefully choose the words I knew would hurt her most.

I did not see what I was doing as abusive; I just thought I had a problem with my temper. I did not think about how it was affecting Karen. I thought only about myself. Even after I had broken Karen's rib, I was ashamed of what I had done more because it went against what I believed about myself rather than because of its devastating impact on Karen.

Karen

It wasn't that I hadn't sought help for what I then thought of as "the problems of our relationship." I had spoken to a number of clergy and counselors. But in my search for understanding, nobody ever used the word *abuse* to describe what was happening in our marriage. Bruce and I also sought couples counseling for several months prior to the big event that resulted in Bruce breaking my rib. Our counselor—trained and certified—pinned the problems of our relationship on me.

- I was not assertive enough;
- I did not put up clear boundaries;
- I did not say no to Bruce.

I was, in fact, following our counselor's advice when Bruce attacked me on April 21. I did what my counselor said, I stood my ground, and Bruce ran over me like a truck.

Bruce

I was very good at hiding my abuse. But even when friends and family noticed behaviour that seemed inappropriate, nobody challenged me. In fact, in most cases, people wrote it off as perfectly normal. I was not held accountable.

Karen

When I was suffering in my marriage, I had no resources to draw on to make sense of my experience. No one had given me language for what I was experiencing. The truth is: the occasional physical assaults were not actually the most difficult to bear. The constant verbal attacks and emotional put-downs were what had the greatest negative impact. But sitting in the emergency room, trying to make up a lie to tell the doctor about my injuries, was a turning point for me. How had we gotten to this point? How could it be that I would need medical attention and yet be fearful about being honest about how I had been injured?

In the days following that event I insisted that we needed to talk to someone about what had happened. Together we decided to tell our two closest friends. The two of them were very clear with Bruce. They told him he had to get himself into a program for abusive men. They encouraged him to do that but also held him accountable over many months to make sure he was doing the work.

Bruce

By the extraordinary grace of God, I found an excellent program for abusive men. It was provided by a secular agency but God worked through it to save me and our marriage.

It was in a group where I learned so much. I wanted to be there because I knew finally that something was wrong. It wasn't just a case of me being a passionate person, which I still am. I learned in that group how pervasive my abuse of Karen was. I learned that my behavior showed a daily pattern of disrespect and controlling behaviour that included many different kinds of abuse—emotional, intellectual, financial, to name a few.

Now something you should know about me was that even back when I was abusive I was a fairly outspoken proponent of equality in marriage. I could talk the talk. But, over time, I discovered that, despite my claims of believing in egalitarian marriage, almost everything in our marriage was tainted by abuse. My actions betrayed my true beliefs about relationship. It was a belief system that left me feeling that I was superior to Karen and that my opinions, thoughts, and needs were more important than hers. I learned that my abusive behavior was not about losing control but was a choice to take control through abusive means.

Karen

Bruce entered the group for men, and he told me that there was a group for women. I was interested but afraid that I wouldn't qualify. After all, I wasn't black and blue all over. I didn't fit the stereotype of what I thought an "abused woman" was. But I did find my way into the group, carrying all my stereotypes with me. There I discovered women very much like me.

The group was one of the most positive experiences of my life. For two hours on a Monday night, the world was turned right-side up. When I was living with Bruce through the week, everything was kind of warped, and distorted, and confusing, and I would go on a Monday night at it was like 'oh, everything makes sense and the world was turned right-side up.' It was like hearing the gospel. I was told that the abuse was not my fault and that I was not alone.

Immediately, from the first night Bruce went to group, I saw a change in him. He brought home the handouts and he showed me the cycle of abuse and he said 'this is what I think is going on.' I saw willingness on his part to change. The physical abuse stopped immediately. But as I was in my group, and I realized all the different ways that he abused me, I realized that I really needed to have my standards very high. I was not going to stop at a half way point and sort of say "this is good enough, it's good enough that you are no longer screaming and yelling and throwing things and hitting me and I'll put up with these put-downs or more subtle kinds of abuse." I got very clear that I needed to be treated as an equal with respect and mutuality. And so I struggled for a couple of months. I did not know if our relationship was over or not. I did not know if Bruce was capable of the hard work I was beginning to realize he needed to do. But I hung in there watching for change.

I lived for about a year with one foot in the relationship and one foot out. I wondered if I was seeing enough change, if it was going far enough. I waited and watched and gathered the evidence as to whether the change was real and lasting or not.

At a certain point I had quite the "ah-ha" experience. I realized what I need in a lifelong partner was someone who not only won't be abusive to me, but who also would realize that I had experienced abuse; someone who would realize I needed time to heal. I needed someone who would give me space for that healing to happen—someone who would let me talk about any past abuses anytime so that I could process them and heal from them. I imagined that if I were to leave Bruce, what I would need in a new partner was a person who would have to have a great understanding about abuse and a willingness to let me heal. A person who would give me lots of time and space to heal. And I wondered, I really wondered, whether Bruce could go from being the perpetrator of the abuse to being a protector. Can a person go from one extreme to the other? Could Bruce go from being the person who wounded me to being the person who helped me heal?

I think it was at that point that I understood what level of change I needed to see from Bruce. And I am happy to say that that has been the case—he has been able to be the person whose protected and helped with healing. He has become my greatest cheerleader in the work that I do with women. But there was certainly a time when I thought, how could that be? How could someone go from being an instrument of hurt to an instrument of healing? It is only by the grace of God that something like this could happen.

Bruce

The key to that change process was accountability. I was held accountable, by Karen, by my counselors, by friends. Gradually we told our story to more and more people—friends and family to help widen that circle of accountability for me. It was a very terrifying process to tell people. But that circle of accountability ended the secrecy of the abuse, which undercut my ability to perpetrate it.

To describe what happened to me in terms of our faith, I needed to move through a process of confession, repentance, and restitution. It was these things that allowed for restoration and reconciliation.

First of all, I had to confess to all that I had done to Karen. I had to admit the full extent of the abuse—all of it. I had to acknowledge the terrible impact my behavior had had on Karen. Confession was not a one-time thing. It involved months of taking stock of all that I had done.

Second was repentance. I needed to repent—to turn around and go the other way. I changed not only my behaviour, but the attitudes behind my behaviour.

Finally, I sought ways of making restitution (or making amends) through acts of love—from the simplest act of doing more than my "share" of cleaning, to praising Karen in front of others rather than embarrassing or humiliating her. None of this can ever erase what I did, but there are ways I can help to restore our relationship, to rebuild trust and to heal the hurt in our lives.

Karen

For me, Bruce seeking to make amends has been important. It was an amazing switch to see Bruce go from the person who took every opportunity to tear me down to being the one who tirelessly encouraged my every endeavour. He continues to encourage and support all the ministry I do. That has been part of what making amends has been for me.

Another important part of making amends has been truth telling. We decided a number of years ago to tell everyone in our lives the truth about our relationship. That meant him telling the people of his congregation and me telling the people of my congregation. That was a hard thing to do.

Bruce

It was a hard thing to do, but we have found that the truth has set us free. For us, it was toxic to live with secrets. We have sought to live in the light and God has honoured that decision by using our story to reach out to other couples struggling with similar issues.

This is an ongoing journey for me. It feels to me like we have left behind the slavery in Egypt but we haven't yet arrived in the Promised Land. Thankfully, it's rare now, but occasionally I slip back into old patterns. But when I do, I address them with my counselor or my spiritual director. As we go along through this journey, that happens less and less.

This has been a long arduous process—one that I assume I will need to be aware of for the rest of my life. But the rewards of doing this work have been amazing. Karen and my counselors have taught me what it means to live in a loving, respectful, equal marriage. What a gift! I have been given a second chance. Ending the secrecy of my abuse, inviting accountability into my life, has not been a burden for me to bear but a gift. It allows me to live in the Kingdom of God—in the ways that God intends us to live together as husband and wife.

Karen

Our relationship is a story of death and resurrection. Our marriage was dead. Bruce broke our marriage covenant when he abused me and the trust and love that are essential in every marriage was eroded and distorted. But through a very long process, God brought about healing and restored our relationship.

The change in Bruce is incredible. He is a completely different person now. It is wonderful to live in a home where I am supported, encouraged, and cared for. Today, Bruce and I have a marriage that is characterized by mutuality, respect, and care.

Although our story of abuse is all too common, the resurrection of our marriage is not. Change is possible, but only when abusers are willing to take complete responsibility for their behaviour. Real change does not happen unless abusive men are willing to learn a whole new way of living in relationship. Sadly, most abusers simply do not care enough to do the hard work and to give up their power.

Telephone interview by Nancy Nason-Clark with Karen and Bruce McAndless-Davis

September 7, 2007

Nancy

Could you tell me a little about your experience of the first evening of attending a batterer intervention program?

Bruce

I walked into this room with a couch and some chairs set up in a circle. There were ten others looking as uncomfortable as I was feeling. There were two leaders; one was a woman, another male. We started with introductions. It was a relief to start talking about this, to finally start doing something about it.

After several sessions, I was feeling impatient, wanting to move forward more quickly. I asked a counselor—the male one—if I could see him privately to move forward faster. "This is not something you can control," he said to me. "You must work through it." He saw, as usual, that I wanted to stay in control. I didn't appreciate it at the time, but this was really helpful.

Nancy

Can you explain what happens in a batterer intervention group?

Bruce

There is a checking in on what happened during the last week. There is a teaching component, something like time out or sometimes looking at beliefs and behaviours. The program attempted to get underneath behaviour and get at attitudes. I talked the talk of egalitarianism but had some underlying beliefs that were not helpful.

Nancy

Karen, can you explain what you were hoping for as Bruce went that first night to group?

Karen

I am not sure I can really remember. But what he showed me, like the handouts, was very reassuring. I had hoped that it would lead to him doing some self-examination and change. I don't think I ever thought it would be immediate. What it did was help me to hang in there when I saw change, week by week. It was not like a honeymoon, immediate but temporary. Rather, it was gradual and ongoing change. I was really glad our friends were so clear with Bruce. He called the program and talked honestly on the phone with the worker.

Bruce

Karen was very anxious when I got home from that first meeting.

Nancy

Can you tell me a little about your present life?

Karen

A really important thing for me is that I feel like I am listened to now. In the past, it was like Bruce was trying to dodge any concern that I brought up. I can remember where I was standing the first day when Bruce finally listened to me.

Now I feel respected and my thoughts and contributions to the family unit are respected. Bruce is encouraging of me. He went from putting me down to building me up. Our book would never have been printed if he hadn't been so supportive. I remember the first night that I did a group [as the facilitator] and Bruce took the family to dinner and bought me flowers.

Nancy

Bruce, what were you thinking as Karen began preparing for a more public role with her story?

Bruce

I was a bit nervous, but seeing her blossom was wonderful. And seeing how much happier she was. It was a kind of redemption because this was a concrete way I could make amends—not tearing her down, but building her up. It was a redeeming activity. It felt wonderful to make restitution in these concrete ways. I was able to restore some of the brokenness I had created.

Nancy

How long have you been married?

Karen

Eighteen years. And we dated six years before that. So when I speak of the first ten years of Bruce's abuse, I am referring to six years while dating, followed by four years while married. The incident involving my rib was when we had been married for four years.

We had a renewal of our vows after one intense year of counseling. It probably was a bit premature, now that I look back on it, but it was more of us saying that we are on the journey. It involved a small gathering of friends and family.

We wanted to say the vows we had made were broken because of the abuse and now we are on the journey again with new vows. It took another year of counseling before we arrived at a more certain point.

Nancy

Listening to the both of you speak, it seems like it has taken so much hard work to bring your relationship to where it is now.

Bruce

It is. I explain it this way: it is like being in a strange land where you don't understand the language or the customs. It was often a bewildering or frustrating experience. I am still working on this. When I get anxious in my work, still there is a tendency to fall back to self centeredness and control. But I see it now. But I am not angry the way I used to be. I have let go of the control, of my expectation of being able to dictate to Karen.

It was not instantaneous, but developed over time. I am very nervous about those Christians who talk of the instant cure. Yes, God can heal us. But it takes us time to receive that healing.

Karen

This is a much better way to live.

Bruce

There were frustrations. There were times I caught glimpses of what a wonderful thing it was to see Karen as she really was. Glimpses of the kingdom. Quite lovely really.

Nancy

Have you had any contact with other couples who have a similar story to yours?

Karen

No, not really, sadly. We worked with one couple where there was some change.

Bruce

Sometimes people come up to us—like at the PASCH Conference—and say that their story is similar to ours. But we really don't know.

Nancy

Over the years, have you had any contact with the other men with whom you attended group?

Bruce

The first group I was a part of had ten or eleven. I had a little bit of contact. After I had completed two groups, that was the extent of my involvement with the intervention program, though I kept seeing the male counselor individually and Karen her female counselor. All four of us met for a while.

I took the initiative to try to keep things going. But it fizzled. Only two or three men were interested initially and then no one. None lived close by.

Karen

I had contact with the other women in my group for a while, two or three years. And I have had ongoing contact with the counselor, with whom I now work.

There is an enormous benefit to keeping the contact. Through our work now we have encouraged this. This can be done through email now, weekly contact.

Nancy

Is there any thing else about your present life that you might wish to pass along?

Karen

It has become a huge part of who we are now. The language and the thinking flows in and through our house now. A day doesn't go by that Bruce and I do not think about how we are going to be in relationship with one another.

Bruce

Yes, we are now integrated. The circle of accountability kept us growing. The people we spent time with knew what had happened. Sometimes there was silent accountability. Sometimes they asked us, because we had given them permission.

Karen

For us it was absolutely critical that we be open about the experience. The secret didn't work for me. I need to live openly and honestly. At a certain point in new friendships—say six months or so—it will come up. I needed to have a circle as Bruce was on the way to no longer being abusive. I needed to know how to deal with this crazy-making. It needs to be brought into the light to be examined.

Bruce

As an abusive man, I could not have done that on my own.

PART TWO

Raising our Voices

Assessing the Contemporary Scene

5

Offering Violent Men Help

Dan Schaefer

IT WAS BY ACCIDENT that I became interested in running groups for men arrested for domestic violence. While I would like to be seen as a visionary champion of this family injustice, my initial training experiences began when a batterer intervention specialist I hired announced plans to move to another state. Since brochures about our small program had already been mailed, I immediately began to accrue domestic violence training opportunities anywhere I could. But, given the fact that referrals continued to be sparse a year later, I began to pursue other areas of interest.

Then the phone rang. A bailiff calmly informed me that in seven days a local judge was going to start referring all his domestic violence cases to our practice. In one month, we were running three groups for twenty-five to thirty men every week, and it has not let up since.

Since that time, I have been struck with how different working with batterers is from my regular general practice as a psychologist. First, most counselors give new clients the benefit of the doubt. They assume that the client is generally telling the truth. With batterers, I rightly assume that they will lie to me in ways that will interfere with the primary purpose of coming to the group. Second, in my regular practice my client is usually the one sitting in front of me. While this may seem obvious, with batterers this is not the case. Although their victims never pay me, and I rarely meet them, the batterer's victim is my real client and is entitled to the highest degree of safety possible. Third, confidentiality, an ethical and legal hallmark in my profession, is hardly applicable in any recognizable way. It is as if the judge and the victim are sitting in the room during the domestic violence group, because it is the right of the victim and the court to call our office at any time and discuss with the facilitators the progress (or lack of progress) that the batterer is making.

This chapter is based on my work with these offenders, my interaction with court systems and police departments, my conversations with family victims, my experience with serving on a county fatality review team, my conversations with dedicated women working in shelters and on domestic violence hotlines, and life-changing encounters with fellow presenters at PASCH conferences. These experiences have changed the way I operate as a male, a Christian, a psychologist, a husband, a father, a friend, and a violence educator/trainer, in that order.

WISELY RESPONDING TO DOMESTIC VIOLENCE

All of us can do something about domestic violence. Statistics throughout the literature on intimate partner violence indicate the severity and pervasiveness of the problem. In fact, the chances are that you already know someone who has been the victim of family violence. If you don't, just wait awhile. You soon will. And when you do, how will you respond? What will you say to the victim? What will you say to the batterer? Will you say anything at all? Responses are often based on two extremes—both of which should be avoided. The first is to demonize the abuser, turning this complex man into a noun (usually a body part), complete with your favorite colorful expletive. Follow this response with ongoing leprous treatment where you sever your connection and conversation with him, you will have effectively excluded yourself from any chance of assisting this man. The other extreme is probably more likely—especially if you are a member of the clergy or involved in a faith community. This overly hopeful response involves minimizing both the offence and its effects. Forgiveness is quickly extended, with little or no accountability required from the batterer. Now I realize that the church is supposed to be a gracious place; a place where sinners are welcome, and where the sick can experience the touch of the Great Physician. However, there are times when it is necessary to be both wise as serpents and innocent as doves. So what might this 'innocent wisdom' look like from inside and outside the church? Let's take a look.

WISDOM IN ACTION FOR MENTAL HEALTH PROVIDERS

It is rare for most couples and individuals to present with domestic violence as their primary reason for entering therapy. It is more likely that it will be discovered along the way, if at all. Unless asked directly, most clients do not bring it up . At our practice, we now screen all adult clients who are married or dating for domestic violence. While there is evidence that just a simple written inquiry on intake forms can render evidence of violence, the combined use of written questionnaires and a clinical assessment tuned in to violence is considered best practice.

In the event that physical abuse in the marriage emerges (especially if the abuse is designed to control, includes emotional abuse, and causes fear and intimidation), the abuser should be referred to a batterers group before re-engaging in marital or family work. If during the course of family or marital therapy it is suspected that a victim is not reporting her partner's violence for fear of reprisals, a separate interview should be conducted to confirm any suspicions. If abuse is confirmed, the victim should be informed of a basic safety plan, and be put in touch with a local victim's advocate. Therapists should also have a working relationship with all batterer programs in the area, and refer the batterer accordingly. Generally speaking, once a man has been court-ordered into a batterers' group, only rare circumstances would dictate that marital work should precede graduation from the group.

I have been trained extensively in family therapy, and have seen the value of making systemic changes in a family. However, domestic violence is a presenting problem to which systemic thinking about the family cannot be routinely applied. Flu-like symptoms should be of concern to any emergency room physician, but if the patient is hemorrhaging profusely, common sense would dictate that the bleeding should be stopped first.

WISDOM IN ACTION FOR PASTORS

Research tells us two important things. First, domestic violence occurs both inside and outside the church at disturbing and identical incidence rates. (Ron Sider, in his book *The Scandal of the Evangelical Conscience*, brings this depressing statistic to light.) Second, people of faith living in violent families are more likely to approach clergy for help than all the other helping professions combined. If anything, this tells us what a key position those called into ministry occupy when attempting to assist people who are impacted by domestic violence.

There is no shortage of information about domestic violence written for clergy members. References in this book alone could keep one busy reading for weeks. Nancy Murphy's *God's Reconciling Love: A Pastor's Handbook on Domestic Violence,* as well as Nancy Nason-Clark's *The Battered Wife,* are excellent starting points. Pastors should know who in their community conducts groups for men who have acted abusively and take those facilitators out for lunch as an opportunity to learn more about their groups.

Opportunities to disseminate information about intimate partner violence within your faith community abound. Men's ministries are perfect places to begin conversations about intimate violence *before* it occurs. Sunday morning sermons, as well as Sunday school classes, should also be considered valuable venues. All church women's bathrooms should have information about local victim's services. Finally, your Board should have a specific written policy regarding how the church will respond to incidents of domestic violence.

I suspect that clergy and church communities generally err in the direction of optimism and togetherness (more grace than truth), and do not provide an 'iron sharpening iron' experience for these men. Clergy must address domestic violence with at least the same seriousness as they would address pedophilia, fraud, embezzlement, or any other illegal behavior.

WISDOM IN ACTION
FOR BATTERER INTERVENTION PROVIDERS

If you are leading batterers' groups you are a vital part of a growing legislative, criminal justice, and community response to a devastating and disgraceful problem. I hope that you are able to keep in touch with others who are running such programs for encouragement, because you aren't likely to get that much from the participants you serve. While this section is likely to be a review for many readers, three key elements are addressed here that stand out in our work with batterers: a) belief structures behind the violence; b) defensiveness; and, c) the use of media.

a) Belief Structures

I remember walking on a Chicago city beach a few summers ago with my family. This beach was 'sandless,' in that the city had poured slabs of concrete at an angle to the shoreline in an attempt to simulate the angle of sand beaches worldwide. As we walked in the middle of the 'beach' and watched the parade of skate boarders, in-line skaters and sunbathers coming our way, we repeatedly and unwittingly found ourselves getting our shoes wet. Unless we consciously picked a point on the horizon and aimed for it, gravity would take over and we would stray into the water. Batterers' groups are similar in that unless you are extremely watchful, the conversations will slowly descend into 'murky water:' comments about 'how women are,' references to the unfairness of the domestic violence laws or the courts, or humor that is seasoned with the very attitudes that allow them to behave illegally in their homes and still live with them-selves. While it is a beautiful thing for another batterer in the group to put a stop to this diversionary talk, it will usually fall on the facilitator to do that. Group leaders will get tired of this and will see eyes rolling on a regular basis. But you must not be satisfied with addressing only the violence committed. The hidden enemy is the host of troubling beliefs that give birth to this violence and fester unless routinely brought out into the light. These beliefs are the very elements that allow these men to behave the way they do without any (or enough) guilt. This allows batterers to put a spin on their stories (if only toward themselves) that serves as permission to continue battering.

"Unless we address the belief system that fuels the abusive behavior we hear about in groups and from partners, we are encouraging merely a cosmetic change" (Adams, 2000, p. 8). These 'supporting' beliefs are as easy to hide as healthy beliefs are to fake. Thus a posture of vigilance is central to any program success.

We often hear batterers who have accompanying mental health or substance abuse problems attempt to blame their violence on their diag-nosis or addiction. While these problems often do accompany intimate violence, particularly in the case of substance abuse, they are only an indi-cation that another problem requires attention in addition to the violence. How else would you explain that fact that there are countless substance abusers all over the country who routinely anaesthetize themselves with alcohol or drugs and who never physically abuse their partners?

b) Defensiveness

Early in Genesis, we learn that to be human is to hide and to blame. However, men in intervention groups have perfected this very human tendency to an art form. Earlier in our development as a program, we were highly confrontational and even had time lines delineated as to when our participants would start telling the truth. We have since found it more effective to establish baseline patterns of blaming, minimizing, and denial before confronting men with their actual (and blessed) police report; a report that batterers usually aren't aware that we have in our possession. A program requirement of every participant is that they introduce themselves every week and describe the behavior that got them arrested. This means that we have twenty-four opportunities to inductively divide their stories into thinner and thinner slices with patient curiosity. Since there is no rush, most of the time (even without the police reports) we can get the full story with respect and persistence. Sometimes it feels 'Columbo-like,' weekly stumbling through the details in our rumpled raincoats to get to the truth.

A second year medical student was in our group years ago. Having finally read the police report, and equipped with numerous details that he had managed to 'overlook,' I spent well over an hour asking about the details of the incident. There were a number of long silences. I barely raised my voice. I never told him that he was minimizing or denying. I simply stuck with the details, somewhat like an archeologist patiently uncovering important details. At one point another group member asked me to "ease up." "What for?" I calmly retorted, and continued. The result was that he finally admitted to key elements that changed the fundamentals of his story (like the marks he left on her throat with his hands). When he graduated seven weeks later I asked him what stood out as being the most helpful parts of the program. He replied (with a wry smile on his face), "The day you grilled me for the whole meeting."

c) Media Clips

The last element is the use of media. We continue to use video clips purchased years ago from the Domestic Abuse Intervention Project which portray scenes from abusive relationships. We also now include scenes from major movie studios that capture central aspects of domestic abuse. For example, *An Unfinished Life* wonderfully depicts a pathetic and dangerously jealous partner, as does *Sleeping with the Enemy*. These scenes generate discussions around questions such as: What exactly is driving these men? What problems do they have and whose responsibility is it to take care of those problems? How would you advise your sister (assuming you like your sister) if she was married or dating a man like that? Do you know anyone like that? Are there ways in which you are like that?

Atticus Finch in *To Kill a Mockingbird* is spit upon (in the face) by a man who is half his size, as Atticus' son watches. After a long tense pause, Finch walks around the little man, gets into his car, and drives away. Questions that follow include: Could you have walked away if you were Atticus Finch? Should he have walked away? Could Atticus have knocked that pencil-necked geek out? Was Atticus afraid? Was his behavior a brand of masculinity that men today ought to strive to emulate? Interestingly, most men in our groups express doubt that they could have walked away in a situation like that, yet readily admit that Atticus was not afraid, and consider his walking away extremely masculine.

We have used clips from *Bonfire of the Vanities* and *Tortilla Soup* depicting reactive arguments between intimate partners and look for ways to diffuse those arguments. Here we confront the absurdity of the phrase, "She pushed my buttons," and emphasize the ever-present element of choice to act decently and nonviolently even if a partner is provocative or unreasonable. We have also used a scene from *Chocolat* in which an abusive husband, separated from his wife, appears at her doorstep with flowers to ask for her forgiveness and for her to move back home. The discussion that follows includes the difference between apology and genuine change, and if reconciliation is possible without the latter. The men in our groups who initially found the wife in that scene too harsh changed their minds a bit when in the next scene the supposedly 'changed' man returns, drunk and swearing, and breaks into her house to assault her.

A surprisingly provocative clip comes from *Monsters Inc.* The monster, Sully, is on a studio set and training other monsters to be scary. A little girl whom he befriends has not seen this side of Sully and becomes terrified during the training. She then hides from him for the first time in their relationship. Sully is hurt but astonished that she is afraid, until he sees himself in the video monitors that have freeze-framed his fangs, claws, and rage. It is only then that he understands her terror and is heartbroken. This scene is an excellent tool to circumvent defensiveness and connect detecting one's own flaws and blind spots to a brand of masculinity that is usually quite foreign to most batterers.

Finally, we use a clip from *What's Love Got to Do With It?* in which the actor playing Ike Turner physically assaults Tina Turner in front of their kids. The acting, by the children in particular, is superb and deeply chilling with respect to the effect family violence has on children.

These media moments allow the men we work with to first view a troubling behavior as 'out there.' They can name it, discuss the behavior's effects on others, ponder what drives the behavior, and even make fun of it. However, the next step requires pure courage—when a participant starts to ask himself, "In what ways am I like that guy?" If we are successful in creating a respectful, non-shaming environment where masculinity is redefined in part as flaw identification and remediation, media selections such as the ones above appear to prove helpful in getting this difficult journey off the ground.

WISDOM IN ACTION FOR MEN OF FAITH

Someday a fellow believer will come to you and confess that he has been physically abusive to his wife or girlfriend. Should that happen, it would be obvious that he trusts you and knows that you are not likely to fire him as a friend for his failure. Most offenders, however, do not confess what they have done to anyone unless they get caught or are arrested. Regardless, however flattered you may be from being sought out, you will miss the only opportunity you have to intervene if his confession to you is the end (and not the beginning) of a long conversation between you two. While there are many scriptures that speak to this situation, you would do well to consider not only the ones that speak to compassion, grace and understanding but also ones that involve more steel, such as "speaking the truth in love" (Eph. 4:25) or "faithful are the wounds of a friend" (Prov. 27:6). Here is an example of what this faithfulness might sound like:

> Frank, I am impressed that you have been so honest with me about hitting your wife again last night. Most men do not have the courage to admit this kind of behavior. I will make sure that this conversation stays between you and me as long as you start to work on this problem. Whether or realize it or not, you have broken the law. Had 911 been called that night, the police would have showed up and interviewed you, your wife, and your children separately. Then they would have arrested you for domestic violence, slapped

handcuffs on you in front of those beautiful kids of yours, and taken you away to jail. Then you would have been sent to a group program for six months to help you with your abusiveness. If you hurt her again during or after the program, you would then be subject to felony charges. That may sound harsh, but if you did the same thing to a stranger on the street, you would be arrested for assault without hesitation. Many men who engage in this kind of intimate violence with their wife or girlfriend do it again in the future. I don't want you to be one of them. I know at this moment that the thought of hitting your wife again seems the most unlikely event in your mind. The truth is, it is now MORE likely that it will happen again. Because of this, I am going to insist that you get some help. Here are some numbers to call.

Your very faith demands that you persist in ensuring the safety of your friend's family by insisting he start and complete a batterers' group. To do nothing begins to approach the cowardice of your violent friend. Love him into action that will help him and extend safety to his family. Go to the pastor together. Pray with some trusted brothers. Begin accountability.

Finally, if you yourself have been repeatedly violent with a girlfriend or wife, your best hope of never crossing that line again is to tell someone, and eventually give that person the right to ask you and your partner about any offences in the future. Find a group that specializes in domestic violence and begin attending regularly. There is hope, all of which is lost through secrecy.

CONCLUSION

We owe a great debt to profeminist thinking and action at the community, curriculum, and legislative level. They had the vision to conceptualize the problem of family violence in a way that has changed the way we as a nation think about battering. Now it is time for these innovators to include the mental health profession at the treatment and research levels in their coordinated community response. Data about the history, attachments, and experiences of the batterer, while potentially available to make excuses for unacceptable behavior by the uninformed, will aid in developing more effective treatment strategies for domestic abuse. To not consider all variables involved in violent behavior is bad science in my view, and a disservice to victims of domestic violence.

I remain hopeful about bringing an end to domestic violence. When we get it right as a nation, victims of family violence will be instinctively viewed and treated as those involved in an automobile accident–as people in need of urgent care. Bystanders to domestic violence, or its more subtle manipulative behaviors, would become at least as offended (and willing to intervene) as non-smokers are now becoming when someone lights up in a smoke-free environment. Prevention efforts will swell. Schools, faith communities, and non-profit organizations working with children will be mentoring their young men with common language and clarity about intimate violence. Thankfully, things are changing, but it is going to take an ongoing persistence at the legislative, community, research, and treatment levels to keep the momentum going. May God help us all to move into the future with courage and compassion.

REFERENCES

Adams, David. "Emerge: Counseling & Education to Stop Domestic Violence." Worcester, MA, 2000.

Aldarondo, E., and M.A. Straus. "Screening for Physical Violence in Couple Therapy—Methodological, Practical, and Ethical Considerations." *Family Process* 33, no. 4 (1994): 425–39.

Bograd, M. "Strengthening Domestic Violence Theories: Intersections of Race, Class, Sexual Orientation, and Gender." *Journal of Marital and Family Therapy* 25, no. 3 (1999): 275–89.

Ehrensaft, Miriam K., Patricia Cohen, Jocelyn Brown, Elizabeth Smailes, Henian Chen, and Jeffrey G. Johnson. "Intergenerational Transmission of Partner Violence: A 20-Year Prospective Study." *Journal of Counseling and Clinical Psychology* 71, no. 4 (2003): 741–53.

Murphy, Nancy. *God's Reconciling Love: A Pastor's Handbook on Domestic Violence.* Seattle: FaithTrust Institute, 2003.

Nason-Clark, Nancy. The Battered Wife: How Christians Confront Family Violence. Louisville, KY: Westminster John Knox Press, 1997.

Sider, Ronald J. *The Scandal of the Evangelical Conscience: Why Are Christians Living Just Like the Rest of the World?* Grand Rapids: Baker Books, 2005.

6

Forgiveness and the Christian Community

Martha Thorson

FAITH FOR CHRISTIANS IS rooted in being forgiven and forgiving others. It is the heart of the gospel; it is the heart of grace. Receiving and giving forgiveness can bring freedom, yet being told to forgive can become a prison that locks Christians in situations where they are repeatedly pummeled with words, fists, feet, finances, and other horrors we do not want to hear about. Women and children have died because they were sent home from church to forgive their abusers. Others walk away from church because they fear forgiving will open them to revictimization.

I am haunted by a vivid memory from a women's retreat I led many years ago. Throughout the weekend we were creating prayer journals based on the Lord's Prayer. Learning this exercise had been helpful to me and I was excited to share the practice. It certainly seemed safe. I know some women have had difficult childhoods so I worked hard on the section "forgive us our debts as we forgive our debtors." As I began that talk, a fragile young woman stood at the back, obscured from general view. She simply made eye contact with me and shook her head. I scrambled to sound deep, profound, and thoughtful. I tried to convey that this would be no simplistic speech. She shook her head and then she was gone. I never saw her again, but her memory follows me wherever I go. I realized when we talk about forgiveness, often we are talking to the wrong people. The Lord's Prayer and the God's grace are given for all believers, but we will see later how interpretations of other texts on forgiveness have been misdirected.

Abuse victims who stay in the church often struggle with their consciences. Some of their abusers will say they are sorry but keep on abusing; other abusers just act like they never did anything wrong in the first place. Virtually all abusers blame their actions on the victim, leaving the

71

victims uncertain whether they themselves are forgiven or whether they have forgiven enough. They struggle to clear their hearts and minds, and forgiveness becomes a very sensitive subject.

Some counselors encourage their clients not to forgive their abusers, while many pastors say forgiveness is the first and final response. Misuse and misunderstanding have made forgiveness the 'F-word' for more believers than we realize. Tremendous healing is possible through God's grace, but forgiveness cannot be forced.

As God in Christ was creating the community of believers to be the church family, God planned ahead for ways to deal with problems that inevitably come. When we are talking out problems, God does not expect things necessarily to be solved quickly and easily, so there is allowance made for multiple opportunities to talk things out again and again as necessary. God knows there will need to be mediation, negotiations, and many occasions for getting a fresh start. (Matt. 18:15–22)

Listening is key to the successful implementation of this plan for solving problems; it is only when people will not listen that the process moves to the next step.

> If a brother or sister sins, go and point out the fault, just between the two of you. If they listen to you, you have won them over. But if they will not listen, take one or two others along, so that 'every matter may be established by the testimony of two or three witnesses.' If they still refuse to listen, tell it to the church; and if they refuse to listen even to the church, treat them as you would a pagan or a tax collector. (Matt. 18:15–17, TNIV)

Jesus repeats the importance of listening as the decisive factor if negotiations need to gradually be made more public.

Listening involves paying attention to the person talking to you, watching their body language, clarifying what the other person means, and caring enough to work towards resolution. When one person confronts the other, a rebuttal often ensues. As two people view the same problem from differing perspectives, each may feel hurt, vulnerable and wronged. The listening process involves both sides.

If Christians can hear each other out, respectfully and responsively, there is a process through which God expects that the Holy Spirit will, over time, help us conform to the image of Christ. This is good news. God is optimistic about how we, and the people with whom we work, will turn out. We may get discouraged, but God looks at us and sees how the very process of working with each other is shaping our character in ways that are more important than if we were just gliding along without a hitch.

In Matthew 18:23–35, the role of the believing community is to report abuse and hold the perpetrator accountable. In abusive situations when Christians work the process of confrontation, safety is a paramount concern. If we attempt the confronting, listening, talking it out approach, safety is jeopardized. The abuser is likely to take advantage of the process, listening to gain information to use against the victim later. In Matthew 18:23–35, there is no model to forgive the abuser, or to tell the victim to forgive the abuser, because none of those things are safe. Forgiveness is to occur only after the abuser has changed both attitude and conduct. When a powerful brother grabs another by the throat, literally or figuratively, the church has often said to the one under attack, "You'll just have to forgive him."

There is no excuse for domestic violence. God has held the principle of accountability since Cain killed Abel and God held him accountable saying, "Listen! Your brother's blood is crying out to me from the ground." (Gen. 4:10b, NRSV)

Elsie, a pastor's wife, explains that forgiveness can only come when the violence, verbal and emotional as well as physical, has stopped. She says her husband used to beat her every Saturday night because he did not think she would call the police. If he were in jail on a Sunday morning, the congregation would find out, he would lose his job, and Elsie was financially dependent on his salary. His logic worked until she began to realize that she was being strangled financially as well as physically; then, by the power of the Holy Spirit, she began to take stock of her own resources.

This pastor is described as torturing his wife by calling her a thief, a liar, a slut, a cheat, a sinner, and any other demeaning thing he knew she would never want to be called. He knew her well enough to exploit her. Everything that mattered to Elsie was under attack, from her character to her dog. If she ever shared a personal thought during a weak moment, thinking one should be able to share with a spouse, it would be turned and twisted into something horribly ugly and dirty. Through constant verbal battering, her inner being began to break down and she did not know the truth of her own value anymore. One night she reports that he literally dumped dirt on her head and said she deserved it. She did not know what she had ever done to deserve this kind of treatment. Hurt fueled hatred in her heart and he did not repent.

Another night, as her husband smashed her nose into the carpet, she thought she would die. She prayed what she thought was her final prayer, relinquishing her soul to Jesus, and then miraculously he released her. Her prayers began to change. Instead of praying for her abuser, she began to pray for herself, asking God what she should do.

The first step was for Elsie to find her own church; God provided that through a part-time church staff position. Encouraged, she found full-time work at a different church as well. The financial strangle-hold began to loosen, but her husband moved to tighten the noose. He began to accrue debt intentionally. Because they were married, she would be held liable for his debts. She could not earn enough to pay a lawyer and pay off his debt. Besides, she didn't want a divorce; she just wanted the violence to stop.

Feeling obligated to keep forgiving seemed to mean not being able to implement any consequences. She felt trapped, but God revealed a way out. She found another job that appeared to be voluntary but which did pay a stipend. This allowed her to meet supportive friends while secretly saving money until she could get away.

Elsie reported her abuser to the denominational authorities, but in this case nothing was done. He simply moved to lead a different congregation. She refused to take his calls and told him only to communicate with her through a lawyer. One day he sought her out at work, intending to harass her. To his surprise and embarrassment, four men came to completely surround Elsie, telling him to leave the premises and never return.

Although her denominational authorities did not provide protection, Christian friends did, and the Holy Spirit equipped her to take necessary action, advocating for herself. That in itself is difficult for many Christians. We "know that the Lord secures justice for the poor and upholds the cause of the needy." (Ps. 140:12, NIV)

David Augsberger suggests new language to use if an offender repents and asks to be forgiven. In his 'Forgiveness Decision Tree'[1] he proposes asking whether the offender is responsible or not. If someone is not responsible, they are exonerated, not forgiven. If the offender is deemed responsible, but begins changing behavior, Augsberger asks whether they are seeking release from consequences or readmission into relationship. The wounded person then has the power to decide the advisability of allowing the offender to in some way "return to moral community," renewing, resuming, recreating, or

---

1. Augsberger, Helping People Forgive, 1966.

renegotiating relationships (Augsberger, 18). Remorse is often feigned to manipulate and regain access to the victim. Discernment and caution are advisable, but when safety is established and the victim becomes a survivor, she may choose to exercise her new power with grace.

Sharon teaches us how this can all come together. She revealed that she had been sexually molested by her mother and father and brothers throughout her childhood. This trauma affected her ability to make safe decisions as she grew older and she was further traumatized by abusive partners. Finally she was able to break free. After years of therapy and living in safety, she was finally able to return to church. At last her abusers did not have power over her. Though they had not repented, at least the abuse had ended.

Sharon was not told she needed to forgive her abusers, but as she received God's grace for herself, she wanted to be able to give it to others. She heard Scripture say, "Be kind and compassionate to one another, forgiving each other, just as in Christ God forgave you." (Eph. 4:32, NIV). She became able to act in kind and compassionate ways toward her abusers, even when she felt the hardness in her heart toward them. As the congregation loved Sharon unconditionally, she began to realize that the hardness was a protection to keep her from getting hurt anymore. No one tried to take it away, but allowed her to keep it as long as she needed it. Everyone knew they had their own people to forgive before they could begin to suggest that others, particularly Sharon, should forgive.

One day during worship Sharon slipped out of the sanctuary, fleeing to the bathroom in tears. After the service, women who came through just gave her a hug. They didn't ask any questions. Eventually she was able to share her experience. God had come to her in the worship and simply overwhelmed her with so much love that the protective barriers went down. No one was even talking about abuse or forgiveness, but in the safe congregation she had finally been ready to receive God's love that was greater than all her pain. At first it was frightening. She didn't want to forgive her abusers, but she realized she wasn't vulnerable anymore. She was safe, physically, emotionally, and spiritually.

Her abusers owed her years of life that could not be reclaimed. It was a debt too great to be repaid; it could only be released. Being filled to over-flowing with the love of God and the power of the Holy Spirit made forgiveness possible.

Jesus said, "Receive the Holy Spirit. If you forgive anyone his sins, they are forgiven; if you do not forgive them, they are not forgiven." (John

20:22–23, NIV) Through the Holy Spirit survivors can find the safety, healing, and power they seek to make spiritual progress. When abusers no longer have power over them, then the survivors can discover the power within themselves to forgive. Through prayer we cooperate with God, asking God to get involved in our lives. Through the Holy Spirit we mend our souls. The Christian community needs to create a safe atmosphere in which survivors can articulate their pain, confronting Christian leaders for our negligence.

As I became increasingly aware of abuse in the Christian community, it began to be reflected in my public as well as private prayers and Bible expositions. Within my tradition, each Sunday there is time for confession of sin followed by an assurance of pardon. This weekly reassurance was important for my own spiritual growth by relieving my anxiety, convincing me of God's constant mercy and unconditional love. With years of experience, however, as I looked out over congregations and saw people sitting there next to their abusers, I began to hesitate as I delivered the assurance of pardon.

Abuse is certainly forgive-able, but I saw the victims repeatedly forgiving the abusers while the abusers dealt harsh penalties for perceived sins, that often were no sins at all. An abuser's remorse was rare, and the genuine, lasting change of repentance invisible. I realized often I was handing out cheap grace, blessing remorse that was not bearing the fruit of repentance. God's grace is unconditional for abusers and victims alike, but the violence must stop. Confession must be linked with the necessary process of purifying sanctification.[2] The purification process often works out as the community prays, reports, and together refuses to tolerate abuse.

---

2. Some Assurances of Pardon Linking Repentance, Sanctification and Forgiveness: The mercy of the Lord is from everlasting to everlasting. I declare to you in the name of Jesus Christ, you are forgiven. May the God of mercy, who forgives you all your sins, strengthen you in all goodness, and by the power of the Holy Spirit keep you in eternal life. Amen.

Hear the good news! If we have died with Christ, we believe that we shall also live with him. So you also must consider yourselves dead to sin and alive to God in Christ Jesus. Friends, believe the good news. In Jesus Christ, we are forgiven.

The God, who judges people with righteousness, defends the cause of the poor, gives deliverance to the needy and cleanses us from sin, for if we turn from our sins, God is faithful and just and will forgive our sins and cleanse us from all unrighteousness.

Hear the good news! Who is in a position to condemn? Only Christ, and Christ died for us, Christ rose for us, Christ reigns in power for us, Christ prays for us. Anyone who lives in Christ becomes a new creation. Live in Christ, for when the old life has gone, a new life has begun. Friends, believe the gospel.

As a community we must verbalize the insidious reality of domestic violence that pervades every culture and every economic level. It will take courage to look at the cumulative effect of centuries of neglect in this area, considering additional ways Biblical interpretation, theology, and church practice have contributed to domestic violence

7

I Am Not Violent

Men's Experience in Group

Barbara Fisher-Townsend
Nancy Nason-Clark
Lanette Ruff
Nancy Murphy

BATTERER INTERVENTION PROGRAMS ARE a key component in the fight to end domestic violence. This is true for both secular and faith-based programs. While all abused women want the violence to end, religious women may hold out more hope for the restoration of the relationship. This is why it is so important to understand the dynamics operating in faith-based batterer intervention programs. In our chapter, we discuss the first-ever exploration of a faith-based program for men who have acted abusively. We ask such questions as: are men who enroll in a faith-based program different in terms of personal characteristics than those in a community-based program? How do men who complete the fifty-two week intervention differ from those who drop out or are terminated? What are some of the central features in the journey of abusive men to develop empathy, take responsibility, and become accountable for their abusive pasts? This innovative study is a partnership between academic researchers and one such faith-based agency, equally committed to ending violence in families of faith.

There has been a plethora of research projects examining the issue of domestic violence from various perspectives. Studies investigating batterers' intervention or treatment programs have included the examination of topics such as standards (Rosenbaum and Leisring 2001; Tolman 2001); the characteristics of men most amenable to change and typologies of batterers (Hamberger, Lohr et al. 1996; Nason-Clark, Murphy et al. 2003; Cavanaugh and Gelles 2005), accountability and change (Bennett and Williams 2002); cultural and gender specific programming (Carney and Buttell 2004; Gondolf 2004); theoretical underpinnings of various program curricula (Healey, Smith et al. 1998; Trimble 2000; Jackson, Forde et al. 2003); as well as recidivism and retention planning (Daly and Pelowski 2000; Scott 2004).

Asking 'when you put faith into the mix what difference does it make?' seeks to incorporate a key contextual element in many peoples' lives that has been absent in previous research. There is no doubt that religion does play an important part in the lives of a majority of North Americans; it is the foundation for the context of their daily living. "Religion is embedded in social norms, in cultural values and understandings, and in arrangements of resources and power that fundamentally shape it and cause it to be the way it is" (Wuthnow 2004:18). According to Warner (1993) religion serves as a fundamental category of identity and association and is capable of grounding both solidarities and identities.

Clearly, the realm of the spiritual lies at the heart of many people's daily living experiences. Another part of the context of daily living for millions of women is, unfortunately, the reality of domestic abuse[1]. Recent Canadian figures indicate that six hundred and fifty-three thousand Canadian women reported being a victim of spousal violence in five years between 1999 and 2004, with twenty-six percent of these women being assaulted more than ten times (Statistics Canada 2006). In the United States, the Centers for Disease Control and Prevention report that nearly 5.3 million incidents of interpersonal violence occur each year among United States women ages eighteen and older, resulting in nearly two million injuries[2] and thirteen hundred deaths nationwide every year (NCIPC

1. The term domestic violence is all-encompassing to denote violence against various parties within a household. Wife abuse is also known as wife assault, battering, domestic violence, family violence, spouse/partner violence and intimate partner violence. These terms are often used interchangeably but whatever term is used women are indeed subject to many forms of violence and thus, for many, their lives rest on a "continuum of unsafety" (Stanko 1990).

2. Battering injuries are reportedly the cause of more women requiring treatment in emergency rooms than muggings, rapes and traffic accidents combined, and are the lead-

2005). On the face of it, it appears contradictory that religion and family violence would be present within the same context. But they are.

In relation to batterers, there have been numerous non-faith-oriented research programs. For example, researchers have sought to examine and compare program outcomes specifically related to secular batterer intervention programs, others have looked at issues of recidivism and drop-out and still others have explored the larger picture of whether family violence can be eradicated. While new approaches and new problems are being examined and considered, the majority of the research has centered on the criminal justice system, the secular therapeutic community and women's rights agendas. Those who do write about the inclusion of faith in the arena of family violence tend to find that it contributes to the problem of abuse. But, as Weaver, Pargament, Flannelly and Oppenheimer (2006) argue, studies that incorporate spirituality may inject new vitality into research and bring new perspectives into the field.

THE CRIMINAL JUSTICE RESPONSE TO DOMESTIC VIOLENCE

Browne (1993) cites a report of the National Clearinghouse for the Defence of Battered Women, which states that domestic violence calls constitute the most prevalent type of call received by the police in the United States. Kantor and Straus (1990) estimate that as few as seven percent to fourteen percent of intimate partner assaults are reported to the police yet Sherman (1992) estimates that police respond to crimes of intimate partner abuse up to eight million times per year in the United States. The enormity of this situation has required various strategies of intervention by the criminal justice system, involving the police, the prosecutors and their supportive infrastructure, the judicial system, and legislative bodies (Loue, 2001). Their responses include mandatory arrest, protection orders, offender treatment programs, liaison with social services agencies, and the prosecution and incarceration of offenders.

Of importance in this paper is the response of the criminal justice system in mandating attendance at therapeutic treatment programs for men who have been charged with and/or convicted of wife abuse—formally referred to as a particular level of assault (Gondolf 2002; Sherman 1992).

---

ing cause of injury to women between 15–44 (United States Senate Judiciary Committee 1992).

This requirement is often a condition of probation, but also may be implemented as a "restorative justice" measure. Bennett and Williams (2002) argue that batterer intervention programs are "but a link in the chain" of the many resources required to end domestic violence, and for the men in this research that link was mandated through the criminal justice system. Like mandatory arrest, however, there is little agreement on the effectiveness of such programs (Daly and Pelowski 2000; Tolman and Edleson 1995). Researchers have identified numerous variables which contribute to attrition and/or recidivism, including demographic characteristics, attitudinal and personal variables, and levels of motivation (Gondolf 2000; deHart et al 1999). Yet, prediction of program effectiveness, including completion rates and subsequent non-violence, remains difficult (Scott and Wolfe 2000; Hanson and Wallace-Capretta 2000; Edleson 1995). While there are various initiatives within the criminal justice system to deal with the issue of wife abuse, including mandatory arrest, diversion to batterer intervention programs, and for some, prison sentences, the effectiveness of these responses remains in doubt. Regardless of the consequences, many men continue to minimize, deny, and/or justify their behavior.

METHODOLOGY

The research initiative upon which this paper is based sought to document in a comprehensive fashion, through the use of closed agency case files, the nature and extent of change in the lives of men who have graduated from a batterers program in the northwest United States.[3] The contents of closed files of men (n=1135) who have been involved in the batterers intervention program since its inception were examined. The contents of the closed case files include the client face sheet, the intake form, the letter of responsibility, the letter of empathy, the graduation checklist and any police or medical reports provided by third parties involved in the case (e.g. probation reports, etc.) Identifying information such as the full names of all clients, victim's names, as well as addresses and telephone numbers, were blackened out before files were made available for research use. Each file was given an identifying number for research purposes by the agency and

3. Our research has not investigated whether or not faith-based batterer intervention programs are more or less successful than their community-based counterparts in reducing domestic violence. Though such questions are imperative, they require a different methodology (longitudinal in nature) and significant funding over an expansive period of time.

only the agency has access to any link between the full name on the case file and the research ID number. The protection of full client confidentiality has been assured throughout the project.

The program under study is offered by a learning and counselling center that has been state-certified to treat perpetrators of domestic violence and to receive court-mandated referrals. It is a faith-based organization. According to the Executive Director, the mission of this agency is "to assist individuals and families in finding hope and healing when facing the pain of domestic violence and related issues." Their primary concerns, both legally and ethically, are victim safety and eliminating violence in the home. Thus demanding standards are set for their staff of between fifteen and twenty, requiring extensive education and experience qualifying them to work in the field of domestic violence.

A requirement for participation in an intervention group is that the applicant acknowledges a need to become accountable for his behavior. He must agree to stop all forms of controlling behavior; not to blame anyone else, including victims, for his choice of actions; to be concerned with victim safety and, the well-being of others; and to learn to care for himself. The intervention process, which makes this accountability agreement possible, consists of a two-hour intake assessment and review of all courts orders and contact issues with the victim(s) to determine the suitability of the program. An eight-hour introduction class, divided into two four-hour presentations, follows that intake. Completion of the introduction class is a prerogative for entrance into a group of up to ten clients who meet together weekly for a minimum of twenty-six weeks. During these groups the facilitator engages the men in required activities and interactions. Those men who complete the twenty-six weeks enter into a monitoring phase wherein they meet individually with a counselor once a month for six consecutive months. The last of those six meetings is an exit interview to summarize treatment and offer post-treatment recommendations. Successful completion of the program requires positive feedback from the victim, the group participants and the facilitator.

WHO ARE THE MEN
WHO COME TO GROUP INTERVENTION?[4]

There are differences between men who have attended secular programs investigated by Gondolf (2002) and the faith-based program under study (Nason-Clark, Murphy, Fisher-Townsend and Ruff, 2003):

Marital Status

- Almost half of the men in the faith-based program were married; one in five was single; one in five was separated; and the remaining one in ten was divorced.

- *More than half of the men in the Gondolf study were not married when they entered their intervention programs.*

- *Comparison*: Men in the faith-based program were more likely to be married, and less likely to be single, separated, or divorced, as compared to men in programs studied by Gondolf.

Age

- Men in the faith-based program ranged in age from fifteen to seventy-six, with a median age of 35.46 years. More than one in three of the men were aged forty or over; with just over one in ten being twenty-five years of age or less.

- *Almost half of the men in the Gondolf study were aged twenty-six to thirty-five. More than one in five had not yet reached their twenty-sixth birthday.*

- *Comparison*: Men in the faith-based program were older than men in other intervention programs.

Ethnicity

- Eight out of ten men in the faith-based program were white, one in ten was African American and the remainder were Asian, Hispanic, Filipino or of other ancestry.

---

4. Adapted from Nason-Clark et al. "An Overview of the Characteristics of the Clients at a Faith-Based Batterers' Intervention Program" *Journal of Religion and Abuse* 5(4) 2003:51–71.

- *Less than half (forty-five percent) of the men in the Gondolf study were white, one in three were African American, one in five were Hispanic, with the remainder of other ethnic origins.*

- *Comparison*: Men in the faith-based program were more likely to be white and much less likely to be African American or Hispanic than men in other intervention programs.

Education

- One in seven men in the faith-based program had eleven years or less formal schooling; one in three had twelve years; while over half had completed some post-secondary education; just under one in four of the men had a minimum of sixteen years of formal education.

- *Slightly more than one in three men had completed some post-secondary schooling in the Gondolf study.*

- *Comparison*: Men in the faith-based program were more likely to have completed some years of post-secondary education or to have attained a university or graduate degree.

Current Employment

- Almost nine of ten men in the faith-based program were currently employed; forty-five percent were white-collar workers.

- *In the Gondolf study, fewer than two in every three men were employed full-time; two-thirds of these men were blue-collar workers.*

- *Comparison*: Men in the faith-based program were more likely to be employed and less likely to be blue-collar workers.

Alcohol Abuse

- Over half of the men in the faith-based program reported alcohol abuse or severe problems related to alcohol use.

- *In the Gondolf study, just under one in three men reported severe behavioral problems associated with their drinking, and more than half showed alcoholic tendencies as measured by the Michigan Alcoholism Screening Test (MAST).*

- *Comparison*: There were no differences between groups in terms of the level of alcohol abuse.

Violence in Family of Origin

- Over half of the men in the current program reported the presence of violence in their family of origin; over half witnessed abuse between their parents or guardians, and two in five men were childhood victims of violence in the home.

- *In the Gondolf study, one in three men reported the presence of violence in their childhood home, and one in four indicated that the violence in their home was directed toward them.*

- *Comparison*: Men in the faith-based program were more likely to have witnessed or experienced violence in their childhood home.

Criminal History

- Over half of the men in the faith-based program had been incarcerated for a criminal offence.

- *In the Gondolf study, more than half of the men had been arrested for offences other than domestic violence.*

- *Comparison*: Men in the faith-based program were similar to men in other programs in terms of whether or not they had ever been arrested or incarcerated for a criminal act.

There were important differences related to many of the contextual characteristics explored in these two research projects. Interestingly, similarities between the two groups of men were most pronounced when examining alcohol abuse and criminal history.

WHO COMPLETES THE PROGRAM?[5]

As we can see, program completion rates were higher when:

- Men were wife referred to the program $p < .024$

- Men were referred by a
  religious source (clergy member) $p < .000$

- Men were older $p < .000$

- Men had higher educational attainment $p < .000$

- Men placed more importance on their religion $p < .000$

- Men were employed $p < .000$

- Men had military training/experience $p < .000$

5. Adapted from an internal report to the agency under study, May 2003.

We know from our research that men who were required by the courts to attend the program under study had significantly higher drop-out rates than men who were pastor or wife referred (Nason-Clark, Murphy, Fisher-Townsend and Ruff, 2003). Completion rates also varied based on demographic characteristics, problems with alcohol abuse and labor force and/or military experiences, and the severity of the abuse perpetrated. They do not vary based on childhood experiences of educational problems or witnessing or experiencing abuse in the family of origin.

UNDERSTANDING MALE BATTERER ACCOUNTS OF THEIR BEHAVIOR

We found that most men rationalized, minimized or legitimated their use of violence when recounting the details of the referring incident that brought them to the treatment program. These men indicated in a variety of ways that they were not violent, while the police reports indicated that they were. This section illustrates patterns of denial regarding the violent behavior of these men.

There is a persistent theme in men's accounts of their behavior and that theme is *I am not violent!* Although men use a variety of phrases to deny their culpability for violence toward their spouses these are all framed by this common theme.

On the intake questionnaire for the batterers' intervention program, clients were asked the question "Is there a pattern to your violence?" Following that question there were several more specific questions related to violent episodes and victims. While this data was missing in many of our research files, which meant that we could not systematically examine these questions, a cursory examination of the responses of the men indicated several patterns.

Many men were forthright about denying the violence. The phrases they used include:

- "I am not violent."
- "I do not recall any event of that nature except to live a very happy pleasant life style."
- "I go quiet, the silent treatment."
- [it was] "not violence."

- "I don't feel the behavior was violent. My behavior is never violent towards people."
- "I don't get upset."
- "I tried to walk away, kept [my] hands in [my] pockets, tried not to raise my voice."
- "I have never hit my wife."

Despite these denials, the file records indicate that many of the men who provided this type of response when questioned were court-mandated to attend the treatment program and some of their victims required medical attention.

A second group of men answered the question, "Is there a pattern to your violence?" with a simple "no," "not applicable," or "no violence," to indicate that they believed they were not abusing anyone. Yet within the files there are various indicators of their levels of violence. When looking at records of their "Domestic Violence Inventory" questionnaire, these men often ranged from medium risk to maximum risk on the violence indicator. Relatedly, on the "Physical Violence Worksheet" the various ways physical force has been abused in their relationship are listed and often these lists are quite lengthy. Finally, throughout the files there are notes made by therapeutic staff regarding the use of violence.

Another group of men who indicated that there was no violence were given a list of options [as part of another question] about how they do respond in difficult situations. They most often indicated "walk away," "withhold sex," and "respond to your partner's questions with one word replies, grunts or silence." This type of response was found throughout the files.

A fourth group of men responded to the question regarding pattern of violence with answers such as "I swear," "verbal fighting with [my] wife," "verbal anger," and "I said severe things," yet again many of them are court ordered and on the "Domestic Violence Inventory" their range on the violence indicator is between problem risk and maximum risk.

All the indicators are that these men are indeed violent, despite their denials. In order to gain a better understanding of factors influencing this violence and to gain insight into how it might be ameliorated, a more systematic examination of the closed case files of a sample of the men who were court-ordered to attend a treatment program for male batterers was conducted.

According to Tolman and Edleson (1995) more confidence can be placed in studies using combined victim-offender-police reports. We have incorporated both the victim's report to police and the batterer's account of the referring incident that was collected on the intake form. Our analysis centers on the discrepancy between these reports. Thus, we focus on what victims say about the violence they have endured and what abusers report to the intake worker at the agency. To be sure, a central feature of any batterer intervention program is assisting violent men in accepting responsibility for the abusive behavior in their past. Men of faith are likely to incorporate elements of their belief system into their responsibility and empathy letters.

CATALYSTS FOR ABUSE

Bilodeau (1990:48) states:

> A man who exhibits violence verbally, psychologically, physically, sexually or financially toward his partner is not losing self-control; on the contrary, he is affirming his power, which he wants to preserve at all costs and which makes him neither monstrous nor sick. If he abuses his wife, it is because he has the privilege and the means to do so.

When women somehow demonstrate independence, whether that entails preparing to leave or seeking assistance, they are often subjected to violence based on male entitlement—named as "prerogative of male authority" by Dobash & Dobash (1979), and "husband-right" by Rich (1979); the violence is meant to curb their attempts at autonomy. This involves an attempt by many abusive men to assert their male authority through a constellation of violent behaviors, including yelling, name-calling and physical force. It is the process by which the abuser attempts to regain the power he once held. Mahoney (1991) refers to this type of violent behavior as "separation assault," meant to keep women in the relationship or terrorize them after they leave. Ptacek (1998) notes that eighteen percent of the women in his research identified "preventing women from separating" as the motive for their partners' violence.

Some would regard the worldview of men of faith as support for their rationalization of patriarchal authority, under which their wives are called to be "submissive." In two secular Texas batterer intervention programs, researchers found that religious men appealed to the Bible to justify their violence. "The most common word they used was submit: She will not submit, she did not submit, she should submit" (Shupe, Stacey and Hazlewood 1987:93).

We offer two examples to illustrate how men in this program understood the issue of male entitlement. In the first example, the man claimed that there were unmet expectations: he expected "subjection and submission" from his wife and when she responded to these demands with a plan to end the relationship he became resentful and, eventually, violent.

> 451—According to the incident description he said: "I reached out to hug her and she backed off. I chased her around the house." She went in the bathroom and he punched a hole through the door.

In his responsibility letter he says:

> I was raised with certain ideals and expectations of what marriage and partnership meant. I felt that my dominance and control through yelling and intellectualizing by slinging bible verses around was the scriptural description of 'subjection and submission.' I perceived you to be wilfully defiant. I was angered that you were not being what I thought you should be as a Godly wife, meeting my expectations.

A second illustration of the issue of male entitlement is captured in the following police report and intake file.

> 004—I got up to call [my friend] and he grabbed the phone out of my hand. He then gestured as if he was going to hit me with the phone. I then asked him what he was doing. He made a fist with his hand and hit me on my shoulder knocking me down. He then again ran upstairs. I knew he was going to get more of my things so I started following him ... I tried to go by him to my room but he was coming toward me as if he was going to push me down the stairs. When he got close to me I tried to hold his shoulders so that he wouldn't be able to push me down the stairs. He then took me by the arms and flung me down the stairs forcefully. I was so scared that I wet myself.

Yet, the batterer claimed that:

> "She was never intentionally pushed. She wouldn't leave and got hysterical." "I was not angry." [There was] "no struggle." "I was having a panic attack." "I raced around frantic."

Stets (1988) identifies this type of response in his research. This abuser's claim was that his response was an irrational involuntary response caused by his emotions being out of control. This emotional loss of control put the violent reaction out of his control.

Sexual jealousy and possessiveness have also been identified as conditions leading to violence (Dobash & Dobash 1979; Gelles and Straus 1988; Stets 1988). These issues work together with the sense of male entitlement as another catalyst for violent behavior. Some batterers in our sample appear unable to recover from relationships that have ended. Several of the men continued to harass, stalk or confront their former partners, and, when confronted with further evidence that the relationship was well and truly over, they became violent in retaliation.

Illustrating this response are two examples taken from case files. The police report stated:

> 405—...she was in the restaurant when he walked up behind and punched her in the right bicep with a closed fist. He then began shouting profanities at her, this incident was witnessed. The victim reported that she tried to ignore the defendant, hoping that he would stop. She stated that the defendant told her that he had parked his car behind her and that he would follow her anywhere she went.

In the words of the batterer to the intake worker:

> I gave my ex-fiancée opera tickets. We met after the opera at a local restaurant. I said several things to intentionally hurt her and that was the end of the evening.

Another batterer accounts for his physically violent and dangerous behavior as resulting from emotional trauma—he found her with another man two years after they had ended their relationship.

The police report records that:

> 007—Victim One advised that she got into an altercation with the suspect. She was very muddy, she was wet, and she had a purple mark on the right side of her face, on her cheek. I noticed that she had mud stains on her legs and on her arms and elbows, because she had been thrown into the mud. She stated that he was jealous over a new boyfriend .... There was information regarding a shotgun that could have been involved in the incident.

Yet, the man involved in this instance tells a different story.

It was his ex-girlfriend's birthday. She wanted another guy in addition to him. She told him about sex with the other guy . . . caused emotional trauma. He got drunk at the party, started pushing the other guy and her. He doesn't remember the incident as he was too drunk.

In both of these examples, the abusive man is attempting to respond to feelings of jealousy. His behaviour might be regarded as a feeble attempt to reverse the scorecard, to pay her back for the loss of relationship.

Dobash & Dobash (1979) identify a pattern that involves violence as a method of enforcing demands for domestic service. We found examples of this pattern in our data also. For one man, the referring incident was related particularly to food preparation:

390—He said [I] assaulted my wife–punched her in the forehead. [We have been] fighting/yelling the whole time we've been married—fighting about the fact that I didn't bring home something to eat. She doesn't cook very often. Junk food. [He] reports he hits her once a month and states that the fights got progressively worse. "In the beginning I'd cry but I stopped feeling bad about it. I didn't think about it." He goes on to state that the lowest point was when she was pregnant. "She stressed me out every day."

The following statement made by a victim to the police also relates to domestic service:

395—[He] started name calling demanding the check book and all the statements—belittling me—telling my daughter in a very rude manner what she was going to do today "you're going to be cleaning the dishwasher out and then clean up the house." She was shaking because he went from yelling at mom to yelling at her. He walked out of the bathroom and said "hey sap, get me a newspaper before you leave." Also that morning he threw our dog against the door and the dog's foot went under it. The dog was screaming. He was laughing . . . we live with stress on a daily basis. In August 1996 after the children and I had been in a rear-end accident I couldn't do much at all around the house. We got into an argument and he said "you want me out of here just say it!" So I did say get out of here. He broke the bedroom door, broke the chest of drawers and a lot of glass decorations. The kids and I were terrified.

Another man recounts how his referring incident was precipitated by the over-commitment of his wife in finishing sewing for the church:

604—[My] wife has several chronic illnesses. The church that we were going to wanted someone to sew jackets for children. They found out my wife can sew and asked her to do that, not knowing she had many health problems. So she volunteered to make them. Meanwhile the house was becoming stressful as the deadline arrived. One night I felt very overwhelmed. We argued and it escalated. I didn't get physical until the foul language [started] coming from my wife for a very long time. That's when I decided to get a dishtowel to muffle her, not to murder her ... she has asthma.

The issue of male entitlement to domestic service is illustrated by cases where men lash out against their partners as a result of unmet expectations regarding housework or other domestic tasks.

We see in this data a variety of circumstances where the reaction of men is to use violence against their female partners. Whether dealing with expectations of submission, issues of personal honor, jealousy and possessiveness, and/or demands for domestic services, the men in this group seem unable to perceive of and utilize appropriate non-violent responses. How can this thinking and behavior be altered? What can a program do to bring a violent man to accountability for his hurtful abusive behavior? In the next section of our paper, we discuss the pivotal role of "empathic understanding" and "taking responsibility" as requirements for abusive men in order to affect change.

DOES ATTENDING GROUP INTERVENTION MAKE A DIFFERENCE?

There are three important elements to be gained from intervention, all of which are intended to make a difference in the thinking and behaviour of men who have acted abusively in the family context. The first of these elements is gaining empathy, the second is accepting responsibility, and the third is becoming accountable for the behaviour.

Gaining Empathy

Wiehe (1997:1992) defines empathy as "feeling into" or putting oneself into another's position. One of the tools for recovery used in the program at United States Agency One is a letter of empathy written by the perpetrator. In this letter the men are asked to describe their violence and its effects from the perspective of their victim. It is necessary for them to put themselves in the place of their victims in order to grasp the impact and consequences of their actions. Two key components of empathy are emotion recognition and perspective-taking (Marshall, Hudson et al. 1995). These involve the ability to know how another feels. In the absence of empathy long-term change may be doubtful. Why would an abuser bother to change if he is unable to recognize and feel the impact of his violence on his victim? In their research on change among batterers Scott and Wolfe (2000) noted that the development of empathy contributed to men's ability to change their abusive behaviour. "Most men indicated that they had little or no appreciation of their partners' affective reactions to their abusive behaviour when they started counseling but that as they progressed, they began to understand the role fear played in their relationships" (835). This rethinking involves a shift from looking inwards at his own experience, to considering his partner's experience (Jenkins 1990).

One important element in the healing journey of the women victims is validation—of both their stories and their right to live violence free lives (Davis and Srinivasan 1995). The empathy letter can be seen as part of this process of validation. By describing their actions from the perspective of their victims the men are in fact validating the victim's experience. As illustrated, some men in the research were more successful in demonstrating sensitivity and understanding than others. While some seem able to place themselves in the victim's position—"to feel into," at times the accounts appear to be based on wishful thinking from the perpetrator's perspective rather than the victim's. Other empathy letters seem to move between the two perspectives. Men who did not complete the treatment program wrote the first two examples, which seem to be a reflection of their own anger and their own self-concept combined with the perspective of the victim:

> 7DT—I thought you were going to kill me. Then I realized you were taking every last vestige of dignity that I had left. *The rage I felt was like nothing I've ever felt. I wanted to kill you! How dare you! How dare you! How dare you!* I am so scared!! I knew you didn't love me, I just didn't know how little. [emphasis added].

> 33DT—Through all of this pain and deliberation, I have made the decision to trust you. I have literally placed both my life and my son's life in your hands. *If I did not feel that deep down you are a kind, loving person and capable of changing your beliefs and your*

life, I would not be engaged to you let alone be in a relationship with you. I am trusting you to continue with your treatment and to use the tools that you are learning as a result of your DV program. [emphasis added].

Men who went on to graduate from the treatment program wrote the following examples, which appear to involve a better grasp of the empathic perspective:

11C—*You took away my life and place to live. You don't know how to communicate that is why you ended up going to jail.* All I wanted to do was see you pay for hurting me. You always use your money to control me. Whenever you give me anything you always expect something in return. You always remind me what you have done for me whenever we get into a fight. I hate feeling like I owe you something [emphasis added].

20C—I will never be able to forgive you for conduct and actions . . . . *I do not think that you really realize how much you hurt me that evening.* You used all of my weakness that I revealed to you throughout our relationship to inflict as much emotional harm as you thought you could possibly inflict . . . . You intimidate me. I can understand why you were hurt but that is not an excuse for your conduct [emphasis added].

Gaining empathy is a process that should evolve over the course of treatment. Hopefully the victim's perspective increasingly will be recognized and understood as men in intervention programs are required to think about their behaviour and to discuss it in circumstances where trained therapists and other batterers can confront their beliefs and attitudes. While the goal of intervention is that all men successfully gain a sense of empathy for their victims, it is evident that for some men this process is more successful than for others.

It seems clear that those who are unable to comprehend their victim's feelings are indeed not likely to complete the program and are thus much less likely to be motivated to change their behaviour. The ability to step into another's shoes to take their perspective is critical to beginning the change process. Those men who successfully learn to "feel into" the views of their victims have made a substantial movement toward violence-free living.

Another element required for graduation from the batterers' intervention program, accepting responsibility, goes hand in hand with achieving empathy.

Accepting Responsibility

Recent research (Heckert and Gondolf 2000a:183) hypothesized that underreporting [referring to disagreement in reports of violence] or minimizing violence by batterers may lessen over time. Yet, their findings did not confirm this hypothesis. Rather, they found that:

> At program intake, most men accurately reported whether an assault occurred but tended to minimize the severity. At follow-up, a large percentage of men underreported assaults in comparison to women. Men would typically report that nothing happened, even when their partners described violent episodes in vivid detail.

While the men in this research do acknowledge responsibility, they are careful to somehow attribute their behaviour to some emotion arising from the relationship. A brief comparison of initial accounts of batterers with later letters of responsibility written as a requirement of the United States Agency One treatment program uncovers a variety of themes—including statements of fear, issues regarding the quality of the relationship and attributions of fault.

DeRuyter (2002:25) states that the meaning of "responsibility" is synonymous with accountability or being answerable. But she adds that only when a person can influence a situation, or has power to change a situation, will they take responsibility. Batterers' treatment programs recognize the necessity of accepting responsibility for one's abusive behaviour as an important step in the treatment process. "Violent and abusive men must begin by admitting that they have in fact perpetrated acts of violence for which they are responsible and are to be held accountable" (Dobash, Dobash et al. 1999:62). Each of the men in the treatment program is therefore offered the opportunity to effect change—to influence their situations. The first step in acknowledging responsibility is to face the feelings of shame, guilt and embarrassment which will accompany the process and "take an honest look" at one's abuse (Jenkins 1990). From a peacemaking perspective (Levrant, Cullen et al. 1999), offenders must willingly and actively participate in their own healing, and that might include both traditional treatment programs and publicly taking responsibility for their actions. Responsibility and change are intertwined—without taking responsibility there will be no change.

On his agency intake form one court-mandated man initially said:

> 4C—I was not angry. There was no struggle.

In his responsibility letter he says:

> I acted in ways that wound up injuring you emotionally and physically. I acted as I did out of sheer panic, because I felt you would not listen to me and do as I asked. I felt helpless and trapped. I just wanted you to be gone immediately and never see you again. With me, when it is over, it is over. I felt that if I did not get your stuff downstairs you would not leave, so I rushed to get everything gone. I remember you being carried out of my house on a stretcher. I later learned you had suffered some degree of concussion. I was glad that you were released so soon and no major injuries occurred, according to hospital records.

Another court-mandated man initially said on his intake form:

> 14C—I'm blown away that I did it. It was out of character.

When accepting responsibility he said:

> No matter what things were said, no matter how anyone behaved, I crossed a line that shouldn't have been crossed. I had no right to yell at you and express the feelings I had in a manner in which I did. I had no right to put my hands on you, nor did I have any right to shove you when you tried to keep a level head and walk away. I shoved you. Although unintentional, it was unfortunate that the direction in which I shoved you, the corner edge of the kitchen entry to the hallway met your forehead. You were cut open and it was because of me.

In almost all states of the United States a required standard is that men enrolled in a batterers' intervention program who wish to graduate must accept responsibility for their actions. Some treatment programs require that men publicly accept responsibility at the very first group session, but that seems counterintuitive. Surely a sense of personal responsibility must be given time to build over the course of the treatment process. As men who have acted abusively assimilate the important elements of the curriculum and develop empathy over time they should begin to move towards accepting responsibility. Some movement between initial denial of personal responsibility and accepting that responsibility is evident in these examples. But clearly these men have progressed only midway along a continuum from denial to responsibility as they continue to partially attribute blame for their actions either to their partner's responses, emotions such as feeling out of control, or the unintentional nature of their behaviour. The men in our examples did complete the fifty-two week program, thus it is hoped that as their treatment progressed they learned to shift responsibility away from factors inappropriate in these situations and toward themselves.

Accepting responsibility has been identified as both a coping strategy and a transition point that is necessary if abusive men are to change. Most certainly it is also an important component of accountability.

Becoming Accountable

Men who do not become accountable during the course of their program, who continue to blame others for their circumstances, probably have little prospect for change in their behaviour (Henning and Holdford 2006). There is a difference between those who continue to blame others for their behaviour and those who have learned to become accountable. The men in intervention groups do attempt to hold each other accountable because they know the power of denial—not only in terms of violence but also in terms of substance abuse.

While the goal of an intervention program is *ending the violence,* female partners of men who are unable to feel empathy and refuse to accept responsibility or become accountable in a meaningful way not only have little hope for change in their lives but they may in fact be re-victimized by continuing to be cast as the "cause" of their partner's violent behavior. These elements are thus critical both for program effectiveness and for offering hope.

CONCLUSION

For many years, we have been investigating the intersection between faith and violence. In this study we explore the emerging story of faith-based batterer intervention programs. Based on an analysis of 1,135 closed case files over a twenty year period, we have found that men who enroll in these programs differ from men who enroll in community-based programs in terms of marital status, age, education, ethnicity, employment status and witnessing or experiencing violence in their families of origin. Moreover, those who complete differ from those men who drop the program or are terminated in terms of referral source, age, education, employment, military training and the importance placed on religion in their lives. The implications of these findings will form the basis of our ongoing investigations of the link between religion and abuse. These data reveal that faith-based programs serve an important constituency of abusers. They also indicate the important role of clergy and other religious leaders in encouraging or "mandating" the attendance of men who seek their help in a state certified program. In this way, the voice of the religious leader works together with the skills of the trained counselor helping to bridge the chasm between churches and the communities they serve.

REFERENCES

Bennett, L. and O. Williams. Controversies and recent studies of batterer intervention program effectiveness. (2002). August 8.

Carney, M. M. and F. P. Buttell. "A multidimensional evaluation of a treatment program for female batterers: A pilot study." *Research on Social Work Practice* 14: 4 (2004) 249–258.

Cavanaugh, M. M. and R. J. Gelles. "The utility of male domestic violence offender typologies: New directions for research, policy, and practice." *Journal of Interpersonal Violence* 20: 2 (2005) 155–166.

Daly, J. and S. Pelowski. "Predictors of dropout among men who batter: A review of studies with implications for research and practice." *Violence and Victims* 15: 2 (2000) 137–160.

Davis, L. V. and M. Srinivasan. "Listening to the voices of battered women: What helps them escape violence." *Affilia* 10: 1 (1995) 49–69.

DeKeseredy, W. S. and M. D. Schwartz. "Definitional Issues." In *Sourcebook on violence against women*, edited by Renzetti, C. M. et al, 23–34. Thousand Oaks, CA: Sage, 2001.

DeRuyter, D. "The virtue of taking responsibility." *Educational Philosophy and Theory* 34: 1 (2002) 25–35.

Dobash, R. P., R. E. Dobash, et al. "A research evaluation of British programmes for violent men." *Journal of Social Policy* 28: (1999) 205–233.

Gondolf, E. "Regional and cultural utility of conventional batterer counseling." *Violence against Women* 10: 8 (2004) 880–900.

Hamberger, L. K., J. M. Lohr, et al. "A large sample empirical typology of male spouse abusers and its relationship to dimensions of abuse." *Violence and Victims* 1: (1996) 277–92.

Healey, K., C. Smith, et al. Batterer intervention: Program approaches and criminal justice strategies. Washington, DC: Issues and practices in criminal justice, 1998.

Heckert, D. A. and E. Gondolf. "The effect of perceptions of sanctions on batterer program outcomes." *Journal of Research in Crime and Delinquency* 37: 4 (2000) 369–91.

Henning, K. and R. Holdford. "Minimization, denial, and victim blaming by batterers: How much does the truth matter?" *Criminal Justice and Behavior* 32: 1 (2006) 110–30.

Jackson, S., D. R. Forde, et al. Batterer intervention programs: Where do we go from here? National Institute of Justice. Washington, DC, 2003.

Jenkins, A. *Invitations to responsibility: The therapeutic engagement of men who are violent and abusive.* Adelaide, AU: Dulwich Centre Publications, 1990.

Levrant, S., F. T. Cullen, et al. "Reconsidering restorative justice: The corruption of benevolence revisited?" *Crime & Delinquency* 45: 1 (1999) 3–27.

Marshall, W., S. Hudson, et al. "Empathy in sex offenders." *Clinical Psychology Review* 15: (1995) 99–113.

Nason-Clark, N., N. Murphy, et al. "An overview of the characteristics of the clients at a faith-based batterers' intervention program." *Journal of Religion and Abuse* 5: 4 (2003) 51–72.

NCIPC. Intimate partner violence: Fact sheet. Centers for Disease Control and Prevention. 2005.

Rosenbaum, A. and P. A. Leisring. "Group intervention programs for batterers." *Journal of Aggression, Maltreatment & Trauma* 5: 2 (2001) 57–71.

Scott, K. L. "Predictors of change among male batterers: Application of theories and review of empirical findings." *Trauma, Violence, & Abuse: A Review Journal* 5: 3 (2004) 260–84.

Scott, K. L. and D. A. Wolfe. "Change among batterers: Examining men's success stories." *Journal of Interpersonal Violence* 15: 8 (2000) 827–42.

Tolman, R. M. "An ecological analysis of batterer intervention program standards." *Journal of Aggression, Maltreatment & Trauma* 5: 2 (2001) 221–33.

Trimble, D. Counselling programs for men who are violent in relationships: Questions and answers for practitioners in the health, social services and criminal justice systems. Health Canada. Ottawa, 2000.

United States Senate Judiciary Committee. Violence against women. Government Printing Office. Washington, DC, 1992.

Warner, R. S. "Work in progress toward a new paradigm for the sociological study of religion in the United States." *American Journal of Sociology* 98: 5 (1993) 1044–93.

Wiehe, V. R. "Approaching child abuse treatment from the perspective of empathy." *Child Abuse & Neglect* 21: 12 (1997) 1191–1204.

Wuthnow, R. *Saving America? Faith-based services and the future of civil society.* Princeton, NJ: Princeton University Press, 2004.

8

Searching for the Missing Puzzle Piece

The Potential of Faith in Changing Violent Behavior

Barbara Fisher-Townsend

THE SCENE OF HOPELESSNESS

Early each weekday morning at the entrance door to the specialized domestic violence court in a large metropolitan city courthouse[1] a roster of the cases to be heard that day is posted by a court employee. As people arrive at the court they move toward the list to check for the daily scheduling of cases. After noting the time of the case they are involved with, they then huddle around one of the many seating sections in the large atrium lobby with those who have accompanied them and speak amongst themselves in whispered tones. Those who are unaccompanied find their own corners of the atrium and sit quietly waiting for the daily proceedings to commence.

The court-appointed defense attorney (public defender) appears from a back room off the lobby and begins to approach individuals to inquire about whether they have representation for their case. If they do, she moves on to the next individual. If they do not, she asks them to follow her to a quiet corner where they discuss the case for several minutes.

Just before 9 a.m. the individuals and small groups of anxious looking people who have gathered around the lobby begin to enter the court-

---

1. Over the past few years I have observed approximately 125 cases in two domestic violence courts, one in Canada and one in the United States.

room. Once inside the doorway, they hesitate momentarily while trying to decide where to sit—seating is important in this court. On the right side of the courtroom sits a small group of advocates whose work involves assisting victims and family members with the court process. Women most often choose to sit near the court advocates. Several distraught looking women sit alone, their shoulders hunched, their arms clasped together and their legs crossed—their bodies turned in on themselves. Most of the men, and those who have come to support them, gravitate toward the left side of the room. The men sit quietly speaking with friends or family members. There are several rows of seats from which to choose, but no one sits in the front row. There is noticeable tension in the room as we await the beginning of the day's proceedings. The facial expressions and demeanor of many of the men and women present display a sense both of fear and of hopelessness.

On the left side of the court room is an area enclosed by railings, where a police officer on guard is seated. Behind that officer is a securely closed door. At the back of the room there is a table, at which is seated a police officer who is there to swear in adjudicated peace bonds. Next to him sits a parole and probation officer who awaits clients who must report to him. These officers of the court confer often between themselves and with the advocates.

At the front of the room, in front of the bar, there is a collection of people—a Crown Prosecutor,[2] various defense attorneys and two court clerks. A low-pitched wave of sound arises from this group as they jostle to speak with each other—questioning the clerks about various procedural issues, negotiating on behalf of their clients, attempting to change the ordering of case presentation and chatting about issues of the day. Occasionally one of the lawyers will signal a client to step forward for a question about some detail of the case.

As the judge enters the room all conversation immediately stops and the court clerk asks those present to stand. Once the judge is seated on the raised bench we once again sit. The clerk calls the name and number of the first case and the busy court day begins. The police officer in the enclosed area opens the door behind him and calls a man's name. Promptly, a man, dressed in an orange prison jumpsuit with shackles on his feet and cuffs binding his hands, appears in the dock. His is the first case of the morn-

2. In the United States this person is a member of the District Attorney's staff, in Canada the term is Crown Prosecutor.

ing. The charges are read very quickly by the court clerk, the prisoner is asked for his plea, and the prosecuting attorney begins to speak. His presentation is followed by the defense attorney, who directs several questions to the prisoner in an attempt to clarify circumstances of the charges. The judge then questions the prisoner, mainly regarding lifestyle stability issues (i.e., are you employed? what is your monthly income? where are you living?). At every given opportunity the man in the jumpsuit turns toward the audience, presumably looking for someone. His countenance is somber, even slightly threatening.

Once satisfied that all relevant information has been presented, the judge proceeds to pronounce sentence. Interestingly, I learn that the provisions of this case will be repeated throughout the day for almost every new defendant found guilty. These include abstinence from drugs and alcohol, treatment for substance abuse, no access to weapons, a no contact order with the victim(s), random urinalysis testing, reporting to the probation officer at specified times, and, importantly, attendance at a batterers' intervention (treatment) program.

Across North America this scene is repeated in specialized and criminal courts on a daily basis throughout the year. Those who have acted abusively are called to account by the criminal justice system and are adjudicated accordingly. It is within this context that their journey toward change must begin.

Specialized Courts

Specialized domestic violence courts, one of a variety of so-called problem-solving courts (Butts 2001)[3], have been established in recognition of the need for an intensive and coordinated approach to the pervasive problem of family violence and with the goal of creating a criminal justice system response to the issue of domestic violence that better addresses the needs of victims (Cook, Burton et al. 2004; Epstein 1999; Dawson and Dinovitzer 2001; Tsai 2000). Other general goals relate to improving the judicial response to the problem by coordinating criminal justice and social service agencies and holding defendants accountable (Gover and MacDonald 2003). To that end there are several specific goals, includ-

---

3. Keilitz 2000 (in Gover and MacDonald 2003) estimated that "over 300 courts in the United States have recognized the need for special attention to domestic violence cases by incorporating specialized processing and structure within existing judicial systems."

ing: expeditious court processing, more appropriate sentencing, reducing case attrition prior to sentencing, and the provision of integrated services to victims (Denham and Gillespie 1999). In taking a social problem approach to crime these courts serve a dual purpose—as agents of social control and of social change (Mirchandani 2005). The argument is that the technocratic approach to justice utilized by these courts mobilizes social control factors related to deterrence, those being effectiveness, certainty, and celerity, in order to facilitate their goals of social change.

Key elements of the specialized court model are identified by Newmark, Rempel et al. (2001:vii):

- a network of criminal justice and social service partner agencies who work together on making the model succeed;
- the specialized caseload of virtually all indicted domestic violence felonies in the jurisdiction, and no other cases than domestic violence felonies;
- trained and dedicated personnel from court, prosecution, offender intervention and treatment, probation, and victim service agencies;
- vertical processing and standard practices to ensure consistency in case handling;
- enhanced case information flow among partner agencies to improve judicial decision-making and partner agency operations;
- an emphasis on defendant monitoring and accountability;
- enhanced protection for, and services to, victims.

The great strength of specialized courts, according to Cook, Burton et al. (2004:E13) is that they "place the victim at the heart of the process." Women are better able to access the multiple and complementary options available to them. An alternative view is offered by Salvaggio (2002), who notes that critics believe public interests have tended to supersede the interests of victims and that the system does not adequately reflect the needs of women.

In Canada, the City of Calgary, Alberta offers a response to domestic violence that is noteworthy largely due to that city's organization called The HomeFront Society for the Prevention of Domestic Violence (HomeFront) which coordinates criminal justice and community responses and has developed protocols with fifty-two agencies, including hospitals, shelters,

Aboriginal organizations, and child welfare agencies (Ad Hoc Federal-Provincial-Territorial Working Group Reviewing Spousal Abuse Policies and Legislation 2003). This coordinated response accelerates resolution of cases, with seventy percent of all cases heard in the Domestic Violence Court (Court 412) being resolved within a month from first appearance date (Van de Veen 2004). The most commonly occurring dispositions (p. 84) were offender treatment conditions (seventy-nine percent); alcohol/substance abuse assessment and treatment (fifty-two percent); conditions requiring the offender to abstain completely from the use of alcohol (thirty-eight percent), and conditions prohibiting contact with the complainant (thirty percent).

The advantages of a specialized domestic violence court are outlined by Helling (undated) in her overview of courts in Seattle, Sacramento and Vancouver, Washington. These are: increased accessibility for victims; specialized expertise of the criminal justice personnel; increased accountability of offenders; renewed commitment to solve problems and work together by criminal justice personnel; consistency in case handling; timely response; and sending a message to the community that the courts take domestic violence seriously. In the Canadian context, the Ad Hoc Federal-Provincial-Territorial Working Group (2003) lists similar elements and adds "the provision of services that recognize the unique needs of spousal/partner abuse victims" (p. 59). Helling also outlines the disadvantages of this type of system. She notes that putting "all the eggs in one basket" does not work if the court makes consistently bad decisions and women have nowhere else to turn. As well, perceptions of bias favoring women may appear, staff has greatly increased workloads, and there is a high burnout rate for all court personnel. These types of concerns are also reported by Newmark, Rempel et al. (2001) who examined the specialized domestic violence court system in Kings County, New York. They note that these system agencies felt workload pressures due to increased prosecutions, insufficient services for victims, and limited resources that serve batterers. Other features subject to criticism in the United States context (Tsai 2000) include peripherally related things such as the indeterminate effect of mandating batterer intervention programs as a condition of probation or sentencing and the questionable deterrent effect of alternative sanctions for domestic violence crimes such as enhanced monitoring and greater enforcement of severe penalties for violating orders of protection.

CASE DISPOSITIONS

As stated earlier, one of the most common case dispositions in specialized domestic violence courts is mandating those found guilty to attend a batterers' intervention program. A brief description of a typical intervention group is provided to enable the reader to visualize the experience of attending a treatment program.[4]

On a mild but rainy fall evening in the Pacific Northwest of the United States, at about 6:30 p.m., men begin to arrive at the faith-based agency where the group is offered. They park their cars or lock their bikes, finish their cigarettes outside, enter the building and come up one flight of stairs to the meeting room. The room, located just steps from the entrance stairway, is large enough to accommodate several tables arranged in a rectangular shape, with seating for approximately twenty men. There is a coffee maker and small fridge in one corner and a television mounted on the wall in another corner that is tuned to a baseball game. The place is warm, comfortable and welcoming. As they enter the room, each man signs the attendance sheet located near the door. The men then sit quietly in the room awaiting the start of group, perhaps having a cup of coffee and often talking amongst themselves about the events of their week. One of the men does look decidedly uncomfortable, seated in the far corner of the room with his arms crossed and his head down—it is later revealed that he is new to the group tonight.

Promptly at 7 p.m. the facilitators (one woman, one man) enter the room and are seated at the head of the table configuration. They welcome everyone to the group (there are seventeen men present that night), recognize that there is a new group participant and interact with him briefly, and then go on to the "check-in" phase of the group. Each person around the room (including the facilitators) checks-in by stating their name and anything of note that happened to them since their last group. One man says proudly that he had the opportunity to visit with his daughter for the first time in six months; another man notes that his hours at work have been cut back and he wonders how he and his family will survive on less income; another man says he has a new woman friend in his life and he hopes this relationship will go smoothly; another man notes rather

---

4. Over the past few years I have observed approximately ten treatment/intervention groups, both faith-based and secular, in two agencies, one located in Canada and one in the United States.

agitatedly that his former wife, who has the kids living with her, has got a new man living in the house; around the room it goes with each person reporting what is significant in their lives. Often participants will offer words of support or solidarity, "sorry about your troubles man," or "I hear you brother." They understand the many issues and concerns and, indeed, have often experienced them in their own lives.

The lesson for the evening involves recognizing emotions and what they mean to each person. A handout is provided and comments and re-actions are solicited by the facilitators. A video clip of an angry response to a relatively minor domestic situation involving a husband and wife is then shown and a discussion ensues regarding the message portrayed. It is obvious that most of the men are familiar with both the type of situation and the inappropriate responses portrayed in the video. The facilitators use that recognition to apply the concept of emotional responses to the lives of the men present. They talk about losing control of one's emotions in volatile situations, about how to STOP and think about your actions, about how to re-direct your emotional responses.

Towards the end of the two-hour session, there is a knock at the door and pizza boxes are handed in. One of the men is graduating, having attended group for the required fifty-two week period, and a celebratory send-off is to take place, complete with pizza and sodas. Congratulations are offered all around. The graduate notes that although he is very pleased to be ending his required time he does have mixed feelings about leaving the group as it has been a source of support and reinforcement for him on his journey toward change.

At the end of group, rather than looking tired, the men are more ani-mated than they were when they entered. Following this two-hour session, each man leaves buoyed by the knowledge he has gained that evening. A message has been given, a lesson perhaps learned, a shift in thinking proposed, an opportunity for change provided, but most importantly, a glimpse of hope—one based on that change—becomes apparent.

Scenes like this happen in cities and towns throughout North America on a daily basis. Although program durations and curricula vary widely the goals of changed thinking and behavior are common.

Batterers' Intervention Programs

Beginning in the 1970s in North America, women's movement activists were successful in focusing public attention on the important social problem of spousal abuse and the lack of sanctions for men who perpetrated violence against their intimate partners[5]. Violence against women in the home began to come out from behind closed doors—the personal became political. As societal awareness of domestic violence increased there was a corresponding recognition of the necessity to respond to questions of how better to assure safety of women and children, and how to assess, manage and treat perpetrators of violence against women. In reaction to this recognition, we have witnessed the implementation of a proliferation of prevention and intervention programs. As this work has progressed it has become clear that the complexity of the issue and the multisystemic origins of battering behaviour warrant multiple responses.

Mears and Visher (2005:204) introduce a recent perspective on the issue,

> Domestic violence is understood to be a critical problem—one that occurs along many dimensions, takes many forms, and arises under a range of different conditions.

One important response of the criminal justice system has been to mandate attendance at therapeutic treatment programs for men who have been charged with and/or convicted of wife abuse (Sherman and Smith 1992; Gondolf, Heckert et al. 2002). This requirement may be imposed as part of a pre-trial diversion program (Johnson and Kanzler 1993); as part of a sentence; is often a condition of probation (Ames and Dunham 2002); but also may be implemented as a "restorative justice" measure (Nova Scotia Department of Justice Victims' Services Division 2001).

Batterer intervention programs (BIPs) have thus become a key element of the programmatic intervention agenda of the criminal justice system. They developed not only in response to the public acknowledgement of wife abuse as a serious social issue, but also because of increased political and legal reaction (Myers 1996; Dobash, Dobash et al 2000; Mankowski, Haaken et al. 2002). As programs evolved, debates developed (Davis and Taylor 1999; Nova Scotia Dept. of Justice 1999; Goldner 1999; Bennett and

---

5. Statistics Canada (2004) report that in 2002, 27 percent of all victims of violent crimes reported to police were victims of family violence and 62 percent of these were victimized by a spouse.

Piet 1999) as to how these programs effectively and efficiently fit into the overall response to violence against women. One of the most widely debated issues is "accountability," as this is often identified in intervention programs as a key theme, yet within most programs there are no resources to assess how this is actually demonstrated (Bennett and Williams 2002).

Since referral of the perpetrator to a batterer intervention program is so prevalent, several issues surrounding referral to treatment need to be addressed. First, we need more information about program effectiveness or outcomes in order to reduce recidivism. Is even a minimal effect sufficient to continue referring violent men to these programs? What program refinements might be made in order to increase effectiveness? Are contextually appropriate programs more effective for certain groups of men? The second issue relates to attrition. Throughout the literature, researchers make note that often there is no follow-up when men drop out of programs, even when they are court-mandated to attend (see for example Gondolf 2000; Aldarondo 2002). While this usually relates to lack of resources for proper tracking, both human and financial, surely programs are fighting a losing battle when men can freely discontinue attendance with few or no consequences. Innovative developments in criminal justice programming and in treatment program delivery are attempting to address issues of attrition and recidivism. As well, recognition of the necessity of providing contextually relevant intervention, such as faith-based programs, offers enhanced possibilities for changing abusive men.

There is a multiplicity of intervention models[6], each utilizing a variety of methods that integrate ideas from different sources in order to understand and intervene to effect change. Yet, despite the eclectic mix of methods found in most interventions there are important core items integrated into the majority of programs, including increasing offender self-esteem and changing sex-role attitudes (Pirog-Good and Stets-Kealey 1985). As well, according to Mankowski, Haaken et al. (2002), the program delivery method, involving a variety of practices based on content differences, may be quite diverse. They identify two major delivery models: (a) the unstructured group model wherein the facilitator remains open to the introduction of unexpected materials, and (b) the more structured Duluth power and control model in which eight specific themes

6. Other formats identified within the literature include Emerge, Manalive, Amend, The Compassion Workshop, self-help, culturally appropriate programs, educational, narrative therapy and grace therapy.

are covered and there is little or no room for unexpected materials to appear. A third method not described by Mankowski et al. is counselling individuals and/or couples, although these methods have been subject to significant criticism.

Recent innovations in batterer programs which require further research include prison programs, integrated substance abuse and offender interventions, focus on attachment disorder, and group leader teams of differing/same gender. As well, issues such as treatment length, conjoint versus gender-specific formats and program standards need additional research inquiry (Aldarondo 2002; Aldarondo and Mederos 2002; Austin and Dankwort 1999; Davis and Taylor 1999; Healey, Smith et al. 1998; Rosenbaum and Leisring 2001).

THE CONTEXT OF HOPE

Believing in what people can become appears to serve as a prime motivator for the offering of a huge range of faith-based services in the United States. Wallace, Myers et al. (2004:12) explain:

> Faith serves as the foundation upon which the [Faith-Based Empowerment] Model is built. For people of faith, the concept means seeing people, situations, and conditions "through the eyes of God"—not as they currently are, but believing in what they can become and acting to realize that vision.

Clark (2005) argues that faith communities can offer those caught in the web of abuse a new paradigm based on mutuality, peace and compassion. Regardless of faith or spiritual orientation, learning to become non-violent is a critical step on the journey towards self-transformation. For many men their faith and/or spirituality assists them on their journey toward change.

A faith-based batterers' intervention program provides the opportunity to include religious beliefs in the therapeutic process. Indeed, Hodge (2005:77) argues that "many consumers desire to integrate their spiritual belief systems into the therapeutic dialogue." He goes on to cite Gallup data, reported in 1998 by Bart, which indicates that "eighty-one percent of respondents wanted to have their spiritual values and beliefs integrated into the counselling process." While this integration is not possible in the majority of batterer intervention programs, for a very small percentage of men who have acted abusively, the possibility of incorporating the spiritual into therapeutic intervention does exist.

During interviews with men currently enrolled in a faith-based intervention program the question was asked—*what is the impact for you personally of being in an agency where faith and spirituality are recognized as being important?* Of the seventeen men questioned, fourteen responded positively about the impact of faith in their lives. The remaining three were not negative, but rather neutral, as to the importance of faith in their lives. Several examples from those who responded positively are offered:

> #06—Um, it's important in my life. I mean I attend church and I study and I have a study group that I am going to . . . . I have been praying about this [relationship]. I have been praying about, you know, my recovery through all this and the answers really haven't came . . . .Without faith there is nothing, and that I, that's what it's all about, it's all about faith.

> #19—I depend on God.

> #07—it just seemed like another piece in the puzzle that had been kind of filtering down from listening, you know, listening to my prayers and listening to the answers.

Reliance on their belief in God is evident in the accounts of these men. Their faith offers structure to their thinking and to their lives. It also may offer them strength through hardship and serve as a source on their road to change (Pargament 1997). Spiritual resources can provide pathways to beneficial outcomes (Hodge 2000a; Kaut 2002). Reading the Bible and praying assist in providing daily motivation and inspiration to keep on "doing the work," to keep on trying to succeed with their life changes, to keep on attending their weekly group sessions. The opportunity to complete their treatment groups at an agency where faith is not only recognized, but also encouraged and modelled, offers great support and meaning to these men. Their lives often seem truly dismal, with broken family relationships, terrible financial burdens, poor living circumstances and work that offers little opportunity for advancement or any kind of creativity. As Hodge (2005:83) notes, "In a forest of troubles, clients can lose sight of the spiritual truth that gives them hope and meaning and helps them endure trials and persevere through hardship." This place, where faith and acceptance permeate the atmosphere, serves as a sanctuary for many of these men where they can come and be welcomed, where their faith is affirmed even when their behavior is not, and where, for a couple of hours a week life seems not so impossible.

Faith-based agencies are uniquely positioned to "tap into" and model certain qualities that are increasingly being recognized as crucial for change (Vandecreek, Nye et al. 1994). In discussing the importance of various therapeutic factors at the beginning of intervention groups for men who batter, Roy, Turcott et al. (2005) found that self-understanding and imitative behavior were considered very important, particularly towards the end of the intervention process. Two therapeutic staff members, one at a faith-based agency and one at a secular agency, believe that the qualities of grace and faith, which are typically part of the culture of faith-based agencies, are essential for this self-understanding:

> Counsellor 1, USA: You can never err on the side of grace so when I come across people … who are going through situations, you can offer them that grace, remind them of all that grace in our faith.

> Counsellor 1, Canada: Without considering faith you would only get part of the person. Faith leads to hope and helps to give them courage to move forward. Also sometimes helps them to take away from that notion of lack of control. It can be very beneficial.

Criminal justice staff in the United States also recognize the importance of a faith-based treatment option for fostering self-understanding, self-respect and movement toward change:

> CJS 1: The people we tend to send there are the people who really do want to see change happening in their lives as opposed to the people that are in major denial.

Gaining Hope

Realistic hope-in-action, as it is humanly lived, is the overriding element contributing to effecting change in the men enrolled in faith-based batterer intervention programs. Roy, Turcott et al. (2005) identify the instillation of hope as a key therapeutic factor in groups for men who batter. Along with developing universality (realizing one is not alone) and imparting information, the instillation of hope is a major issue for establishing trust both between members and with regard to the group program. The therapeutic value of hope is also identified by Bergin and Walsh (2005) who state that, particularly at the beginning of the therapeutic process, clients invest the therapist with the role of being 'an ambassador of hope.' Hope is engendered in the interaction (Eliott and Olver 2002).

But what is hope, and specifically what is hope-in-action? The diverse array of definitions, frameworks, models and characterizations make it difficult to arrive at a concise definition. Yet a common theme that links all of these approaches is that hope is intrinsically adaptive and positive (Babits 2001 in Bergin and Walsh 2005). The word *hope* appears frequently in a spiritual context. It is seen as an abiding Christian characteristic, along with faith and love, in the New Testament (Ai, Cascio et al. 2005). Additionally, numerous definitions of hope are found in the literature, particularly related to health or mental health issues. Eliott and Olver (2002) identify fourteen different scales designed to objectively measure hope and three measuring hopelessness. They also suggest that the grammatical uses of the word hope or its derivatives, as a noun, a verb, an adverb or an adjective, confound its definition.

According to Snyder, Harris et al. (1991) hope is the belief that one has the means or ways to do what is required to realize one's desired expectations and that one is able to sustain movement along those selected pathways. A slightly different definition is provided by Meadows, Kaslow et al. (2005:110) who describe hope as "positive expectations about the future and positive ways of assigning causality to events. . . ." Thus hope, particularly linked with faith, engenders positive attitudes and serves as a potential protection against despair, giving up, failing to meet goals. Additionally, a person's entire sense of well-being is affected by the ability to perceive positive effects following negative experiences (Park and Folkman 1997).

Hope as it is used within my research is a subjectively defined term with a variety of versions based on individual meaning. But it is meant to signal a warrant for action and thus is conceived of as a process based on personal agency or determination. It helps to provide the 'why' for behavior. Mascaro, Rosen et al. (2004:846) cite Nietzsche [1888] in reference to 'why,' "If we have our own why of life, we shall get along with almost any how." For these men who have acted abusively, hope is not based on a hoped for 'thing,' but rather on a 'state of affairs,' that being the prospect of 'tomorrow being a better day,' leading to the outcome of change. The 'why' leads to the 'how.'

Men from a United States therapeutic agency were asked—*Do you consider yourself a man of hope and what gives you hope?* Only one man of seventeen said he had no hope. His reply was "no, I am put here." He felt that he had been victimized by the "system" and because he was incarcerated he had lost all his worldly possessions and his relationship with his ex-partner's children. He saw no way back, and thus had no hope. We later learned that this man had left the program and been re-incarcerated for his behavior. The other sixteen ranged from subdued to effusive in their descriptions of hope in their lives. One man said he has always preferred to keep his goals to "one day at a time" but that is changing:

> #11—I was thinking the other day if I make it to two years and eleven months this time that's almost six years of sobriety that I have had in my adult life. People get degrees in less. I have always kind of romanced this kind of idea, it was always to be like a [helping profession].

Their children were central to hope in the lives of men. The men often mentioned their hope that they would have the opportunity to reunite and have healthy relationships with their children, who were often in the care of others. But these men do realize that the only way that might happen is for them to be recognizably changed, both in the eyes of the law and in the eyes of their children's caregivers.

> #05—So I am mainly here trying to get my [child] back.

> #13—It's important for [my son] to see me being a good man and a different person too cause it helps him to know that he needs to do that you know.

> #08—...see because Department of Human Services got involved, well they came to talk to me and I told them the truth for the first time.... Since then we have had the child removed from her mother's custody and at the same time because of my violence and prison and all that they had to take my custody too, but I had her placed and I knew all this, I had her placed, she is with my [relative].... I mean it's just all, it's been a blessing, the Lord has blessed me and I am on the verge of getting custody of my daughter back.

Sustaining hope requires support as its resilience ebbs and flows depending on the often moment-by-moment context of men's lives. An example of the shift in hope from exuberance to despair was found in interacting with one man participating in the program. In a morning interview he was exuberant about his hope for reunification with his son but several hours later that hope turned to despair when he was told by Child Protection Services personnel that he was not likely ever to be reunited. He failed to attend a scheduled interview later that day and we were subsequently told that he had dropped the program entirely.

Because hope is vulnerable to the vagaries of life, the therapeutic influence is critical to its sustenance. The tools for change offered within the therapeutic treatment program contribute to the lived experience of hope in the men, but these tools are especially useful when partnered with their faith in God as "backup."

> #05—If you can have backup it might as well be God. That's some good back up right there.

> #01—. . . It's given me a great degree of hope. Um I don't know, it's really I don't think you could explain to somebody all the changes that I have seen happen in the last few years. It's too remarkable . . . I don't know if it's because of Him [God], I just believe that it is. It's what drives me so much I guess, cause it's amazing. There isn't very much at all that He hasn't changed completely, completely around for me and that's about it. I don't know how else to say it.

> #08—Hope is to me, it's like this is my thing on hope—helping other people everyday. That gives hope. It's hard, every individual is different, you know I see this a lot going to AA and NA meetings, people relapse and keep going back and keep going back. I don't know, I really don't know, until you have lost everything, until you have totally surrendered, I think it takes total surrender to the Lord, total surrender of heart, and when you have totally surrendered that heart the Lord will start healing and when you totally surrender that will, that's the problem, most of these guys that say they have no hope, you got to do the work.

> #16—The hope, my hope really is 100 percent in God and Christ. . . . With Christ you have all the hope and if you do get thrown in prison then Joseph is your example and that's just how you accept it.

Without hope for a changed future, why bother? Being in a state of no hope, hopelessness, inhibits action. Meissner (1973:121) argues, "In his hopelessness, the patient makes a basic presumption that he possesses no inner resources to bring to bear on the solution of problems or the fulfillment of wishes—or at least that his inner resources are completely inadequate." Thus the process of hope leading to change is stymied. The nurturing of hope as an action process in men who have acted abusively is a key to changing their behavior. It is the carrot dangling in their vision and they can keep moving forward because of rays of hope that come both from within themselves and from those with whom they interact. Hope can offer improved self-esteem and personal empowerment to men who have very difficult lives.

The issue of these difficult lives is important. In talking with many of the men about something as simple as what they do for relaxation on the weekends it was evident that any concept of enjoyment or relaxation just for the sake of it is foreign to their experience and they were unfamiliar with ideas about how they might enjoy a few hours on the weekend with their children. Often their lives have consisted of working on weekdays, or living on the good will of others, and partying every spare moment–using both alcohol and drugs to fuel the "good" times. As well, the cast of characters that have passed through the lives of some of these men have not been great role models for the development of qualities needed for change. Having hope is thus really important as the qualities it evokes can help to counteract much of what has come before with the prospect of 'tomorrow being a better day.'

Once into the program, within the faith-based setting, the Biblical or faith component of the curriculum is of interest to many of the men. None of the men interviewed felt uncomfortable with bringing these issues into the therapy. In fact, from their perspective, talking about the Bible and its directives reinforces the deeply felt beliefs of many of them and offers new perspectives to those who are not so familiar with faith tenets. The men at both agencies acknowledged the importance of their faith in assisting them to alter their ways—to be accountable, to let go of violence and walk the world in a peaceful way. According to them, their faith also gives them hope—a quality necessary to maintain focus on their goals, providing resilience on the journey toward change. Perhaps this sense of hope is what is missing in those who, after months of treatment, are unable to achieve empathic understanding of their victims' feelings or take responsibility without somehow attributing blame to others.

Hope-in-action, a characteristic subjectively imbued with the expectation of a good that is yet to be, is clearly linked with faith. The men discuss the relationship between their faith and hope and its importance in changing their lives, and the therapists find hope in small changes amongst the men. Those changes nourish their reserves as 'ambassadors of hope.' Hope for those men interviewed is not based on unrealistic optimism. It does set in place an action scenario because of its emotional and motivational characteristics and it is strengthened because of its connection to their faith or sense of spirituality. Perhaps it can thus nourish "the seed" of change.

The demonstrated potential for faith and hope-in-action to facilitate change amongst violent religious men can either be challenged or supported by a number of correlated factors. Issues that can challenge plans for change, if not gradually overcome during the treatment process, include denial of the violence, substance abuse problems, learned behaviors, and problematic friendship and living arrangements. Unless men develop the ability to start accepting culpability for their behavior and then maintain the motivation to overcome myriad contributing factors, change is unlikely.

But there are also factors that may outweigh the impact of those challenges to provide resilience as men of faith journey toward change. Those include the essential support of faith communities and the acceptance and assistance of other men within both the criminal justice system and group therapy settings.

During the early stages of therapeutic intervention many men attempt to maintain a normative identity (Buchbinder and Eisikovits 2004; Henning and Holdford 2006) through offering socially desirable responses, impression management, and, perhaps, self-deception. While faith serves an important role in starting and keeping men on the road to changed thinking and behavior, it is, of course, necessary that they acknowledge their violence so the journey can be profitable. Unfortunately, many men never reach that stage of acknowledgement. Their emotional residue of anger, shame, denial, minimization, and attributions of blame is so deeply entrenched and they have dedicated so much effort to mitigating culpability that they remain unable to develop a new behavioral paradigm based on relational equality and respect. These men are court-mandated to enroll in the program, they attend on a weekly basis, they listen to the information, they interact with other men, and yet some never get to the point of accepting responsibility for the violence.

While the faith component is demonstrably important for many men participating in batterers' intervention programs, participants stress the necessity of "doing the work," acting on your beliefs, practicing different behavioral techniques, making sure you get to classes, or asking for and offering appropriate support. As one man said, "My dad always told me that no one is going to do it for you, you just got to get up and take care of it." The actualization of the work might mean numerous things, such as participating in therapy to overcome alcohol and/or drug addiction, attending to social interactions to ensure appropriate responses, seeking additional professional help as necessary, providing support, and setting examples for your children. But this actualization is also very much related to a sense of hope for a better tomorrow. Hope instills the motivation and reinforces the action required for "doing the work." Mills (1979) posits that hope implies participation in what we hope for, thereby establishing some possibility for the realization of the hope.

The concept of hope, or more specifically *hope-in-action*, is a key intersection point for those working with violent men of faith. For the men themselves, hope signals a warrant for action. It is conceived of as a process based on personal agency or determination. The men cling to the belief that tomorrow can be a better day, a necessary element in working toward change. For those working with abusive men, faith and hope can strengthen and bolster the resilience they offer the men for the long and difficult journey ahead, a journey that begins with one day at a time. Women of faith who are victims of abuse look for hope that the violence will end but they may also look for hope that there can be reconciliation of their relationship within the context of their faith community.

REFERENCES

Ad Hoc Federal-Provincial-Territorial Working Group Reviewing Spousal Abuse Policies and Legislation. Final report: Prepared for the Federal-Provincial-Territorial Ministers responsible for justice. http://canada.justice.gc.ca/en/ps/fin/reports/spousal.html (2003).

Ai, A. L., T. Cascio, et al. "Hope, meaning and growth following the September 11, 2001, terrorist attacks." *Journal of Interpersonal Violence* 20: (2005) 523–548.

Aldarondo, E. "Evaluating the efficacy of interventions with men who batter." In *Men who batter: Intervention and prevention strategies in a diverse society*, edited by Aldarondo, E. and F. Mederos, 3–1—3–20. New York: Civic Research Institute, 2002.

Aldarondo, E. and F. Mederos. *Programs for men who batter: Intervention and prevention strategies in a diverse society.* New York: Civic Research Institute., 2002.

Ames, L. J. and K. T. Dunham. "Asymptotic justice: Probation as a criminal justice response to intimate partner violence." *Violence Against Women* 8: 1 (2002) 6–34.

Austin, J. B. and J. Dankwort. "Standards for batterer programs: A review and analysis." *Journal of Interpersonal Violence* 14: 2 (1999) 152–168.

Bennett, L. and M. Piet. "Standards for batterer intervention programs: In whose interest?" *Violence against Women* 5: 1 (1999) 6–24.

Bennett, L. and O. Williams. Controversies and recent studies of batterer intervention program effectiveness. (2002). August 8. http://www.vaw.umn.edu.

Bergin, L. and S. Walsh. "The role of hope in psychotherapy with older adults." *Aging & Mental Health* 9: 1 (2005) 7–15.

Buchbinder, E. and Z. Eisikovits. "Between normality and deviance: The breakdown of batterers' identity following police intervention." *Journal of Interpersonal Violence* 19: 4 (2004) 443–467.

Butts, J. A. "Introduction: Problem-solving courts." *Law & Policy* 23: (2001) 121.

Clark, R. R., Jr. "Submit or else!: Intimate partner violence, aggression, batterers, and the Bible." (2005) Society for Biblical Literature, www.sbl-site.org/article.aspx?articleId=530.

Cook, D., M. Burton, et al. Evaluation of specialist domestic violence courts/fast track systems. London, England: Crown Prosecution Service 2004.

Davis, R. C. and B. G. Taylor. "Does batterer treatment reduce violence? A synthesis of the literature." *Women & Criminal Justice* 10: 2 (1999) 69–93.

Dawson, M. and R. Dinovitzer. "Victim cooperation and the prosecution of domestic violence in a specialized court." *Justice Quarterly* 18: 3 (2001) 593–622.

Denham, D. and J. Gillespie. Two steps forward . . . one step back: An overview of Canadian initiatives and resources to end woman abuse 1989–1997. The National Clearinghouse on Family Violence, Health Canada. Ottawa, 1999.

Dobash, R. E., R. P. Dobash, et al. *Changing violent men.* Thousand Oaks, CA: Sage Publications Inc., 2000.

Eliott, J. and I. Olver. "The discursive properties of "hope": A qualitative analysis of cancer patients' speech." *Qualitative Health Research* 12: 2 (2002) 173–193.

Epstein, D. "Effective intervention in domestic violence cases: Rethinking the roles of prosecutors, judges, and the court system." *Yale Journal of Law and Feminism* 11: 3 (1999) 3–50.

Goldner, V. "Morality and multiplicity: Perspectives on the treatment of violence in intimate life." *Journal of Marital and Family Therapy* 25: 3 (1999) 325–36.

Gondolf, E. "A 30-month follow-up of court-referred batterers in four cities." *International Journal of Offender Therapy and Comparative Criminology* 44: 1 (2000) 111–28.

Gondolf, E. W., D. A. Heckert, et al. "Nonphysical abuse among batterer program participants." *Journal of Family Violence* 17: 4 (2002) 293–314.

Gover, A. R. and J. M. MacDonald. "Combating domestic violence: Findings from an evaluation of a local domestic violence court." *Criminology and Public Policy* 3: 1 (2003) 109–32.

Healey, K., C. Smith, et al. Batterer intervention: Program approaches and criminal justice strategies. Washington, DC: Issues and practices in criminal justice, 1998.

Helling, J. A. Specialized criminal domestic violence courts. www.vaw.umn.edu/documents/helling.html (1990). December 9.

Henning, K. and R. Holdford. "Minimization, denial, and victim blaming by batterers: How much does the truth matter?" *Criminal Justice and Behavior* 32: 1 (2006) 110–30.

Hodge, D. R. "Spiritual Genograms: a generational approach to assessing spirituality." *Families in Society—The Journal of Contemporary Human Services* 82: (2000a) 35–48.

Hodge, D. R. "The spiritually committed: An examination of the staff at faith-based substance abuse providers." *Social Work & Christianity* 27: 2 (2000b) 150–67.

Hodge, D. R. "Spiritual lifemaps: A client-centered pictorial instrument for spiritual assessment, planning, and intervention." *Social Work* 50: 1 (2005) 77–87.

Johnson, J. M. and D. J. Kanzler. "Treating domestic violence: Evaluating the effectiveness of a domestic violence diversion program." *Studies in Symbolic Interaction* 15: (1993) 271–89.

Kaut, K. P. "Religion, spirituality, and existentialism near the end of life: Implications for assessment and application." *American Behavioral Scientist* 46: 2 (2002) 220–34.

Mankowski, E. S., J. Haaken, et al. "Collateral damage: An analysis of the achievements and unintended consequences of batterer intervention programs and discourse." *Journal of Family Violence* 17: 2 (2002) 167–84.

Mascaro, N., D. H. Rosen, et al. "The development, construct validity, and clinical utility of the spiritual meaning scale." *Personal and Individual Differences* 37: (2004) 845–60.

Meadows, L. A., N. J. Kaslow, et al. "Protective factors against suicide attempt risk among African American women experiencing intimate partner violence." *American Journal of Community Psychology* 36: 1/2 (2005) 109–21.

Mears, D. P. and C. A. Visher. "Trends in understanding and addressing domestic violence." *Journal of Interpersonal Violence* 20: 2 (2005) 204–11.

Meissner, W. W. "Notes on the psychology of hope: The psychopathology of hope." *Journal of Religion and Health* 12: 2 (1973) 120–39.

Mills, R. "An anatomy of hope." *Journal of Religion and Health* 18: 1 (1979) 49–52.

Mirchandani, R. "What's so special about specialized courts? The state and social change in Salt Lake City's domestic violence court." *Law & Society Review* 39: 2 (2005) 379–418.

Myers, K. An overview of Corrections research and development projects on family violence 1996–03. Solicitor General of Canada. Ottawa, ON, 1996.

Newmark, L., M. Rempel, et al. Specialized felony domestic violence courts: Lessons on implementation and impacts from the Kings County experience. Urban Institute, Justice Policy Center. Washington, D.C., 2001.

Nova Scotia Department of Justice. Framework for action against family violence. Department of Justice. Halifax, NS, 1999.

Nova Scotia Department of Justice Victims' Services Division. A review of the effectiveness and viability of domestic violence interventions as an adjunct to the formal criminal justice system. Nova Scotia Department of Justice. Halifax, NS, 2001.

Pargament, K. I. *The psychology of religion and coping*. New York, NY: Guilford Press, 1997.

Park, C. L. and S. Folkman. "Meaning in the context of stress and coping." *Review of General Psychology* 1: (1997) 115–44.

Pirog-Good, M. and J. Stets-Kealey. "Male batterers and battering intervention programs: A national survey." *Response to the Victimization of Women and Children* 8: 3 (1986) 8–12.

Rosenbaum, A. and P. A. Leisring. "Group intervention programs for batterers." *Journal of Aggression, Maltreatment & Trauma* 5: 2 (2001) 57–71.

Roy, V., D. Turcott, et al. "Therapeutic factors at the beginning of the intervention process in groups for men who batter." *Small Group Research* 36: 1 (2005) 106–33.

Salvaggio, F. "K-Court: The feminist Pursuit of an interdisciplinary approach to domestic violence." *Appeal: Review of Current Law and Law Reform* 8: (2002) 6–17.

Sherman, L. and D. Smith. "Crime, punishment, and stake in conformity: Legal and informal control of domestic violence." *American Sociological Review* 37: (1992) 680–90.

Snyder, C. R., C. Harris, et al. "The will and the ways: Development and validity of individual differences measure of hope." *Journal of Personality and Social Psychology* 60: 4 (1991) 570–85.

Tsai, B. "The trend towards specialized domestic violence courts: Improvements on an effective innovation." *Fordham Law Review* 68: 4 (2000) 1285–1327.

Van de Veen, S. L. Some Canadian problem solving court processes (excerpt). Excerpt of article published in the Canadian Bar Review 83(1): 91-158. 2004.

Vandecreek, L., C. Nye, et al. "Where there's life, there's hope, and where there is hope, there is . . ." *Journal of Religion and Health* 33: 1 (1994) 51–59.

Wallace, J. M., V. L. Myers, et al. Holistic faith-based development: Toward a conceptual framework. The Nelson A. Rockefeller Institute of Government. Washington, DC, 2004.

9

The Role of Regret

Lanette Ruff

EVANGELICAL FAMILIES ARE CONFRONTED with mixed messages on an ongoing, daily basis. Everywhere they turn they see evidence of a world where they must live, yet not fully belong. The secular music that blasts from their car radio, television programs that enter their home every evening, and conversations that they overhear in the workplace—all these are messages reinforcing that they are 'in the world, but not of the world.'

The constant reminders of the separation from mainstream society are particularly troubling for many evangelical couples when they have a family. They are faced with the difficult challenge of raising children who will recognize and embrace distinctions between 'the world' and the Christian community (Wilcox 1998; Wilcox, Chaves, et al. 2004). How do they raise children to grow up with goals of post-secondary education, a successful career, and a happy family life, yet shelter them from the evils feared to be lurking around many corners?

Without question, the foundation of the evangelical family is built on the notion of being separate from the world (Ammerman 1987; Ammerman 1991). And, as families work to ensure that boundaries are maintained within the walls of their home, there is an increased risk of harsh family practices (Capps 1992; Straus 1990; Straus 1991b). Recent decades have shed light on the abuse that occurs in Christian families (Nason-Clark and Kroeger 2004). While projecting an image of a good Christian family, many Christian women are being abused by their husbands (Kroeger and Nason-Clark 2001; Nason-Clark 2000b; Nason-Clark 2004; Nason-Clark and Kroeger 2004). And, although there is an image of a child-centered happy home (Smith and Kim 2003a; Smith and Kim

2003b), far too many evangelical parents have excessively punished their children (Capps 1992).

Women, who are at the heart of the home, experience incredible pressures to project an image of a perfect Christian family (Gallagher 2003; Gallagher 2004). Not only must they have a perfect Christian marriage, they also bear most of the burden of raising the next generation of evangelicals. The enormity of this responsibility no doubt creates incredible anxiety for many mothers. How can women consistently be an example of a Christian wife, mother, and nurturer at home as well as in the community? Does the pressure to be a shining example create an environment where family life may suffer? And, how do women reflect on their mothering experiences after the children have left the nest?

These very questions were at the heart of my graduate research. I wished to explore more fully the incredible mothering pressures that evangelical women face each and every day. Over the past couple of years, my dissertation research has provided me with opportunities to examine mothering experiences of evangelical women in New Brunswick, Canada—a region of Canada that has a sizeable conservative Protestant population (Statistics Canada 2003a; Statistics Canada 2003b; Statistics Canada 2005). Not only did I collect questionnaires from church women of many denominations in the province, including Baptist, Church of Christ, Independent, Pentecostal, and Wesleyan, I also had many occasions to interview women at various stages of the lifecycle and hear the challenges of raising children first hand.[1] Based on the thoughts and experiences of these women, this chapter will explore the demands on evangelical women, pressures often resulting in harsh practices that will be regretted later in life.

PERFECTION

To be like Jesus—this is a motivating goal in evangelical circles. After all, Jesus has provided a perfect example of human behavior and the Bible gives its followers the ultimate guidebook. Evangelical women reinforce this desire in all aspects of their life. Such statements include:

---

1. My dissertation, entitled Religiosity, Resources and Regrets: Religious and Social Variations of Conservative Protestant Women, is based on the data collection and analysis of 131 questionnaires and fifty-one interviews.

> ... to follow the role model, the perfect role model which is the Lord Jesus and ... how he dealt with people ... if we could only be more like Him. We pray that we are everyday.... God is moulding us into what He wants us to be (Participant #44, 1115–1119).

While Jesus provides humanity with extraordinary examples of kindness, forgiveness, and love, even the most devoted Christians realize that human nature causes each and every one of us to fail time and time again. Yet, despite human disappointments, the evangelical community encourages a goal of perfection in thought and action.

Pressure from Churches

Local church communities provide platforms where affiliates are encouraged to work towards following the faultless life examples of Jesus Christ. In order to attempt to follow in His footsteps, families often focus on their differences from mainstream society (Ammerman 1987; Beaman 1999; Berliner 1997). And enforcing this separation from mainstream society puts an enormous pressure on many evangelical women.

The faith community reinforces that message the motherhood is the highest calling—far more important than education or career aspirations. Unlike their individualistic, selfish counterparts in the world, evangelical women are destined for life as a mother where they can be a living example of self-sacrifice and separation from the world (Bartkowski 2001; Bartkowski 2004). And while female labor force participation is common in many evangelical families, young women continue to experience and witness a pressure for motherhood:

> Well, that's my struggle. Because I would kind of like to work outside of the home, but a family is really important to me. And I really want to be home with my kids, if I have kids, too. . . . So, I wouldn't want to work full-time. . . . It's kind of affecting my whole decision about what I want to do as a profession, is that fact that I want to be a mother. So, I thought about medicine, but then, and it was something that I was kind of really interested in. But then when I thought about my priorities and a family, it was more important to me (Participant #33, 116–29).

> But my biggest thing was I couldn't realize how many young girls, their focus was getting married and having children. That was all they wanted to do. It was something that I wanted to do, but it was

one of, like if you put them hierocratic, like it was one of my top priorities. It was their only top priority. . . . I think you can serve Him in many different aspects, in sports, in everything else. I see the streamlining of women. And that your role is a stay-at-home, which is fine, if that's what she chooses to do . . . I don't think that's wrong, I just think it's wrong if your heart is somewhere else. If, you know, if your heart is a veterinarian, and you are a stay-at-home mom because that's what you think was expected of you. I think it's wrong to close the doors for kids. (Participant #6, 37–50).

Making the decision to have children is not enough to satisfy the desire for perfection. Evangelical mothers also feel pressure to raise their children in a manner that will appease those in their local church congregations. There is a fear of judgment from other evangelicals and women openly admit to criticizing the parenting practices of other women within their church:

Well, I would disagree with people who, you know, people who basically let their kids do whatever they want, you know. Like that are very lax and stuff or you know, or I see qualities or things maybe in their kids that I would not like to see in my own, so there's just certain people that I wouldn't even ask because I see those things. You know, maybe within their family. And I don't want to be judgmental, but it's just things that I wouldn't particularly, you know, want in my own family (Participant #2, 211–220).

Like, lots of people in our church right now, they don't come sometimes at night . . . I'm saying they don't go at night because the children. Like they're noisy. Seeing them come Sunday morning, and then go down in their class. Our children were always in church, up sitting on the seats. And, and, if they didn't listen, they were there anyway. You know, and, and I never, we never let a small child off our lap. We never let them on the floor because they were under the seat and gone. We saw others. That happened to others, so we just kept them all together. And they weren't allowed to talk or chew gum. I see adults chewing gum in church. That was things we taught the children not to do (Participant #42, 389–400).

. . . well, I would say that the time that that Christian lady said to me, 'You give your kids too many choices,' probably ah, probably was reflective of my listening and thinking about Spock. And you know, giving kids liberty and freedom, and that kind of thing . . . what I caught from him was the idea of letting them develop as their own entity, sort of thing. You know, let them be their own person. Encourage that (Participant #15, 436–445).

While churches may appear to be places that are family friendly, women find that they are also places which are highly critical of parenting practices. While the church is known for the child-centered focus on family life, rarely is there acknowledgement of the common problems that are faced by everyday Christian families. Since women seldom hear messages that childrearing can be frustrating, and sometimes even exasperating, many feel compelled to hide their own experiences, sensing that they must be alone (Ruff 2006).

Women on Themselves

Not only do mothers feel pressure from their church community but they also place incredible pressures on themselves. Evangelical women are convinced that God has provided them with the perfect manual for life, and that includes covering any childrearing issues that they might have:

> Well, of course, our greatest resource is the Bible. And we have ah, in our church, always had excellent teaching, practical teaching on ah, you know the roles of the father. The roles of the husband. The mother, the wife, the children. And throughout, of course, the Word of God there's all kinds of teaching on how people are to react to one another and their responsibility to God (Participant #44, 1108–1114).

Not only do women believe that they should be perfect as mothers, because of their dedication to Biblical teaching, but evangelical women also believe that they have additional support through prayer and their relationship with God.

> I think maybe one of the misconceptions is if you're a Christian parent, then you know, you've got it all together. You know, that's, you have the same, same problems you know, only you have a counselor. You have, you know, a built in counselor that you can go to (Participant #6, 1197–1203).

They have been told that mothering 'just comes naturally' (Ruff 2006) and whatever struggles they might have can be rectified through Bible reading and prayer. If they struggle with parenting, perhaps they have not spent enough time reading their Bible, or perhaps they need to strengthen their relationship with God. They tell themselves that as a Christian woman, they must be the perfect mother, they must do everything right. And when they do struggle, women learn to hide any misgivings they might have, fearing that these may question their religious commitment. How can a good Christian woman, who loves the Lord, struggle with her 'calling' to be a mother?

Women on Their Children

As a result of the pressures from the church and the responsibilities they place on themselves, mothers place incredible pressures on their children. First and foremost, they do not want to lose their children to 'the world.' Time and time again mothers insist that their primary goal for their children is that they will make a personal commitment to Christ (Ruff 2006), that they will become a 'born-again' Christian. They fear that they will lose control over their children if they are lenient (Ellison, Bartkowski, et al. 1996; Ellison and Goodson 1997; Ellison and Sherkat 1993).

In addition to the concern that they have for the souls of their children, mothers want their children to do their part to contribute to the image of their perfect Christian family:

> . . . I always wanted to have kids that people would like. You know, instead of, you have birthday parties and all the kids come over, and you think, man alive, there's somebody . . . that is worse than mine. I didn't want my kid to be the one that was worse than everybody else (Participant #15, 539–542).

> Um, I guess before you have kids, you think that everything is just going to be hunky-dory, all the time, you know. And you just kind of have this vision of, you know, peace and everybody getting along all the time. (laughs) . . . But . . . reality is not that (Participant #3, 363–367).

While women of all backgrounds can be embarrassed by the behavioral choices of their children, evangelical women may believe that their worth as Christian mothers is in question. When things are not 'hunky-dory' in the home, the children misbehave, or the pressures of motherhood become too much to bear, women naturally turn to the strategies that they know best. And for many in the community, these solutions often come in the form of discipline. After all, conservative interpretations of Biblical scriptures are well-known for their emphasis on punishment. While punishment is a tool used to steer children towards 'the path of righteousness' it can also be used to avoid parental embarrassment.

DISCIPLINE

Evangelical Christians are often depicted by their unwavering worldviews on evil and humanity. Well-known for their beliefs about the sinfulness of human nature, it is such views that lead parents to believe that all children are born in sin (Bartkowski 1995). Many within the evangelical community believe that physical punishment is not only recommended, it is in fact required, in order to drive out this sinful nature. One mother uses the typical justification for physical punishment, "the famous scripture in the Bible, 'spare the rod and spoil the child'" (Participant #5, 464–465). Many evangelical parents believe that without the use of physical punishment they risk not only losing their children to the world, but also jeopardizing their very souls and eternal salvation. Their views on the secular world, beliefs about directives from Biblical scriptures, and religious convictions about heaven and hell, lead many parents to the conclusion that the use of physical punishment is an appropriate form of discipline.

Support for Physical Punishment

Evangelical families not only believe that the Bible instructs them to use the 'rod' on their children, but that view is reinforced by many well-known figureheads within the community who support the use of physical punishment (Bartkowski 1995). Perhaps one of the most well-known within religious circles is James Dobson, founder of *Focus on the Family*. Although careful in his instructions on the use of spanking, he nonetheless is a clear supporter of this form of punishment (Dobson 1994). Countless books, magazines, articles, and other resources available through *Focus on the Family* reinforce that physical punishment is fitting—particularly for children who willfully defy the authority of their parents.

While the Word of God is viewed as the ultimate guide, Dobson's voice is also heard loudly and clearly in evangelical circles:

> I couldn't have lived without James Dobson . . . I read all of his books. Any resources that he offered. The magazines and everything (Participant # 46, 246–256).

> I respect him as a scholar and I respect him as a person. And um,
> he's perspective for me, I guess, it satisfies. The kind of . . . author-
> ity in the Christian world that I always liked (Participant #15,
> 361–365).

As mothers state, he is a respected voice—a voice whose opinions of family life and childrearing are incredibly influential. When evangelical parents spank their children, they have the comfort of believing that they are
following the will of God and have the support of prominent figures in
the community. While far from endorsing abusive practices, the approval
of prominent Christian figureheads provides justification for parents who
use excessive discipline with their children. With the exception of specialized sporting events, it is the only circumstance in our cultural context
where striking another individual is deemed socially appropriate.

Discipline Practices in the Home

While many experts in society debate the impact of physical punishment,
it is apparent that this form of punishment has the possibility of crossing
the line (Straus 1991a; Straus 2000a; Straus 2000b; Straus, Larzelere, et al.
1994; Straus and Yodanis 1996). Experts in support of spanking clearly
understand it can be excessive—parameters such as identifying appropriate ages, instruments used, and suitable body parts are examples of
suggested limitations. Yet, even within the confines of these limitations,
spanking can be excessive. According to the following participant, even
bruising and leaving marks seems open to interpretation:

> You can give a child a good, hard spanking and sometimes leave a
> mark without it being excessive. Maybe that child happens to bruise
> easily . . . And my idea of a hard spanking and somebody else's idea
> of a hard spanking . . . depending on the age of the child, too. So . . .
> where's the cross over line? (Participant #20, 1352–1452).

Parents who believe they have the God-given authority to physically pun-
ish their children acknowledge that there are many grey areas with this
form of discipline. Certainly many dedicated church women admit going
too far with their children:

> . . . on the last day of school, on the bus stop and they didn't get
> off, and I had no way of knowing. But their bus driver felt that he
> did the wrong thing. And when he got home, he called me. I got in
> the car, and I took the belt with me . . . and they knew I was angry.

And we got home, I gave them the belt. . . . I beat them so many times. But, I should never have beat them in anger (Participant #31, 558–567).

Although they believe that the Bible instructs them to use 'the rod' in punishing their children, many women recognize that there is a risk of excessive discipline. Not only do they recognize the danger, mothers also have experience in going over the line. Many acknowledge using harsh discipline out of frustration (Ruff 2006), a practice that they will most definitely later regret.

REGRETS

Undoubtedly, all mothers have regrets (Berndsen, van der Pligt, et al. 2004; DeGenova 1996; Groat, Giordano, et al. 1997). Yet, when evangelical women look back on their childrearing years, the regrets that they face are unique to their religious beliefs (Ruff 2006). Even though they believed that they should teach their children to be 'separate' from the world (Berliner 1997; Ruff 1999), in reflecting on their mothering experiences women indicate that they regret the limitations they placed on their children. Women regret forbidding their children to participate in numerous secular activities:

> . . . there's some things that I didn't allow my kids to do that, maybe I should have. Because it really wasn't going to hurt them. Like the school dances . . . I've tried to make them live my life, the way I wanted it. And it really wasn't fair to them (Participant #47, 519–526).

> Um, be a little bit more lenient, um, as far as activities and things. You know, um, allow them to participate in things that are not morally wrong, . . . They didn't really have anybody to, you know, to chum around with, say. You know, best friend, type thing. (Participant #13, 510–20).

> Well, for instance, going to movies (Participant # 20, 746).

> There are some things that I do regret, you know. Ah, I could have let them listen to different music. Just because in my head, rock music was wrong, Christian rock, or whatever. I don't agree with that today (Participant #51, 587–591).

> And ah, and I remember one of our boys played hockey. And ah, of course, they had hockey games on Sunday. We wouldn't allow him to go to his games on Sunday. We wouldn't allow him to play. I don't think I'd do that now (Participant #43, 328–331).

Evangelical mothers must feel an incredible tug-of-war as they assess the messages they hear from mainstream society and their church community. On one hand, they want only the best for the children; they want their children to be happy and want to provide memories for them to cherish for a lifetime. Yet, on the other hand, their faith community tells them that if they want to see their children saved, they must sacrifice earthly pleasures. If they allow their children too much involvement in the world, they are certain to lose them. Sadly, years later, it is these very choices that will result in regret for many women who have had only the best of motherly intentions (Ruff 2006).

Not only are mothers troubled by their decisions regarding social activities, they are particularly disturbed by the disciplinary practices that were used in the home. They recognize the pressures of being a mother in an evangelical family, yet understand other choices could have been made. It is the physical punishment of their children that empty-nesters regret the most:

> I feel that I should have had a better support system, when my husband was away. Um, because I was a very frustrated person at that time. And I dealt with things more harshly than I should have. And that's one of my regrets. And I'm sure all mothers do have, but ah, that would be the thing that I, if I were to be able to go back, I think that's the one thing that I would try to do differently (Participant #28, 638–645).

> But ah, my views on parenting have definitely changed. Yeah they have. I would, as far as discipline, I would not use spanking as much as I did. Now, when you have grandchildren, you don't want to spank your grandchildren. I will do everything but that unless it's absolutely necessary. . . . Ah, spanking, when my children were growing up was used far too much. Not far too much, I think, but that was what we did. You got a spanking, you know (Participant #31, 656–667).

When evangelical women become empty-nesters, and again when they become grandmothers, they often reflect on the choices they made.

Perhaps the saddest part of the evangelical mothering narrative is the level of secret sorrow, the regret that is rarely acknowledged within their church community, and the feelings that must remain hidden. After all, as mothers they believed they were following the directives of the faith community when they made parenting choices. Although well-intended, church emphasis on family life has sometimes led to harsh practices within the home, and to a deep sadness for many women in their later years.

SUPPORT

Without question, evangelical women identify family life challenges that threaten the safe sanctuary of home. While all Christians aim to live a life like Jesus, the journey for perfection leads parents to be overly harsh with themselves and their children (Ruff 2006). Church communities, although on the surface providing a supportive environment for families, too often have been negligent in recognizing and identifying signs of families who are in need of assistance (Nason-Clark 1999; Nason-Clark 2000a). Just as church families are beginning to acknowledge incidents of wife abuse, they also need to consider the welfare of children. Based on research findings, this section will highlight some suggestions for church communities:

Acknowledge that family life is not easy

From my research with evangelical women, I found that women report a need for support with family life from their church and its leadership. In fact, of the women who participated:

- Ninety-one percent want support in providing religious training for their children;

- Seventy percent want assistance in finding personal time for themselves;

- Sixty-nine percent want assistance in determining appropriate discipline for their children;

- Fifty-three percent want support in resolving parenting differences with their spouse; and

- Forty-two percent want assistance with family budgeting.

As these women indicate, mothers are in need of a support system. Churches have an incredible opportunity to address the varied issues that families face on an ongoing basis. Family members will struggle as they negotiate their roles as husbands, wives, and parents. And, while mothering may be 'blessed,' faith communities should be diligent in acknowledging that mothering can also be very exasperating. As one woman states, as a young mother she was overwhelmed by the responsibilities she faced:

> I relied, in all honesty, on what I was taught as a child . . . but I didn't feel that I had enough. I can't lie and say I felt I had enough. I didn't, I didn't feel I had enough. I didn't feel that I had any place that I felt I could reach out and get what I needed. I felt that there was so much need and I didn't know what direction to turn to get it (Participant #16, 508–515).

If churches insinuate that all answers are readily available in the Bible and through prayer, struggling families may question their personal faith and be hesitant to reach out for help. Although family life can be tremendously rewarding, it can also be very challenging.

Provide supportive environments

Not only can local churches acknowledge the struggles that families face, they have a unique opportunity to provide an environment that is supportive of parents and children. Evangelical women have many suggestions on ways in which faith communities can nurture family life and 'help each other along the way:'

> I guess supporting me . . . I think it would be good if they had little seminars . . . for mothers, with kids, you know, how to deal with certain situations. . . . I guess, especially with the upcoming years, like, with mine coming into their teen years. I would, I would like to see more support for how to handle certain situations (Participant #5, 603–618).

> . . . there's . . . older ladies that are often . . . home and don't have enough to fill their day. And there's people like I was . . . when my children were young, and I had three real little kids. And I just had no time to myself. Even just to nurture myself, you know. Just to sit down and read the Bible, or have a nap, or go for a walk or something. It just wasn't happening (Participant #32, 709–718).

By arranging opportunities for young mothers to share and social-
ize with other young mothers, or opportunities where elder mothers can
share their experiences and expertise, young mothers can flourish in an
understanding environment where they are free to address common frustrations and workable solutions. Mothers who struggle need the affirmation of the faith community:

> Well, I've actually talked to a pastor . . . about the children, raising
> them up. After you've raised them up in a Christian home, and
> they stray away, whose fault is it (Participant #42, 302–306).

Evangelical women need the supportive environment of their Christian
community. In fact, based on the responses of the participants in this
study, next to family members, evangelical women are most likely to turn
to Christian friends when they need advice or assistance.

Condemn not only wife abuse, but child abuse

As we challenge the church to recognize all forms of family violence,
faith communities must recognize that punishment and discipline can
be forms of abuse. In fact, statistics show that excessive discipline is the
most common form of child abuse (Statistics Canada 2001). Parents need
to hear that while God may have given parents authority over their children, God has not given them permission to abuse their children (Straus
1991a). Behind closed doors, evangelical women acknowledge that this is
a problem, and they long for the church to recognize it:

> I think it should be addressed. I think there's people that are doing
> it [abusing their children] that don't even realize that they're doing
> it. And it might not be physical, it may be physical . . . abuse should
> be addressed, because that's what you don't see. . . . I think people
> are abusive and nobody knows about it. Or they don't think that
> they've crossed the line. . . . I would bet that there's kids in the
> church that are verbally abused. I wouldn't be surprised at all. I
> would like to be surprised, but I wouldn't be surprised (Participant
> #27, 714–726).

Just as it can be difficult for some to imagine that a God-fearing man would
strike his wife (Nason-Clark 1997; Nason-Clark, Fisher-Townsend, et al.
2005; Nason-Clark, Murphy, et al. 2004), it can be even more difficult to
imagine that Christian parents would abuse their children (Wilcox 1998).
After all, when we think about coverage of child abuse in the media, we

often recall appalling situations of starvation, abandonment, and captivity. Yet, excessive discipline is another form of abuse and the consequences are harmful not only to the child, but to future generations (Heyman and Slep 2002). Silence should never be mistaken for condemnation of abuse. It must be openly addressed.

Churches need to be safe places for all family members. Faith communities have many opportunities to minister to all, from the youngest to the oldest. In nursery services, in Sunday School classes, in senior quilting bees—local churches have many opportunities to model true Christian love. Not only can faith communities work toward providing a safe environment through the proper screening of all workers, it is imperative that church officials be aware of the signs of child abuse. What better way to be the hands and feet of Jesus than by rescuing the vulnerable from the hands of an abuser?

Understand that families will struggle

Faith communities not only need to recognize the call for help and assistance, they also have an opportunity to reach out to families who struggle. Evangelical women identify stresses encountered in taking their children to church:

> Um, it's funny because every once in a while there will be a kid crying. Or I mean the pastor is strict, I think, when it comes to church and kids running around or talking or whatever. If there's somebody talking, he'll say, 'Ok, I'm talking.' Like, I mean, like last Sunday morning, I think it was, he says, 'Ok, I'm talking and I'm going to wait for a couple of people to get done talking.' . . . And ah, if a kid cries, he'll say, 'We have a nursery' (Participant #5, 549–564).

When women sense there is a lack of understanding related to children's behavior during church services, how much more difficult it must be to acknowledge other, more pressing problems, as mothers.

In an environment where all are encouraged to strive for perfection, those who struggle the most risk feeling like failures. Acknowledging that although 'being changed in an instant' is the ultimate goal of all sinners, perfection is difficult to achieve. Being a good Christian does not mean that someone will be a good parent. Just as on the surface, a man who abuses his wife can appear to be dedicated to his faith, other family members can struggle with countless personal issues:

So, yeah, so, it's a little confusing sometimes when you think about it because, we went to church, we're learning, you know, things about how to live a godly life and stuff, and yet, at the same time, my Mom had troubles with temper. And um, when it came to disciplining, a lot of times, I think she acted out of anger instead of when the punishment was needed, you know. To make sure that that behaviour wasn't continued, sometimes it was probably just you're driving me crazy and I'm mad, so, you know getting back at you, that's what I felt anyway. So, it's taking me a whole lot to sort of get over that and not have any resentment. So, I usually tend not to think about it (Participant #11, 100–111).

Um, ah, our house was, I would say, quite dysfunctional. Very, we were all very isolated from one another. Um, there was very strong discipline. No not discipline. Punishment. And it was basically, you are punished for everything that you ever did wrong. Or that was not up to standards. And there were rules. And sometimes you didn't even know what the rules were. And the rules seemed to change. And there was very heavy handed, corporal type punishment . . . because the punishments were um, like they were severe. And there was not, there was no offsetting or touching in a positive way, to offset it. In any way. And so, it just instilled fear as opposed to learning changed behavior. Obviously you change your behaviour, you change it not because you understand it to be incorrect, but because you are scared to death. What will happen if you ever do it again? So, I don't think it was, no, it was not positive (Participant #51, 7–30).

Although Christian families may have goals of salvation for their children, those goals do not necessarily equate to a healthy home environment. Far too often, parents are not only unable to live up to societal expectations, but they also must struggle to ensure that their parenting practices are in line with their religious convictions.

Refer to experts

Far too often, religious families have been reluctant to seek assistance outside of the church community. Researchers find that evangelical parents have been hesitant to consider mainstream parenting advice, fearing that such experts do not share their values. Instead, evangelical women are turning to numerous Christian resources, from parenting books, to magazines, to online parenting websites (Ruff 2006). While Christian resources may be a priority, evangelical women indicate that they are also familiar with the resources provided by mainstream experts, such as Dr. Phil. Younger women are more likely to make use of the growing access to parenting resources.

While church communities can acknowledge the challenges of striving for a perfect life and provide supportive environments for parents, churches also have the opportunity to direct families to mainstream experts, as needed (Nason-Clark, Mitchell, et al. 2004). Certainly, many churches are not equipped to respond to the various needs of families. While prayer may be appropriate and helpful, it does not replace the need for a physician to attend to a sick child. Nor does it replace the need for mental health experts for those who have been traumatized by horrific events. Similarly, there are times when parents may need to enroll in parenting classes, seek the assistance of a social worker, or reach out to intervention workers. By becoming familiar with local resources, churches can demonstrate approval of selected community expertise. Acknowledging personal weakness does not represent a crisis of faith—it symbolizes a strength of character.

CONCLUSION

Evangelical families are often portrayed as nurturing and loving, child-friendly homes. But, does the rhetoric match the reality of everyday experiences in evangelical families? As the women in this study demonstrate, we cannot assume that the polished, smiling family that attends the local church has a perfect family life. Instead of being sanctuaries, under the guise of nurturing the soul evangelical homes can hide harsh family practices. The regrets of many women who participated in this study demonstrate that childrearing practices can be and have been excessive. While as Christians we strive to live like Jesus, the focus on perfection has left many women being overly harsh on themselves and their children. Yet, as we begin to address the secret burdens of evangelical family life, we can learn from past mistakes and work toward a better tomorrow. The regrets of evangelical women clearly demonstrate that reconsidering long-held beliefs can enhance the experiences of Christian families and need not sacrifice eternal salvation.

REFERENCES

Ammerman, N. T. Bible Believers: Fundamentalists in the Modern World. New Brunswick, NJ: Rutgers University Press, 1987.

_____. "North American Protestant Fundamentalists." In Fundamentalists Observed, edited by Marty, M. E. and R. S. Appleby, 2–4. Chicago: University of Chicago Press, 1991.

Bartkowski, J. P. "Spare the Rod ... Or Spoil the Child? Divergent Perspectives on Conservative Protestant Child Discipline." Review of Religious Research 37: 2 (1995) 97–116.

_____. Remaking the Godly Marriage: Gender Negotiations in Evangelical Families. New Brunswick, NJ: Rutgers University Press, 2001.

_____. The Promise Keepers: Servants, Soldiers, and Godly Men. New Brunswick, NJ: Rutgers University Press, 2004.

Beaman, L. G. Shared Beliefs, Different Lives: Women's Identities in Evangelical Context. St. Louis: Chalice Press, 1999.

Berliner, D. C. "Educational Psychology Meets the Christian Right: Differing Views on Children, Schooling, Teaching, and Learning." Teachers College Record 98: 3 (1997) 381–416.

Berndsen, M., J. van der Pligt, B. Doosje and A. S. R. Manstead. "Guilt and Regret: The Determining Role of Interpersonal and Intrapersonal Harm." Cognition and Emotion 18: 1 (2004) 55–70.

Capps, D. "Religion and Child Abuse: Perfect Together." Journal for the Scientific Study of Religion 31: 1 (1992) 1–14.

DeGenova, M. K. "Regrets in Later Life." Journal of Women and Aging 8: 2 (1996) 75–85.

Dobson, J. Parenting Isn't for Cowards. Nashville: Word Publishing, 1994.

Ellison, C. G., J. P. Bartkowski and M. L. Segal. "Conservative Protestantism and the Parental Use of Corporal Punishment." Social Forces 74: 3 (1996) 1003–28.

Ellison, C. G. and P. Goodson. "Conservative Protestantism and Attitudes Toward Family Planning in A Sample of Semarians." Journal for the Scientific Study of Religion 36: 4 (1997) 512–30.

Ellison, C. G. and D. E. Sherkat. "Conservative Protestantism and the Support for Corporal Punishment." American Sociological Review 58: (1993) 131–44.

Gallagher, S. K. Evangelical Identity and Gendered Family Life. New Brunswick, NJ: Rutgers University Press, 2003.

_____. "Where Are the Antifeminist Evangelicals? Evangelical Identity, Subcultural Location, and Attitudes Toward Feminism." Gender and Society 18: 4 (2004) 451–72.

Groat, H. T., P. C. Giordano, S. A. Cernkovich, M. D. Pugh and S. P. Swinford. "Attitudes Toward Childbearing Among Young Parents." Journal of Marriage and the Family 59: 3 (1997) 568–81.

Heyman, R. and A. S. Slep. "Do Child Abuse and Interparental Violence Lead to Adulthood Family Violence?" Journal of Marriage and the Family 64: (2002) 867–70.

Kroeger, C. C. and N. Nason-Clark. No Place for Abuse: Biblical and Practical Resources to Counteract Domestic Violence. Downers Grove, IL: InterVarsity Press, 2001.

Nason-Clark, N. The Battered Wife: How Christians Confront Family Violence. Louisville, KY: Westminster/John Knox Press, 1997.

_____. "Shattered Silence or Holy Hush: Emerging Definitions of Violence Against Women." Journal of Family Ministry 13: 1 (1999) 39–56.

_____. "Has the Silence Been Shattered or Does the Holy Hush Still Prevail? Defining Violence in Religious Contexts." In Bad Pastors: Clergy Malfeasance in America, edited by Shupe, A., Albany, NY: New York University Press, 2000a.

_____. "Making the Sacred Safe: Woman Abuse and Communities of Faith." Sociology of Religion 61: 4 (2000b) 349–68.

_____. "When Terror Strikes at Home: The Interface Between Religion and Domestic Violence." Journal for the Scientific Study of Religion 43: 3 (2004) 303–10.

Nason-Clark, N., B. Fisher-Townsend and L. Ruff. Changing Abusive Religious Men: Notes from the Field. Violence Against Women: Partnering for Change—Muriel McQueen Ferguson Center for Family Violence Research Day, Fredericton: 2005.

Nason-Clark, N. and C. C. Kroeger. Refuge from Abuse: Healing and Hope for Abused Christian Women. Downers Grove, IL: InterVarsity Press, 2004.

Nason-Clark, N., L. Mitchell and L. Beaman. Bridge Building Between Churches and Community Resources: An Overview of the Work of the Religion and Violence Research Team. Fredericton: Muriel McQueen Fergusson Centre for Family Violence Research, 2004.

Nason-Clark, N., N. Murphy, B. Fisher-Townsend and L. Ruff. "An Overview of the Characteristics of the Clients at a Faith-Based Batterer Intervention Program." Journal of Religion and Abuse 5: 4 (2004) 51–72.

Ruff, L. "Homeschooling: A Response to a Perceived Moral Crisis in Education." Ph.D. diss., University of New Brunswick. Fredericton. 1999.

_____. "Religiosity, Resources and Regrets: Religious and Social Variations in Conservative Protestant Mothering." Ph.D. diss., University of New Brunswick. Fredericton. 2006.

Smith, C. S. and P. Kim. Family Religious Involvement and the Quality of Family Relationships for Early Adolescents. Odum Institute. Chapel Hill, NC, 2003a.

_____. Parents in Religious Families with Teens More Likely to Express Affection or Love to Each Other. http://www.youthandreligion.org/news/2003-0121.html. (2003b). May 20, 2003.

Statistics Canada. Family Violence in Canada: A Statistical Profile 2001. Canadian Centre for Justice Studies. Ottawa, 2001.

_____. Populations by Religion, 1981 and 1991 Census, Canada. www.statcan.ca/english. Pgdb/demo32.htm. (2003a). January 30, 2003.

_____. Selected Religions, for Canada, Provinces and Territories—20% Sample Data. http://www12.statcan.ca/english/census01/products/highlight/religion/Index. cfm?land=E. (2003b). May 14, 2003.

_____. New Brunswick: Second largest proportion of Roman Catholics. http:// www12statcan.ca/english/census01/Products/Analytic/companion/rel/nb.cfm. (2005). January 9.

Straus, M. A. "Family Patterns and Abuse: The Social Causes of Child Abuse." In Physical Violence in American Families: Risk Factors and Adaptations to Violence in 8145 Families, edited by Straus, M. A. and R. J. Gelles, 248–263. New Brunswick, NJ: Transaction Publishers, 1990.

_____. Advising Parents About Corporal Punishment: The Research Evidence And Its Implications for Pediatric Practice. Family Research Laboratory. Durham, NH, 1991a.

_____. Beating the Devil Out of Them: Corporal Punishment in American Families. New York: Lexington Books, 1991b.

_____. "Corporal Punishment and Primary Prevention of Physical Abuse." Child Abuse and Neglect 24: 9 (2000a) 1109–14.

_____. "Corporal Punishment by Parents: The Cradle of Violence in the Family and Society." Virginia Journal of Social Policy and the Law 8: 1 (2000b) 7–60.

Straus, M. A., R. E. Larzelere and J. K. Rosemond. "Should the Use of Corporal Punishment by Parents be Considered Child Abuse?" In Debating Children's Lives: Current Controversies on Children and Adolescents, edited by Mason, M. A. and E. Gambrill, 196–222. Thousand Oaks, CA: SAGE Publications, 1994.

Straus, M. A. and C. L. Yodanis. "Corporal Punishment in Adolescents and Physical Assaults on Spouses in Later Life: What Accounts for the Link?" Journal of Marriage and the Family 58: November (1996) 825–41.

Wilcox, W. B. "Conservative Protestant Childrearing: Authoritarian or Authoritative?" American Sociological Review 63: 6 (1998) 796–809.

Wilcox, W. B., M. Chaves and D. Franz. "Focused on the Family? Religious Traditions, Family Discourse, and Pastoral Practice." Journal for the Scientific Study of Religion 43: 4 (2004) 491–504.

10

Overcoming Sexual Addictions

Marjorie P. Kroeger

NAOMI IS A BRIGHT, successful physician's assistant who came to me for treatment to cope with her husband's increasing demands on her to participate in sexual behavior that made her uncomfortable. She met her husband, Stephen, when she was fifteen, soon after her mother evicted her from their home. Naomi took refuge from the abuse of her childhood with Stephen, who was in his early twenties, and his family. She had suffered sexual abuse at the hands of her stepfather from the time she was five years old until she was twelve, at which time she told her mother about the abuse. Naomi's mother initially forced her to sleep in the car to protect her, but eventually kicked her out of the house, as she posed too much of a threat to her marriage.

At the beginning of their relationship, Stephen was protective and eager to take care of Naomi, showering her with gifts and providing her with the attention she craved as a child. As the relationship progressed however, he became increasingly controlling and began to push her to have sex in more demeaning ways. He frequently pressured her to take off her clothing while they were driving so he could fondle her as he drove. At home he would wake her up in the middle of the night to have sex, which was particularly alarming for Naomi as it triggered flashbacks of her abuse. Stephen frequently watched pornographic videos in the house, even when their two young children were playing nearby. Meanwhile, it became clear that Stephen was having extra-marital affairs. Stephen was never very vigilant about hiding his affairs, but Naomi chose to ignore the evidence, even when people told her of his actions.

With the advent of the internet, Stephen began to advertise for group sex, and demanded that Naomi accompany him to "swinging" parties. He insisted that Naomi have sex with other men, while he watched, at parties or in parking lots outside of strip clubs. In desperation, Naomi sought therapy with a psychologist who told her to "call [her husband's] bluff," and go along with his behavior to see how far he would really take it. Every week Naomi would recount the details of the sexual exploits to her therapist, and every week he would encourage her to continue to participate. This went on for three years.

Naomi found my name on a website for the Society for the Advancement of Sexual Health, an organization dedicated to treating sexual compulsivity. When I first met Naomi, I was struck by the fact that such a bright, capable and professionally successful woman possessed no power and no voice in her own marriage. It immediately became clear that Naomi's fear of saying "no" to her husband originated in her sexual abuse history. Her stepfather had told her that if she exposed him, she and her siblings would be taken away from their mother. Thirty years later, Naomi was almost literally paralyzed at the thought of standing up to her husband. When I told her that she absolutely did not have to have sex with her husband anymore, Naomi cried with relief. I explained that healthy sex is based on relationship, connection, intimacy, and trust. Unhealthy, addictive sex is selfish and demanding rather than mutually satisfying. Naomi was able to recognize that her sexual relationship with Stephen was continually triggering within her the shame of her childhood abuse.

In my work as a psychotherapist, specializing in the treatment of sexual addiction, I find that the spouse/partner of the sexually addicted person requires her/his own program of recovery. Many, if not most, of the partners of sex addicts come from families in which addiction, abuse and neglect are common. In the case of Naomi and Stephen, both have histories of childhood sexual abuse. It is not uncommon for two people with significant trauma histories to come together in what is referred to as "traumatic bonding" or a "betrayal bond." Many partners of sex addicts resist doing their own work because they feel that sex addiction is "his problem, not mine." At a minimum, however, the partner needs to explore how he or she ended up in a relationship with a sex addict, and what impact the relationship has had on his or her own emotional, physical and spiritual welfare, as well as that of their children. Most partners maintain some level of denial around their spouse's behavior, as well as their own behavior. Partners are particularly reluctant to address how the addictive system has impacted children. They maintain the stance that what the children don't know can't hurt them. But children often do know, on some level, and inherit the intimacy difficulties their parents possess. This is why it is common to see sexual addiction passed down from one generation to the next. At a minimum, children learn inappropriate ways of communicating and being intimate with each other, or absorb subtle but inappropriate sexual messages.

Partners also need assistance in addressing other co-existing addictive or compulsive behaviors which enable the addictive system. For instance, a partner may become enraged over her husband's compulsive online pornography use, but ignores or even encourages his compulsive work habits, alcohol or other drug consumption, or compulsive spending. My treatment of the sex addict includes treatment of the whole person, including all of the ways that his or her life has become out of control and out of balance. Likewise, I assist the partner in addressing the ways in which her life is out of control. Typically, when I meet a partner of a sex addict, she has spent many years trying to control her husband's behavior. She may monitor his computer use, read his email, check his cell phone bill or grill him as to his whereabouts. She likely spends most of her time and energy focused on him, thereby neglecting her own needs. She is often out of control with food, spending, exercise or numbing behaviors like compulsive business, television watching or internet use. Often she believes that if she was prettier, smarter, taller, or had a body more conforming to media standards, her husband would not engage in these behaviors. She works overtime trying to anticipate her husband's every need to prevent him from pursuing other sources of sexual satisfaction. It is not uncommon for the partner to engage in sexual behaviors with which she is uncomfortable in order to keep him satisfied. This is by far the most difficult part of my work with the partner. Until she understands that there is literally nothing she can do to control her partner's behavior there is little chance that she can become healthy or that this couple can recover successfully.

The bulk of my work with the partner is to encourage her to attend to her own needs. I have often said that treating the partner of a sex addict is more difficult than treating the sex addict. The reason for this is that the partner has enormous difficulty taking the focus off of her husband and placing it on herself. She is certain that if she doesn't direct all of her energy on him, he will betray her again. So she remains in a heightened state of anxiety and distress at all times. The issue of focusing on self-care is especially difficult for female partners, and, I would submit, most especially difficult for Christian women. Women are socialized to take care of the needs of others first and endure hardship and suffering for the sake of their loved ones as well as strangers. Christians are taught that it is selfish and sinful to put oneself before others. Growing up in Sunday School we learned the following song:

> Jesus and others and you
> What a wonderful way to spell joy
> Jesus and others and you
> And the life of each girl and each boy
> J- is for Jesus for He gets first place
> O- is for others we meet face to face
> Y- is for you and what ever you do
> Put yourself last and spell joy
> (Source Unknown)

I maintain that this song and other teachings like it has created generations of Christians who have difficulty with self-care and end up in abusive or addictive relationships. To redress the core issues that contribute to the partner's co-addictive or co-dependent behavior, I urge all of the partners I treat to get involved in a twelve-step meeting for co-addicts. These groups include COSA, COSLAA, S-Anon and Al Anon. Unfortunately, specific groups for partners of sex addicts are not available everywhere, so I encourage partners to attend Al Anon because its principles are identical. The twelve-step community offers her support for managing her anxiety around her husband's recovery process. Typically the partner tries to micromanage her partner's recovery, monitoring his twelve-step meeting attendance and grilling him about the details of his therapy. She often interrogates him as to his activities both inside and outside the home. Needless to say, over involvement in the addict's recovery process only increases his shame, and may sabotage his recovery, since he often wants nothing more than to placate his wife. In some cases, I may recommend a "therapeutic separation" for couples who are so focused on each other that they are unable to address their own recovery needs. A therapeutic separation is designed to be a highly structured, contractual arrangement, whereby both parties agree to various terms outlined by their therapists and each other. These terms may include a minimum number of individual and couples therapy sessions, meeting attendance for both, and scheduled conversations for mutual accountability. The goal of the separation is to move toward reconciliation, and therefore dating outside of the relationship is not advised.

Once the partners achieve a healthier level of self-care, they are ready to reunite and work on their relationship. During this phase the couples' therapist works with the couple on trust building, healthy intimacy and parenting issues. Building trust requires time and a dedication to honesty in communication. Often the partner wants a detailed account of the addict's 'acting out' history, but details are never helpful to building trust. The partner needs to know the essence of the truth but not the details. I have one client who found a picture of her husband's mistress on a social networking site. Despite her husband's resounding success in recovery, the image of the other woman haunted their relationship, and especially their sex life, for several years. Learning to let go of the details of the addict's past is an important recovery milestone for the partner.

Most sex addicts do not have a clue what constitutes healthy intimacy, and their partners may not either. In fact, sex addiction is really considered an intimacy disorder. That is, the addict cannot tolerate emotional connection and vulnerability. Chances are, like the addict, the partner grew up in an addictive or otherwise dysfunctional family in which communication and intimacy were limited or inappropriate. Therefore the partner may recognize that she doesn't feel connected to her husband, but may not know what to do about it. She is likely more comfortable blaming him for the problem rather than taking responsibility for her own part in their dysfunctional dynamic.

Frequently, the addict is out of control with pornography or extramarital sex but is not interested in physical, emotional or sexual intimacy with his spouse. This is because addictive sex is based on fantasy and self-gratification. Healthy sex is grounded in a real relationship, requiring acceptance of the imperfect. Healthy sex requires vulnerability, connection and patience. Learning healthy intimacy is usually the most difficult task for the addict and can be a source of intense frustration for the partner. Finally, for partners who need a higher level of care than is available in an outpatient setting, there are residential treatment centers specializing in the issues of the partner. The Meadows, in Wickenburg, Arizona, is one such program. As with residential treatment centers for the sex addict, these programs provide the partner with a safe, supportive environment away from the toxic dynamics of her marriage, in which to address her own issues.

Christians are often shocked to discover that many of my colleagues in the sex addiction treatment community refer to sex addiction as the "addiction of choice for Christians." I believe that the reason for this is that so much of Christian teaching emphasizes shame, sin and self-deprivation. Since shame is at the core of sex addiction, and deprivation rituals are used in every religious tradition to achieve purity, it makes sense that well-intentioned Christian pastors and educators may be unwittingly reinforcing the messages that contribute to sex addiction. Throughout the country laypersons and pastors have started up Christian recovery groups dedicated to helping people with pornography addiction. If these programs primarily emphasize the repentance of sin, then they are likely to fail. As one of my clients noted after trying such a program, "focusing on sin only increased my shame, self-loathing and my failure to God, and never did anything to reduce the behavior." There are many qualified Christian psychotherapists who understand the importance of shame reduction in the treatment of both the addict and partner. Dr. Mark Laaser, founder of Faithful and True Ministries, helped to coordinate the American Association of Certified Sexual Addiction Therapists, Inc. in order to address the unique needs of Christian families facing sex addiction.

REFERENCES

Beattie, Melody. *Codependent No More*. Center City, MN: Hazelden, 1986.

_____. *The Language of Letting Go*. Center City, MN: Hazelden, 1986.

Carnes, Patrick. *Don't Call it Love*. New York: Bantam, 1991.

_____. *Out of the Shadows: Understanding Sexual Addiction*. Center City, MN: Hazelden, 1983.

_____. *The Betrayal Bond*. Deerfield Beach, FL: Health Communications, 1997.

Earle, Ralph and Gregory Crow. *Lonely All the Time*. New York: Pocket Books, 1989.

Ferree, Marnie C. *No Stones: Women Redeemed from Sexual Shame*. Longwood, Fl: Xulon Press, 2002.

Maltz, Wendy. *The Sexual Healing Journey*. San Francisco: Harper Collins, 1991.

Schaeffer, Brenda. *Is It Love or is it Addiction?* Second Edition. Center City, MN: Hazelden, 1997.

Schneider, Jennifer. *Back From Betrayal: Recovering From his Affairs* New York: Ballantine, 1988. [The classic book for women involved with sex-addicted men.]

_____. *Sex, Lies, and Forgivness: Couples Speak on Healing From Sex Addiction*. Second Edition. Tucson, AZ: Recovery Resources Press, 1999.

Schneider, Jennifer and Deb Corley. *Disclosing Secrets: When, to Whom, and How Much to Reveal*. Center City, MN: Hazelden, 2002.

11

It's Everybody's Business

Irene Sevcik and Marlette Reed

If I had been given this (domestic violence) information years ago, I wouldn't have shook for three years after leaving my husband.[1]

. . . in the social services agencies—for so long spirituality, religion, any of those sort of things was sort of a bad word. We can't talk about it. And so I think the first thing (FaithLink) did was to de-stigmatize the whole area. And I think that it de-stigmatized on a lot of different levels, because it allowed colleagues to talk about it with each other. So all of a sudden you're talking with your colleagues about spiritual, religious beliefs—whatever you want to call them—issues.[2]

INTRODUCTION

DOMESTIC ABUSE AFFECTS EVERY community, including those which are religiously/spiritually-based. It cannot be effectively addressed without a broadly-based, multi-faceted community response. FaithLink is an organization which formed from the realization that religious/spiritual leaders and communities needed to be—and indeed could be—engaged with the broader community in addressing issues of family and sexual violence. This chapter will outline the development of the program and

1. The words of a Christian woman who experienced abuse in her marriage; she said this after being a part of a FaithLink focus group. Calgary, AB, March 2006.

2. A service provider speaking about the work of FaithLink in the domestic and sexual violence sector. Interview, Calgary, AB, May 2006.

the services offered, the rationale upon which they are founded, and will conclude with some of the lessons learned in the past ten years.

Domestic abuse affects every person in our society. It is therefore incumbent upon us all to find ways to prevent its occurrence and to take action when it does occur, lessening its impact on victims, and holding accountable those who act in abusive ways. Violence within the context of intimate relationships and families *is* everybody's business.

BEGINNINGS AND FORMATION

FaithLink developed, in Calgary, Alberta, Canada, from the desire of key religious and service agency leaders to establish a coordinated, systems-wide community response to family and sexual abuse. In 1998 a planning group began the work of developing a dedicated domestic violence court. The proposed model would bring together: police; Crown Prosecutors and defence lawyers; victim services; probation officers; and those offering treatment services to individuals who had acted abusively. The Very Reverend Robert Pynn, then Dean of the Anglican Cathedral Church of the Redeemer, and Karen Walroth, Executive Director of the Action Committee Against Violence (ACAV), were key members of these discussions. They recognized that, to achieve a full realization of the goal of a broadly-based community response to family and sexual abuse, the inclusion of religious/spiritual communities was necessary. Events in the next two years would lay the foundation for their dream to become a reality.

To explore the question of how religious/spiritual communities could be engaged, a small committee was formed and therein FaithLink was born. One of its first initiatives was to sponsor, in April 2000, a workshop that brought religious leaders and service providers together to discuss the possibilities of working together. This weekend event was sponsored by the Anglican Cathedral Church of the Redeemer and facilitated by Drs. Nancy Nason-Clark and Lori Beaman. Through presentations and discussions, recommendations emerged that formed the foundation for a long-term initiative to build bridges between religious/spiritual communities and secularly-based domestic and sexual violence servicing agencies. The work of what was to become FaithLink was beginning to take shape.

A mission statement was articulated: *Spiritual/religious communities and service providers working together to prevent domestic violence and to provide healing and hope to all those affected by it.* The term 'religious/ spiritual communities' was, and continues to be, interpreted broadly to include a wide variety of religious traditions, spiritually-based groups and ethno-cultural communities. The original FaithLink committee continued to meet and expand in membership. As the work developed and broadened, it became evident that it could not be sustained through volunteers alone. A small staff complement was employed. The Very Reverend Robert Pynn, an initiator of the work, continues to act as 'Advisor' to FaithLink and to cast its vision.

FAITHLINK TODAY

The work of FaithLink continues to evolve. The original FaithLink committee has developed into a Steering Committee with a representative membership of various constituent groups: spiritual leaders from different religious traditions; women's shelters; counselling and family violence intervention services; the Faculty of Social Work, University of Calgary; and interested individuals. Though our work began, and continues, with Christian congregations, it has expanded to include the Jewish, Khmer Buddhist (Cambodian), Laotian and Hindu communities within the city. FaithLink has also engendered provincial, national, and international interest; its work is being discussed and its resources obtained from groups across the continent. But the fundamentals remain: the work of FaithLink is a community initiative, grounded within collaboration among those confronting family and sexual violence—whether from a spiritual or a secular perspective.

As the work has developed five interlocking areas of focus have emerged:

- Raising awareness within religious/spiritual communities of domestic and sexual abuse and building capacity to respond when it occurs within congregant families;

- Raising awareness and building capacity with service providers and spiritual leaders in responding to the impact of abuse on the spirit,

- Facilitating opportunities for religious/spiritual leaders and secularly-based service providers to discuss issues of mutual concern and develop collaborative working relationships;

- Offering to front-line responders to abuse victims opportunities to enhance their self-care practices; and

- Conducting relevant research which explores the interface between the spiritual and the secular, as it relates to domestic abuse.

Each of the areas of focus is grounded in best practice principles:

As awareness of domestic violence increases within a given population or community, disclosures will result. Therefore the work of raising awareness within religious/spiritual/ethno-cultural communities must be done in concert with enhancing the capacity to respond effectively to it.

Experiencing abuse affects the whole person, including the spiritual, necessitating a multi-faceted response. Given that most service providers are limited in the range of services they can provide, taking a holistic perspective requires coordinating across professional disciplines and across secularly and spiritually-based domains. Clients who desire spiritual support and counsel should have access to spiritual leaders of their own choosing who understand the dynamics of domestic abuse.

Collaborative working relationships are built on trust and mutual respect. Secularly-based professionals and spiritual leaders can work effectively together when there is mutual understanding and recognition of the unique contribution made by each.

First responders to traumatized individuals are at risk of experiencing vicarious trauma. This includes those who respond and give support to individuals impacted by domestic and sexual violence. Maintaining personal wellness is therefore of importance to service providers working within this sector.

When program development and practice are grounded in empirical evidence and a broad knowledge base, they are stronger and more effective. When research is grounded within the rich soil of practice, the knowledge base is enhanced and deepened.

WHAT WE DO

Work with Religious/Spiritual Communities

Religious/spiritual communities play an important preventive and practical role in addressing issues of family and sexual violence. Through speaking out against, educating about domestic abuse and sexual violence, and making known the resources that are available within the broader community, spiritual leaders can raise awareness and create a culture of safety for all congregants. It has long been understood that within such a culture, victims of domestic abuse are likely to look first to their spiritual leaders to offer assistance.[3] When confronted with disclosures of abuse, leaders can ensure the safety of the victim and take action to hold accountable the person who has acted abusively.

FaithLink offers assistance to spiritual leaders in these efforts in a number of ways. First, we offer presentations to congregations, groups within congregations, seminary students and faith leaders. These seminars offer basic information about domestic violence: *Domestic Violence 101*. They are also geared to the receiving audiences. Roman Catholic deacons and their wives received a presentation on the basics of family violence, plus material on premarital mentoring for their work with soon-to-be married couples. *FaithLink* will do workshops for teens on dating violence. We have provided seminars on "Raising Safe Kids"—an informational presentation for parents on how to raise children that are safe *towards* others and safe *from* the violence of others. Every presentation is age-appropriate and theologically sensitive.[4] "This class has saved me from a lot of mistakes in ministry!" was the comment of one seminary student after hearing a presentation about domestic violence and boundaries in ministry.

FaithLink develops and distributes informational, education and resource-based material for faith communities. A comprehensive manual—*Hope and Healing: Domestic Violence Resources for the Church (2004–2007)*—is available for Christian congregations in Calgary; at the present time, this resource has been distributed to individual congregations from the Canadian west coast to its eastern shores. A Khmer-Buddhist group in the city, with the help of FaithLink, is adapting portions of this manual for members of their own community. A similar resource, specifically for the Jewish context, was purchased and made available to that community. Brochures have been developed for Jewish, Christian, and Cambodian Buddhist groups. The pamphlet for the

---

3. Hong and Wiebe, *Psychology and Theology* 2 (1974): 291–97. See also Clemens et al, *Religion and Health* 17 (1978); 227–232 and Clark and Thomas, *Psychology and Theology* 7 (1979): 48–56.

4. The mandate for FaithLink is to educate about domestic violence. We work within the paradigm of each faith tradition; it is not our purpose to change foundational beliefs within their system.

Cambodian group provides information in both the Khmer and English languages. Shortly, a brochure outlining the basics of domestic violence as well as listing local resources will be published for the Laotian Christian community. This document will be in both Laotian and English.

In the development of resources specifically for communities, FaithLink is sensitive to the needs of the communities within which it works. A brochure was developed specifically for Roman Catholic and Anglican groups who requested it. It covers basic information, with the faith language geared towards people of liturgical traditions. (It has proved popular with non-liturgical churches as well.) When translation work is required, such as with the Khmer and Laotian materials, great pains are taken to make sure that the information in these respective languages accurately reflects the concepts presented. This work is both labour-intensive and costly.

As raising awareness invariably leads to disclosures, FaithLink assists churches and denominations in developing protocols consistent with their theology, as well as best practices in the domestic violence field. We will provide leadership with training in the implementation of the protocol. There is also much informal support for faith leaders who are dealing with specific incidences of abuse within their congregations. A phone call to FaithLink, or a conversation at the end of a meeting asking for advice, is a regular occurrence. As well, individuals within congregations will disclose after informational presentations. A recent presentation to forty women in a fundamental congregation led to three disclosures. Awareness-raising and the provision of helpful resources break the "holy hush" [5] by openly naming and describing what is a reality in every faith group. We welcome the opportunity to provide support for congregations seeking to increase their capacity to handle disclosures!

FaithLink also seeks to create relationships between religious leaders and service providers. Faith leaders have sometimes been unaware of, or hesitant to use, secular services. By bringing these two groups together, and engaging them in discussion, trust is built. Both groups are more likely to access the unique services of the other when there are human faces attached to 'institutions.'

---

5. This term was coined by Dr. Nancy Nason-Clark.

Working with Service Providers

For those who are spiritually committed, life's meaning is viewed though a spiritual lens. Thus when abuse becomes part of one's life—either as a victim or as someone who acts abusively–the search to understand, to heal, and to modify the spiritual perspective becomes central.[6] Secularly-based service providers are increasingly recognizing the importance of this dimension in their work with those who access their services.

> We recognize . . . across the board that spirituality—broadly defined—is something that gets so badly damaged in family violence issues. I mean, just really, really damaged. And you need to be encouraging clients to . . . rediscover their own sense of spiritual connection.[7]

> Most of the people who are immigrating come from sacral societies, and if you're going to deal with them, we have to deal with their religion. You cannot just deal with it in a secular manner. So it's requiring a whole new . . . learning for our social system and FaithLink is one of those organizations that's doing this.[8]

FaithLink seeks to assist service providers acknowledge and validate their clients' spiritual dimension in several ways. First, we offer workshops that assist staff members to be more aware of their own spiritual journey, and thus more comfortable in raising spiritual issues with their clients. These workshops provide sound clinical evidence to service providers of why they need to be aware of their own spiritual perspectives, and of the need to be sensitive to the spiritual needs/paradigms of their clients.

"Sensitization process—excellent" stated one workshop participant on an evaluation form. "I learned some new things that were unexpected" stated another. As a part of this workshop, participants are asked to reflect upon the impact of their own experiences upon their spirits. A few have said that they find this difficult, due to their own experience of trauma. This type of response from caregivers reinforces the depth to which trau-

6. Victims of abuse often ask, "How could God let this happen to me? Where was He when I was being violated?" These questions can precipitate a spiritual search and a change in one's paradigm.

7. A service provider's perspective regarding the importance of spirituality. Interview. Calgary, AB, May 2006.

8. A service provider who works specifically with diverse ethno-cultural communities. Interview, Calgary, AB, May 2006.

ma impacts one's spirit, even many years after the event; it also highlights the necessity for 'wounded healers' to experience a significant degree of healing within their own souls, as well as to receive ongoing support in the difficult work they do.[9]

FaithLink has developed a brochure for women's shelters within Calgary, which highlights the impact of abuse on the spirit. *Spiritual Support for Victims of Domestic Violence* is written to victims, and states "All abuse is spiritual abuse!" It describes the impact of abuse upon the spirit, speaks of the power of spirituality to aid in one's healing process, and indicates that there is spiritual help available in the community.

To this end, FaithLink has provided service providers with a list of spiritual leaders within Calgary who understand family violence, will accept referrals from, and work with, secularly-based professionals. These spiritual leaders come from a number of faith traditions: Christian, Jewish, Muslim and Buddhist. A variety of denominations within each faith are represented. When a woman in a shelter indicates that she would like spiritual support, she will be provided with a faith leader of her paradigm, who will, in conjunction with the secular services, offer her the spiritual support she needs.

At a recent luncheon with spiritual leaders and service providers, the ministers present asked for a copy of this list. As Calgary is a multi-cultural and multi-faith city, and as spiritual leaders encounter violated people of many faiths, they asked for names of faith leaders from other traditions to whom they could refer victims. This is consistent with the philosophy of FaithLink—to offer victims spiritual support from *their* tradition—and the list was made available to these pastors.

We also provide relevant research findings pertaining to the spiritual, as it affects the work of service providers. In one situation, a children's counsellor in a shelter was dealing with a spiritually traumatized child. The counsellor anticipated that this situation would go to court and contacted FaithLink for relevant research on the effect of spiritual abuse on children.

> [FaithLink] was the key here . . . was struggling for . . . a
> published authority to go into a report concerning a child
> who was being . . . um . . . I would use the word 'tortured.'
> [FaithLink] spoke to me about a book . . . and I've been

---

9. The term "wounded healer" was coined by Henri Nouwen. See Nouwen, *The Wounded Healer.*

able to take a portion of that to incorporate in a legal report.[10]

Building Collaborative Bridges

There is often limited trust between spiritual leaders and secularly-based service providers. There are many reasons for this, including a lack of mutual understanding. Family and sexual violence issues are complex and carry an inherent lethality to them. They cannot be adequately addressed solely by spiritual leaders and their faith communities. The services provided by the family and sexual violence sector seek to address these complexities at varying levels (e.g., legal, justice, safety and shelter, counselling, housing, financial support, child custody). These services, however, may take positions that marginalize the importance of the spiritual dimension of their clients. Spiritual leaders have rich wisdom as well as experience with religious practices that can address the spiritual dimension of clients—knowledge and understanding that may enhance the work of the service providers.

In the interest of those who are most directly affected by family and sexual violence (the victims, those who have acted abusively, and child witnesses), FaithLink seeks to bring together the rich resources that are represented by both religious/spiritual communities and secularly-based service providers. To this end FaithLink sponsors conferences and workshops which provide opportunities for spiritual leaders and service providers to learn from each other, to build collaborative working relationships and to discuss issues of mutual concern.

These collaborative bridges are built intentionally; for example, FaithLink regularly sponsors luncheons to which spiritual leaders and service providers are invited. Here they discuss together practical concerns, such as how to effectively conduct mutual referrals. Collaborative bridges are also constructed incidentally; breaks at workshops and lunch times at conferences provide excellent opportunities for both groups to intermingle and develop connections. The incidental bridges that result may be as or even more effective than the exercises we provide to build intentional bridges; when caring, competent people of different disciplines get together, good things happen!

10. Interview, May 2006, Calgary, AB.

As a new clergy, I'm just beginning to gather information/gain an understanding of this whole issue of domestic violence. This conference has given me a great foundation. Thank you![11]

Caring for the Caregiver

It is widely accepted that first responders to traumatized individuals (emergency medical technicians, fire fighters, police, criminal defense lawyers, medical personnel, counselors) experience negative effects as a result of their work. Figley refers to this as 'the cost of caring.'[12] "The effects of vicarious trauma extend to all realms of anti-violence workers' lives and are cumulative, unavoidable and applicable to everyone uniquely."[13]

FaithLink considers it important to recognize the work and experience of those individuals working within the family and sexual violence service field. It does this by validating the experience of front line and management level workers. As well, we provide opportunities for enhanced personal self-care. One such opportunity, offered to front line workers and others working within the family and sexual abuse sector, was an introduction to, and training in, a centered meditation practice. A series of workshops, meetings and mini-retreats was the means. Over the space of a week, Dr. Cynthia Bourgeault, a well known contemplative, made herself available to small and large groups, within a variety of settings and time periods.

Conducting Relevant Research

FaithLink seeks to ground its development and services within a tested knowledge base. It also recognizes the importance of building the knowledge base as it relates to the interface between the spiritual and service providers. To this end it joins with other groups and individuals to conduct relevant research. One project, conducted with Dr. Nancy Nason-Clark, examined the efficacy for domestic violence service providers of a centering meditation practice in handling work-related stress, work with clients, and relationships with colleagues.

---

11. A response on a March 2007 FaithLink conference evaluation form.

12. Figley, (ed.). *Compassion Fatigue: Coping with Secondary Traumatic Stress Disorder in Those Who Treat the Traumatized.*

13. Richardson, *Guidebook on Vicarious Trauma: Recommended Solutions for Anti-Violence Workers.*

I think that the responses were amazing. In terms of the impact that meditation made. Six weeks practice is a very short time, and I was amazed in the difference people felt. It clearly did deal with the three areas that we were talking about: the capacity to deal with stress, and vicarious trauma, and being more clear and able to respond to clients—and also to be more open to collaborative work. Because it set a kind of atmosphere of . . . um . . . surrender of turf and an openness to a much larger, inclusive sort of engagement.[14]

A second, multi-year project, being conducted in collaboration with Dr. Nancy Nason-Clark and RESOLVE Alberta, is using surveys, focus groups, and interviews to track the impact of FaithLink's work within religious/spiritual communities and among secularly-based service providers. Research participants include: religious/spiritual leaders; service providers; and women from three different religious traditions.

Initial data is confirming. Sevcik and Rothery indicate that this research "highlights the differences between the various communities, and the need for a differential response from programs such as FaithLink— what is highly useful with one community could be entirely inappropriate with another." [15] These findings are providing excellent insights into the complexity of FaithLink's work, strong support for much of what has been done, and suggestions for future initiatives.

WHY WE DO WHAT WE DO

As discussed, FaithLink works with faith communities, service providers and with the two groups together. Initially, the project began with spiritual communities as our focus, to bring them into the process of working with victims of domestic violence. This continues to be a primary emphasis. The following section delineates the rationale for our work, but pertains only to our work with faith communities.

14. A service provider speaking about the impact of the centering meditation project on them personally and professionally.

15. Sevcik and Rothery, Actions and Achievements: Program Evaluation 2006, 13.

Domestic Violence and Religious Communities

Research is confirming the long held assumption that family violence is as prevalent within religious/spiritually-based communities as it is within the general population.[16] Women of religious/spiritual communities often remain in abusive relationships longer.[17] Spiritual leaders are called upon to both intervene in domestic disputes and to counsel those who have been abusive within intimate relationships.[18] Victims of violence, however, report the counsel they receive from spiritual leaders has not always been helpful to them.[19] It is in this unique setting that religious and spiritual communities play a key role.

> Walking alongside each other may be the most effective
> ministry we can provide anyone—in the name of Christ.[20]

FaithLink's *raison d'etre* is vested in this conviction. The role of the faith community is fulfilled both within the specific community of a congregation and within the broader community within which the congregation finds itself. Spiritual leaders can be both preventive and practical in their responses to family and sexual violence within their own communities. Their faith community can be a place where victims of violence feel safe and can experience spiritual healing.[21] And for men within the church who are abusing, the pastor's strong stance to hold this individual accountable and support the community treatment he is getting have proven to keep men in their programs for the duration.[22]

---

16. Nason-Clark. *The Battered Wife: How Christians Confront Family Violence.* See also Beaman-Hall and Nason-Clark, *Affilia,* 12(2) : 176–196.

17. Nason-Clark, *JSSR* Vol. 43:3 (2004): 304.

18. Nason-Clark, *The Battered Wife,* 14.

19. Giesbrecht and Sevcik, *J. Fam Viol,* 15(3): 229–248. See also Nason-Clark, *The Battered Wife,* 14.

20. The authors are referring to the key role the church has in being present with those who have experienced abuse. See Toews with Loewen. *No Longer Alone: Mental Health and the Church* 1995, 134.

21. Research shows that women caring for women within the church is a powerful way in which spiritual women who are experiencing abuse can be supported within a faith community. The church environment, however, needs to be safe for them in order to facilitate this. See Nason-Clark, "When Terror Strikes at Home: The Interface Between Religion and Domestic Violence," 307.

22. Ibid., 305.

Faith communities have access to vulnerable individuals across the life span. They minister to children, the elderly, disabled people, members of minority cultures, women, and teenaged girls, to mention a few of these at-risk populations. By raising awareness about the issue through presentations and educational programs, and making available information about resources within the broader community and how they can be accessed, faith communities play a key preventative role. Spiritual communities also create safety in their midst through ensuring that their places of worship and communal gatherings are safe, and by being alert to signs of abuse, and available to receiving disclosures.

Spiritual leaders who are knowledgeable about abuse issues, and address them openly, clearly signal their congregants that they are willing to receive disclosures of abuse. When receiving a disclosure from a victim, a child witness, or a person who has acted abusively, they can take practical actions to ensure the safety of the victim, hold accountable the person who has acted abusively, as well as report to and work with Child Welfare authorities and/or the police. They also can facilitate the access of resources within the broader community that are designed specifically for abuse victims, those who have acted abusively, and witnesses of the abuse. Faith communities can work collaboratively with resource personnel to ensure that congregants continue to receive spiritual support alongside the counsel they receive through secularly-based services. They may provide support within the congregation and facilitate opportunities for spiritual healing for affected congregants. This type of response facilitates a powerful, holistic approach to domestic violence within the church.

Beliefs Matter

The tenets of any religious/spiritual system will be reflected in how adherents apply them within their daily lives. Beliefs about suffering, justice, repentance, forgiveness, and reconciliation significantly influence how conflicts are defined and resolved.[23] Roles, responsibilities, and boundaries between men and women are often clearly defined in faith systems. Father-son, mother-daughter relationships, modeling, and education may be prescribed.

Specifically within the domestic violence realm, the paradigm influences one's decision to disclose abuse, when and to whom, whether or

23. Ware et al., *J. Religion and Abuse*, 5(2) (2003): 71–72.

not this person can/should leave the relationship, as well as if and when to reconcile. Beliefs also sway whether a victim should access secular community services, the extent to which the sanctions of the courts are accepted, and the degree of commitment given to secularly-based intervention regimes. The status of children within the community and their future opportunities for marriage and career success may be jeopardized by a family separation.

The impact of the belief system—the paradigm of an individual, a family or a faith system—cannot be overestimated. One woman who was raised in a family where divorce was never an option ("You've made your bed, lie in it!") spoke of the difficulty of leaving her abusive marriage. Though her church gave her permission, the faith paradigm of her childhood remained on her internal 'hard drive.' Nevertheless, the spiritual counsel in her adult life had enough impact to move her to act towards safety for herself and her children.[24]

Trauma Impacts the Spiritual

Abuse strikes the very core of one's being. Current research is increasing our awareness of the negative impact trauma can have on the spiritual component of one's life.[25]

> Abuse strikes at the heart of a person's selfhood, self-concept and sense of the sacred.[26]

> Concerns about identity, the value of suffering, the importance of justice and the appropriateness of forgiveness [are suddenly front and center].... Questions of identity proliferate.[27]

Who am I? Am I worth anything? These questions are frequently asked by victims of abuse.

For victims who place importance on 'experiencing' God, the emotional numbing that results from the on-going abuse may be interpreted as abandonment by their Source. Others may interpret the abuse itself as

24. This comment was shared at a FaithLink presentation in rural Alberta in the Spring of 2007.

25. Barrett, Healing From Trauma in *Spiritual Resources in Family Therapy*, 1999:193–208.

26. Nason-Clark, *The Battered Wife*, 14.

27. McKernan, *Radical Relatedness: Exploring the Spiritual Dimension of Family Service Work.* 2004.

divine punishment for past failures and/or actions.[28] Has God left me? Has His blessing been withdrawn from me? Who is God?! Does (He/She) even exist?

Spirituality Aids the Healing Process

Faith fuels the resilient spirit. [29]

Spiritual belief and community can provide a rich reservoir of healing and support for victims of violence. Rituals, ceremonial rites and prayers are potential sources of support and healing.[30] One victim of sexual assault said that her baptism was a source of profound healing: "When I came up from the water, I felt clean." Spiritual practices can/should be seen by practitioners as spiritual assets, available to them during difficult times, as sources of strength in times of struggle.[31]

Spiritual practices provide a framework for individual experiences to be placed within a wider perspective: to see the 'reality' of a larger whole; to draw strength from the realization of new and different possibilities. Spiritual leaders offer to victims of abuse a unique wisdom about the Christian spiritual journey and experience in Christian practices that can aid healing. Spirituality may help answer the 'why did this happen to me?' question.

Fear Hinders Accessing Resources

There is, within the broader community, an array of services available to those who are impacted by family and sexual violence: emergency and long-term shelters for women and children; treatment/intervention programs for those who have been abusive; counselling services to individuals/families struggling with the reality of violence becoming a part of their lives. Notwithstanding the efforts on the part of these service providers to be sensitive to cultural norms and spiritual practices held by those accessing their programs, fear keeps many away.[32] These fears can include that

28. See Toews with Loewen, chapters 3 and 4.

29. Walsh, Religion and Spirituality: Wellsprings for Healing and Resilience, 24.

30. Barrett, 193–208.

31. Ibid.

32. Ringel and Bina. *Research on Social Work Practice*, 17 (2), (2007): 277–286. See also Nason-Clark (2004), 304.

the value of their spirituality may be under-estimated or not validated, that their beliefs will be misunderstood, underappreciated or ridiculed. When secular-based counsellors fail to validate the importance of the spiritual, clients may feel that a vital component of their beings and an authentic avenue for coping, healing and change is not being recognized.

Victims of abuse may also fear that it may not be possible to accommodate spiritual practices and/or religious requirements, or that they will lose support and/or standing within their religious community. The stigma of violence within the family exists in faith communities—and often the victims bear it.

Fear may also be at the base of the denial by some spiritual leaders that domestic abuse occurs within their congregants. This may be a fear of not knowing how to respond to disclosures and/or trepidation of what the repercussions within the congregation could be when disclosures are made. Fear also hinders the accessing of educational and supportive resources. "We don't do domestic violence here; we do worship!" was the comment made by a minister when offered FaithLink resources and information.

Community Ties can Support; They can Bind

Religious/spiritual communities are just that—communities—that offer friendships and family connections, a sense of identity and 'place.' They are a source of practical help and emotional support. They provide a sense of 'mission' and offer avenues for meaningful volunteer involvement.

But the ties that provide meaning, support, and connection can also be ties that bind. There may be hesitancy on the part of community members to disclosure abuse for fear of not being believed or because of the shame and blame that may result if the disclosure becomes known within the broader congregational community. Congregants may also fear the possible loss of friendships, family connections, and support networks; the thought of they and their children being isolated from their community is intolerable when the home situation is abusive.

When leaders of religious/spiritual communities address issues of abuse knowledgeably, directly, and openly, their community's capacity to offer support and comfort is strengthened.

LESSONS LEARNED

Although FaithLink continues to be 'a work in progress' there are a number of lessons we have learned over the past decade:

Mistrust is Deep

One of our first realizations was that a deep mistrust exists between religious/spiritual leaders and secularly-based service providers. Spiritual leaders are concerned that secularly-based counselors will invalidate the spiritual paradigm of their parishioners. They also fear that secular counselors will counsel divorce and/or deny them access to the victim.

Service providers have their own fears, and often misconceptions, about the responses of spiritual leaders when receiving disclosures of abuse from a congregant. They are concerned that the safety of the victim will not be the first priority. They feel that the abusing partner may not be held accountable and/or that the victim will be counseled to reconcile with, and return to, the abusing partner. The following is a statement from a service provider, who felt that religious commitment may be used by one who is abusing as an excuse to avoid consequences and accountability for his violence:

> And then they [those who have acted abusively] would end up in some kind of faith community . . . and then they would find that as justification—'I am a reformed person now' and 'Look, it says in my faith that it was okay to do that. My pastor says yes, my wife is a [difficult woman].'[33]

Differing Analyses Result in Differing Responses

How an issue is understood and defined determines the response to it. Secular wisdom has understood family and sexual violence as a 'power and control' issue. This analysis has shaped approaches to service development and intervention. Spiritual leaders, while acknowledging that the exercise of power and control are present, often take a broader, existential perspective, viewing abusive behaviour as an expression of spiritual estrangement. As such, their response may be to foster intra-personal connectedness and openness to the Source (however this may be defined).

33. A service provider speaking of his/her mistrust of distorted religious doctrine and the potential response of a faith leader. Interview, Calgary, AB, May 2006.

This perspective and response does not negate their taking action to ensure the safety of the victim or accountability for the person who has acted abusively. It may, however, not be appreciated by those who take a more secular perspective and may result in distrust that the abusive situation is being taken seriously by the spiritual leader.

On Building Bridges

It may appear that with the differing ways in which family and sexual violence is understood by secularly-based professionals and the wide variety of religious/spiritual communities represented within our society that the 'divide' is too great to be 'bridged.' Our experience, however, has been that bridging the divide is possible. But constructing the bridge requires a number of things. First of all, the commitment of strong leaders from both the spiritual and secular communities is essential. FaithLink began, and continues, through the efforts of respected individuals representing secularly-based services and religious/spiritual leaders.

Clarity of purpose is essential. There must be a common vision. The issue is family violence and a broadly-based community response to it. The work is not about re-interpreting sacred texts.[34] It is not about asking denominational distinctions to be erased. And it is not about asking secularly-based counselors to become spiritual counselors.

Rather, it is about raising awareness and capacity building on both the sacred and the secular sides. It involves developing respect between various parties engaged in the discussion through providing opportunities for discussion of mutual concerns and developing relationships. Bridges are built when resources are developed that take into account the particular context of the intended users.

A crucial part of the work of collaboration across the 'divide' is for any given religious/spiritual community to have an individual, who has credibility within that community, championing this cause; someone who can 'speak the language,' who knows the belief systems, and understands how the community works. This individual also needs to understand family violence and the services available to those affected by family violence. And individuals from both the secular and the sacred realms need to be

---

34. FaithLink will, however, work with the paradigm of a faith group to place safety of victim(s) as priority. Within *every* religion is the belief that the vulnerable and innocent must be protected.

able to think and work outside prescribed perspectives; collaboration between the two sides is definitely groundbreaking work!

As with any new venture, time, patience, and perseverance are necessary. Within Calgary, it took several years of hard work within a particular religious community to be able to have a conference. When the attendance was good and the day successful, it may have appeared 'easy.' However, there were several years of 'soil preparation' before this event (and the foundational work) took root. In Calgary and the surrounding area, these bridges *are* being built!

> For collaborative ventures between the steeple and the shelter to be successful, personnel operating from a secular or sacred paradigm must be willing to see that the condemnation of domestic violence requires both the language of contemporary culture and the language of the spirit.[35]

> . . . we found a lot of secular service providers (are) able to come out of the religious closet and they're able to claim their own motivation—which for many started in churches or synagogues or whatever, and the teaching they received about loving your neighbour, etc. So it turned out the gulf was in some ways an unreal gulf.[36]

CONCLUSION

Religious/spiritual communities have a significant role to play in a broadly-based community response to domestic and sexual abuse. As the bridge between the spiritual and the secular is constructed, FaithLink is seeing the ever-increasing involvement of spiritual communities and a greater dialogue between faith leaders and service providers. With deepening relationships between members of the two groups, trust is beginning to be established. Domestic and sexual abuse affects us all and therefore confronting it is *everybody's business*.

35. Nason-Clark, *The Battered Wife*, 304.

36. The remark of a service provider about the common ground shared between service providers and spiritual leaders. Interview, Calgary, AB, May 2006.

REFERENCES

Barrett, Mary Jo. "Healing From Trauma: The Quest for Spirituality," in *Spiritual Resources in Family Therapy*, edited by Froma Walsh, 193–208. New York: The Guilford Press, 1999.

Beaman-Hall, Lori and Nancy Nason-Clark. "Partners or Protagonists: The Transition House Movement and Conservative Churches." *Affilia,* 12(2) (Summer 1997) 176–96.

Clark, S.A. and A.H. Thomas. "Counselling and the Clergy: Perceptions of Roles." *Journal of Psychology and Theology* 7 (1979) 48–56.

Clemens, N.A., R.B. Corradi and M. Wasman. "The Parish Clergy as a Mental Health Resource. *Journal of Religion and Health* 17 (1978) 227–32.

Figley, Charles R. *Compassion Fatigue: Coping with Secondary Traumatic Stress Disorder in Those Who Treat the Traumatized,* edited by Charles Figley. New York: Brunner Mazel, 1995.

Giesbrecht, Norman and Irene Sevcik. "The Process of Recovery and Rebuilding Among Abused Women in Conservative Evangelical Subculture." *Journal of Family Violence* 15(3) 229–48.

Hong, B.A. and V.R. Wiebe. "Referral Patterns of Clergy." *Journal of Psychology and Theology* 2 (1974) 291–97.

McKernan, Michael. *Radical Relatedness: Exploring the Spiritual Dimension of Family Service Work.* Canada: The Muttart Foundation, 2004.

Nason-Clark, Nancy. *The Battered Wife: How Christians Confront Family Violence.* Louisville, KY: Westminster John Knox Press, 1997.

Nancy Nason-Clark. "When Terror Strikes at Home: The Interface Between Religion and Domestic Violence," *Journal for the Scientific Study of Religion* Vol. 43:3 (2004) 303–10.

Nouwen, Henri J.M. *The Wounded Healer.* USA: Doubleday, 1972.

Richardson, Jan I. *Guidebook on Vicarious Trauma: Recommended Solutions for Anti-Violence Workers.* Ottawa: National Clearinghouse on Family Violence, 2001.

Ringel, Shoshana and Rena Bina. "Understanding Causes of and Responses to Intimate Partner Violence in a Jewish Orthodox Community: Survivors' and Leaders' Perspectives," *Research on Social Work Practice* Vol. 17, no. 2, (2007) 277–86.

Sevcik, Irene and Michael Rothery, "Actions and Achievements: Program Evaluation 2006." Calgary, AB: FaithLink, June, 2006.

Toews, John, with Eleanor Loewen. *No Longer Alone: Mental Health and the Church.* Waterloo, ON: Herald Press, 1995.

Walsh, Froma "Religion and Spirituality: Wellsprings for Healing and Resilience," in *Spiritual Resources in Family Therapy,* edited by Froma Walsh, 3–27. New York: The Guilford Press, 1999

Ware, Kimberley N., Heidi M. Levitt and Gary Bayer. "May God Help You: Faith Leaders' Perspective on Intimate Partner Violence Within Their Communities," *Journal of Religion and Abuse,* 5(2) (2003): 55–81.

Words of Hope

RAVE seeks to shatter
the silence surrounding
abuse, particularly in
families of faith. Our
use of stained glass is a
constant reminder that
beauty can be borne out
of brokenness.

www.theRaveProject.org

PART THREE

Raising Our Voices

The Prophetic Call for Future Action

12

When Terror Strikes the Christian Home

Nancy Nason-Clark

INTRODUCTION

A BUSE CAN NEVER BE justified. It is always wrong. It is never part of God's design for family relationships. It shatters dreams and distorts family life. In its wake, there is pain and despair. Domestic violence is inappropriate, harmful, and—illegal.

We must not be stuck with our heads in any celestial sand when it comes to this issue. As believers we need to be informed about the nature, prevalence and the severity of abuse that characterizes our churches, our neighborhoods, and our world.

The Spirit filled life should never include abusive acts, nor should it involve turning a blind eye to the suffering of another. Surely increasing our knowledge will lead to action.

Did you know:[1]

- The World Health Organization says that one in five women around the globe is physically or sexually abused in her lifetime;

- Gender violence causes more death and disability among women aged fifteen to forty-four than cancer, malaria, traffic accidents or war;

---

1. For reference citations see: Kroeger, C. C., & Nason-Clark, N. (2001). *No Place for Abuse: Biblical and Practical Resources to Counteract Domestic Violence.* Downers Grove, IL: InterVarsity Press, and Nason-Clark, N. & Kroeger, C.C. (2004). *Refuge from Abuse: Healing and Hope for Abused Christian Women.* Downers Grove, Il: InterVarsity Press.

- Women worldwide tell governments that family violence is one of their biggest concerns;

- Canadian women with a violent father-in-law are at three times the risk for spouse abuse as women with a non-violent father-in-law.

Violence against women is a pervasive reality across the world. It exists in every nation, and within every congregation. Violence occurs amongst the rich and poor alike. Its boundaries cross language, culture, religious and social barriers.

Governments are beginning to wake up to the devastating reality and consequences of violence for their people, their economies and particularly, for the most vulnerable, their children. Large sums of public money are starting to be directed toward understanding the issue of violence in the family context, reforming the criminal justice system to respond with greater efficiency and effectiveness, and providing health and other social services to ensure a coordinated community response.

Yet, amidst growing recognition of the everyday fears of abused women, the bruises and battering they have endured, and the need for safety, security, and shelter for survivors, where are the churches? Where are the prophetic voices? Where can we find the *healing balm of Gilead?* Are we—like the disciples in the Garden of Gethsemane—sound asleep?

By and large a holy hush engulfs us when it comes to the relationship between abuse and faith. Sometimes the silence is unintentional. Sometimes it is willful. Yet, it is always wrong. Just because the issue makes us feel uncomfortable, or we are unsure as people of faith how to respond, we should not—dare not—forget its victims.

We need to wake up, crawl out from under the proverbial church carpet, see the horror of violence for what it is, and then proclaim loudly and often: every home a safe home, every home a shelter. *There is no place like home.* For many women and children—after abuse strikes—there is no home.

CONSIDERING THE RESEARCH

I am a sociologist by profession, but a Christian by commitment. Over the last fifteen years, my program of research has involved mailed questionnaires, personal interviews, community consultations, telephone surveys, congregational studies, case file analysis and fieldwork in many parts of the globe. Our team has collected and analyzed data from thousands of

Christians. In the process, I have come face to face with the suffering, the pain, the reality and the despair of abuse.

And what have I learned? Christian women who are abused have told us about their fear—fear for their safety, fear for their children, fear that others will find out, fear that the future may be worse than the past, fear of retribution if they leave or seek help, fear that they cannot support their own children financially. The stark reality is this: many, many women—believers in Christ—live in fear because they are married to a violent man.

Christian women also experience guilt. Guilt that the relationship did not work out, feeling that somehow they are responsible for the abuse they have suffered. Battered Christian women could write a book on guilt—after all, they believed they promised God until death drew their last breath that they would love and cherish this man, for better, for worse.

We have also heard women in church life talk about the abandonment they feel when others turn a blind eye to their suffering. Where is God in the midst of their pain? Where are other believers? Doesn't anyone care, not even the pastor?

Although abused religious women want the battery to stop, they may not wish to terminate their relationship with the abuser, either temporarily or forever. Consequently, the resources these women seek in the aftermath of violence in part differentiate them from their sisters not in the church. Simply put, the stakes to keep the marriage together are much higher for women who are believers.

You and I can do something about this horror. We need to understand that abuse exists in every nation and in every neighborhood. We must learn to recognize the signs of abuse and develop the skills to discern when relationships are not healthy. Then we can answer the prophetic call: to speak out against violence whenever we have the opportunity to do so. When believers around the world accept that challenge, the horror of violence will no longer be hidden in the church closet.

THE IMPACT OF VIOLENCE

Abuse leaves emotional scars that can last a lifetime. Fear is the most common response to violence in the family. Victims also experience shame, betrayal, and a sense of hopelessness.

Witnessing violence harms children, even if they're not the ones being struck or cursed. When abuse occurs in a family, everyone is impacted. From our clergy data[2] we have learned:

- Pastors believe one in five couples in their congregation is violent;
- Nine percent of pastors have counseled five or more abused women in the last year;
- Eighty-three percent of pastors have counseled at least one abused woman;
- Eight percent of pastors feel well equipped to respond to domestic violence;
- Thirty-one percent of pastors report they have preached a message on abuse;
- Forty percent of pastors discuss violence in premarital counseling.

From our church women data[33] we have learned:

- Ninety-five percent of church women report that they have never heard a message on abuse;
- Fifty-eight percent of church women have personally helped an abused woman—of these, one in four have offered her a bed for the night;
- Seventy percent of conservative Protestant women have sought the help of another woman in their church regarding a family-related problem;
- Many Christian women who have been violated by abusive acts do not feel that the term "abused woman" applied to them.

The challenge—for you and me—is to never underestimate the long and difficult journey for survivors. We need to think about the children—and do everything we can to ensure that their needs are met and that the

2. Nason-Clark, Nancy. 1997. The Battered Wife: How Christians Confront Family Violence. Louisville, KY: Westminster/John Knox Press.
3. Ibid..

cycle of violence is broken. As religious leaders it is important to emphasize for the entire church family that there needs to be non-violent ways of dealing with the frustrations and disappointments of life. We must attempt to spread this message throughout all of the programs and groups that operate under the umbrella of congregational life.

HOPE IN THE MIDST OF CRISIS

There are many hurdles to be overcome on the journey towards healing and wholeness for a religious survivor of domestic violence.
Here are some points we have learned through our fieldwork.[4]

The lie of worthlessness

So many abused women have been told that they are stupid, ugly, or useless. These are lies. But it is very hard to come to a place where you stop believing what you have been told, especially since you may have heard this message for so long. As a result, an abused woman feels her life is of little value. When she stops believing the lie, the first hurdle is overcome.

Fear that the future could be worse than the past

Facing reality is very hard work, especially difficult for an abused woman who has few marketable skills or limited education. Without the support of family or friends, an abused woman may have great difficulty believing that anybody cares. There is very little trust left. But to start a new life, or to look for help, she must believe in the promise of a better tomorrow.

The difficulty of taking action

For all of us, there is a wide gap between insight and action. But for those who have lived with the lie of worthlessness, the pain of betrayal and the fear of violence, this is all accentuated. Often abused women do not know where to turn either for practical advice or for help in sorting out all the spiritual and emotional questions that surface. It takes a lot of courage to tell your story to someone else and then to consider what options you have for change.

---

4. Nason-Clark, Nancy. 1997. The Battered Wife: How Christians Confront Family Violence. Louisville, KY: Westminster/John Knox Press.

Reluctance to figure out what's wrong

Abuse can happen to any woman, at any stage of the life course. One of the ways women differ, however, is whether or not they are prepared to break the silence surrounding their abuse. Assessing risk is imperative. Most women—even if they have suffered at the hands of their partner—are reluctant to think of themselves as abused women. Safety must be the first priority, for a woman and her dependent children.

The struggle to figure out what help you need

Once a woman has realized that safety cannot be guaranteed in her home, it's time to develop a safety plan that will allow her to escape next time there is danger. Often there are physical needs, emotional needs, financial needs, and spiritual needs. Thinking through all of the immediate and longer-term requirements can seem daunting, especially for someone who has been told all her life that she can do nothing right.

RELIGIOUS WOMEN AND THE DECISION TO SEEK HELP

Deciding whether or not to disclose your abuse to a religious leader is an important question that many women of faith face. Sometimes the question is posed like this: is my church a safe place to talk about the abuse I have suffered? Deciding whether or not to disclose the importance of your faith is also important for many religious survivors when they have sought respite or services within community-based agencies. Here the question may be posed like this: Is the shelter a safe place to talk about my church or the importance of my faith?

Yet, there are signs that congregational life is open to the subject of abuse in the family context. Here are several signs you might look for, or questions you might ask yourself: In the women's washroom, is there information about local shelters (or transition houses) and how I can contact them? Has my pastor preached a sermon in which abuse was condemned and violence-free family living was celebrated? Have there been fundraising efforts at my church for a local battered women's shelter? Have there been any church-sponsored events to highlight the issue of abuse in our community or times when a community leader has spoken in our church about family violence?

As men and women of faith—and as faith leaders—our challenge is to offer safe places to talk about life's disappointments and problems, at our kitchen table, or in the privacy of the church office. We need to be a *listening ear*. In our fieldwork, we learned that women survivors defined a listening ear as "someone in the church whose ear was bigger than their mouth!" The challenge is to practice this. It is also important to practice empathy and to keep confidentiality. And finally, it is imperative to make referral suggestions. It is never a good idea to be a solo supporter.

Violated women and their children need support from a wide range of people in the community and in the church. Referrals put those in need directly in contact with those who can help. Of course, it is vital that church leaders are clear on what local community resources have to offer. And we in the church need to be clear on what our community of faith has to offer an abuse survivor. We must never forget that referrals offer choices to a woman about her own emotional, practical, and spiritual needs. However, she alone must determine the course of her journey. It is our job to offer accurate information, support, and encouragement.

Shattering the silence surrounding abuse is no small matter—for survivors or for congregations. From our research[5] we have learned that breaking the silence usually involves:

- *Reflecting on how much pain you have suffered;*
- *Remembering the broken promises of your partner;*
- *Considering the level of fear you feel;*
- *Gathering your courage to take action;*
- *Realizing that your children are being affected by the violence too;*
- *Knowing there is hope for a life free of abuse.*

Once the silence has been broken, an abused woman can begin to consider what kinds of assistance will help her on the road to wholeness. For religious women, there are often spiritual issues to be resolved and many unanswered questions. *Where is God in the midst of my suffering? What does God expect of me? I promised for better, for worse: does that mean I can never leave the relationship? What did I do to deserve this?*

5. Nason-Clark, N. & Kroeger, C.C. (2004). *Refuge from Abuse: Healing and Hope for Abused Christian Women.* Downers Grove, Il: InterVarsity Press.

CLERGY AS A SPIRITUAL RESOURCE TO ABUSED WOMEN

Since many pastors feel ill equipped to respond to the needs of abused women, it is a good idea for a woman who is hurting to let her pastor or other spiritual mentor know what kinds of assistance would be helpful. Here are some ideas I have learned from our fieldwork that can be incorporated into the emotional and practical support offered by religious leaders to those whose lives have been impacted by domestic violence.[6]

- Help her reflect on the nature of God;

    It is important to remind a survivor that God cares about human misery. Assist her to meditate on the value God places on human life. Use Scripture verses and prayers that affirm this message.

- Help her reflect on her need of God;

    Just as Jesus looked to God for strength, a woman survivor needs guidance in reflecting on her need of God at this difficult juncture in her life. Help her to see that calling out to God opens the doors for God to help her. Use Biblical stories, like that of Hagar, to reinforce this truth.

- Help her reflect on God's ability to meet her needs;

    She will be experiencing fear and guilt. Help her to pray for courage even as you offer practical suggestions and referral sources to ensure her safety and security. Suggest Bible passages that speak of God's provision in the midst of crisis.

- Help her condemn abuse using the language of the spirit;

    It is one thing for a secular professional to say to a survivor that violence is wrong. For a woman of faith, it is even more impactful for her religious leader to say that violence is wrong. Point her in the direction of Scripture passages that condemn violence. Help her to see that resources are available—even in her own congregation—to offer her strength at this time.

- Affirm the use of secular resources;

    Church leaders need to support community based resources. Of course, they cannot affirm that which they know nothing about, so it is imperative that pastors find our what indeed is available in their local

6. Nason-Clark, N. & Kroeger, C.C. (2004). *Refuge from Abuse: Healing and Hope for Abused Christian Women.* Downers Grove, Il: InterVarsity Press.

region to assist survivors and their children—and also to be aware of national resources, like the domestic violence hotline. After referral suggestions are made, it is important that religious leaders maintain contact with those who have come to the church looking for help. Often it is advisable to consider additional spiritual resources to supplement those services received in the wider community.

- Offer her supportive services from church people.

  Many religious survivors of domestic violence report how important it is to be connected to a supportive faith community during their crisis involving domestic violence and its aftermath. In time, as healing takes place, survivors like others in congregational life want to be given ministry opportunities so that they can reach out to others.

For those who have been violated, the challenge is to be silent no longer. To shatter the silence on abuse, though, is a responsibility all of us in church life must assume. We must be determined to be silent no longer—to speak out whenever an opportunity exists so that awareness might be raised both within the walls of our congregations and beyond. For those who suffer, the challenge is to search for help and, if you do not find it where you first look, keep on searching. There are many who want to walk alongside you as your journey toward healing and empowerment. In time, both the language of contemporary culture—with its focus on safety and practical resources—and the language of the spirit—with its focus on the words of comfort and encouragement from the Scriptures and other religious symbols—will be able to assist you.

HOLY HUSH OR SHATTERED SILENCE?

For many years, I have been arguing that there is a holy hush that pervades religious organizations when it comes to the subject of abuse in the family context. The evidence is overwhelming:[7] most pastors have never visited the transition house in or near their local area; most pastors do not know by name any of the workers in the local shelter; most pastors have never preached a message that explicitly condemned wife abuse and/or child abuse; and clergy are reluctant to refer to outside community resources those that come to them for help.

7. Nason-Clark, Nancy. 1997. The Battered Wife: How Christians Confront Family Violence. Louisville, KY: Westminster/John Knox Press.

Let us consider this last point in more detail—the lack of referrals from clergy to community-based resources. What we know from the data we have collected over the last twenty years[8] is that most clergy do not feel equipped to respond to the needs of abused women, men who act abusively or other situations related to violence in the family context.[9] In fact, in one of our studies involving a sample of over five hundred clergy, only eight percent of religious leaders reported that they felt well prepared to offer assistance in cases of domestic violence. Yet, in this same study we learned most clergy are called upon to respond to such situations—often. At first blush, you would think that with a lack of prior preparation to respond to the needs, religious leaders would seek out community-based resources. Not so. In fact, referrals occur amongst those who know most about the subject and least from those with limited training. Thus, where referrals are needed most—from pastors who report they are ill-equipped to assist abused women—they are least likely to occur. This endangers women who seek their help and compromises the role of the church in assisting with the spiritual needs of those who suffer.

Yet, things are beginning to change. There is a rumbling in the church closet that cannot be silenced. It occurs when you least expect it and from some unlikely corners. There are a growing number of church leaders and followers who are determined to shatter the silence, to speak out, to proclaim from the church roof-tops that peace and safety must prevail in families of faith. Such women and men of courage are paving the pathway from the steeple to the shelter, ensuring that there is coordination and collaboration between church-based and community-based resources.

Lest I be accused of being overly optimistic, let me remind you that this too is evidence-based.[10] Most clergy have counseled a woman who has been battered. Most Christian women have helped an abused woman they know. Most church women's groups have supported in some way

8. Nason-Clark, Nancy. 1997. The Battered Wife: How Christians Confront Family Violence. Louisville, KY: Westminster/John Knox Press.

9. Including situations where the man is the victim, the child is the victim, both partners are violent one towards the other, or the victim is an elderly parent.

10. Nason-Clark, Nancy. 2007 Christianity and Domestic Violence. Essay in *Encyclopedia of Domestic Violence*, edited by Nicole Jackson. New York: Routledge, pp. 161–166; Nason-Clark, N. (2005) Linking Research and Social Action: Violence, Religion and the Family. A Case for Public Sociology, *Review of Religious Research*, 46(3): 221–234; Nason-Clark, N. (2004) When Terror Strikes at Home: The Interface Between Religion and Domestic Violence. *Journal for the Scientific Study of Religion* 43(3): 303–310.

their local transition house, by either financial, or in-kind donations—like taking food, giving clothing or bedding, or sending school supplies to the children living there. Some churches have information provided in church washrooms or other safe places that outline what to do and where to go if you are a victim of abuse.[11]

DEVELOPING A PASSION FOR PEACE AND SAFETY IN THE CHRISTIAN HOME

For me, researching violence has had an enormous impact on my personal life. In an essay I wrote several years ago entitled *From the Heart of My Lap-top*, I began to think about how my abuse work had altered who I was, how I spent my time and what I considered important. I am a field researcher with a very important sociological story to tell. It is my responsibility to understand it well—its overarching themes and subtle nuances. When we translate research for a wider audience, we face a number of specific paradoxes. For this enterprise to be successful there needs to be sufficient flexibility to accommodate both the rigors of the academy and the passion of an activist. While passion without data can be misguided or even dangerous, passion based on empirical validation can be powerful. And that power has the potential to shape not only the path the data travels but also the heart of the researcher.

So too for the believer. Knowledge and social action go hand in hand. I would like to use the structure of my garden to illustrate what I mean. For the sake of brevity, a garden has some high interest structures, some developed beds, stairs and height, background context, waves of colour and texture, bushes and evergreens for year round interest, and grass, mulch and fragrances to pull it all together. Some perennial plants or shrubs signal a new season, others are very showy but die fast. Dead wood becomes the mulch that retains the water that helps the new plants to grow.

Violence knows no religious boundaries—it is a global issue. Breaking the cycle of violence requires both the language of secular culture and the language of the spirit. For our collaborative garden to grow, we must respect our differences and honour each other's contribution. A cultural language that does not pay attention to religious symbols, meaning and legitimacy is relatively powerless to alter a religious victim's resolve to stay

11. Information, like this, is available on our website at www.theraveproject.org.

in the marriage no matter what the cost. Correspondingly, the language of the spirit, without practical resources from the contemporary culture, compromises a victim's need for safety, security and financial resources to care for herself and her children.

It should alarm us to know that evangelical family life can be dangerous to your physical or emotional health. Statistically speaking, you and I are more likely to be harmed or hurt by someone within the confines of our own home than we are to be attacked by strangers. Sounding the alarm bell should motivate us to action. But, like the priest and levite in the story of the Good Samaritan, it is so much easier—so much less painful, so much less anxiety-producing—to look the other way. Looking the other way does not challenge our pocket book, our time or our ideologies. Pew potatoes always look the other way.

For the Christian believer, Jesus' experience in the Garden of Gethsemane offers us some important insights into the link between God and human suffering. Think of some of the images from this familiar scene: Jesus' prayer to God for strength, the sleeping disciples unaware of the support they may offer, the "kiss" of betrayal, the soldiers, the exchange of coins, the arrest. Gethsemane was a garden, across the Kidron Valley from Jerusalem. Jesus and the disciples went there often, for it was a safe place, a place of refuge, a place to rest, pray, and receive spiritual renewal. Yet, it is best known as a place of betrayal, the spot where the guards came to arrest Jesus of Nazareth. The garden that offered shade in the heat, refuge from the crowds, sustenance for the human spirit and privacy to communicate with God was the place where Jesus received the kiss of betrayal, wounded by someone who was loved and trusted.

The story reminds us that even where we feel the greatest refuge from the strains and pressures of contemporary life, we can also be the most vulnerable. The Garden of Gethsemane serves as a warning for us all—but especially for women and children—that we can be wounded and betrayed by those to whom we are closest, those who are loved.

But Gethsemane represents more than just pain and anguish. It also signals hope, renewal, and strength to combat even the greatest challenges that betrayal can bring. Here we are reminded that there are resources both within and beyond the human person that can transform a woman or man, girl or boy, from vulnerability to strength, from fear to calm, and from desperation to hope.

To respond with the mind of Christ to a victim of domestic violence is to support that woman in finding the inner strength to leave the garden—and to work through the pain and betrayal to wholeness. Such a response offers hope while never diminishing the reality of the pain; it provides the basis for growth and independence without denying the fear of the unknown.

Betrayal and hope—themes of the Garden of Gethsemane—help us to understand in part the journey for a religious woman from victim to survivor.

Her journey is long and arduous and many traveling companions are required? Are you willing to walk alongside her?

13

Theological Reflections on the Prophetic Call

Elizabeth Gerhardt

A CHURCH APPROACH THAT places *theology first* provides the foundation for the church to be a strong prophetic voice that counters violence against women. In general, there has been a halting appropriation of defining the problem of domestic violence as a doctrinal or confessional issue. The approach of many mainline churches is to place an emphasis on practical pastoral counseling resources and educational efforts. Christian publications on the subject of domestic violence also reflect the trend toward individual and counseling issues. This is due to the tendency to define violence against women as a moral and ethical problem. There lacks a theological framework for addressing the problem as a confessional issue.

The prophetic call to end violence against women and children becomes more clearly defined when rooted in a confessional theology of the cross. The work of ending violence must first begin with an appropriation of the proclamation call of the gospel. Through the revelation of Christ we can begin to define violence as sin due to the violation of human integrity that belongs to all human beings as bestowed by a gracious Creator. Within a christocentric theological model violence against women is defined as both sin *and* a human rights issue. In addition, a *theologia crucis* is a relational theology in that it provides a description of how women and men are called to relate to each other. In addition, a theology of the cross is a *theology of life* that exposes and opposes the false Christian claim that abused women ought to "bear their cross" in silence. It rejects theologies that maintain that suffering "builds character," victims should "turn the other cheek," and all other maxims used to oppress others by religion.

Martin Luther's dialectic of law and gospel is helpful in its description of the tasks of the individual Christian *and* the church as both *kerygma* and *diakonia*, that is, proclamation and service.

A theology of the cross offers the most useful content, approach, and methodology by providing a perspective that grounds social ethics in faith. It also provides a correction to the misuse of Christian tradition. From this viewpoint, violence against women is defined in both legal and spiritual language, and challenges the church to engage in both realms. There is a danger of pursuing one without the other. In preaching against violence as sin without also working for justice Christians may fall into a trap of believing that love alone will change the individuals and, subsequently, end violence. This "superspiritualism" is optimistic in its idealism but ignores the reality of the systemic nature of violence. Love rooted in a pietistic individualism is, in the end, ineffective in ending violence. On the other hand, pursuing justice work without faith based proclamation becomes a type of works righteousness. It is easy to be deceived into believing that human effort at social transformation will establish a sort of Christian kingdom on earth. Justice building without a firm establishment in the faith of Christ's power and love becomes divorced from the gospel.

Dietrich Bonhoeffer's theology and ethics offers a contemporary example of the application of Luther's theology of the cross to the problem of institutional violence. Bonhoeffer offers a model of a practical application of Luther's theology that results in a social ethic grounded in proclamation. Christ is the starting point for his commitment to social and political justice. A study of Bonhoeffer's practical application of a theology of the cross can act as a guide when considering what prophetic call the church needs to make concerning violence against women. However, before further reflections on the relevance and application of a theology of the cross for the church, it is important to acknowledge the most prevalent and influential modern theologies that have provided a paradigm for the work of ending violence. It is important to note the important contributions some feminist theologies have made in this area, and recognize their theological limitations.

FEMINIST THEOLOGIES

On the topic of violence against women, feminist theology has dominated the literature. It has strongly influenced contemporary church practice.

In general, feminist theologians identify the church's problem as a lack of support for women who have been subjected to domestic violence. They reject theologies that blame women for violence in the home. They rightly argue that a refusal to hold perpetrators accountable helps to maintain an institutional structure that colludes with a culture of violence against women and children. Feminist theology correctly identifies domestic violence as an ethical and a legal problem that needs to be addressed within the church. Feminist descriptions of church practices that revictimize women by holding them accountable for their partners' behavior is, generally, quite accurate.

Radical feminist theologians strongly criticize Christian traditions and doctrines which they perceive are behind church practices that silence the pain of women. Specifically, they indicate that church teaching on suffering and the cross has exacerbated wrongful practices. The problem with this view is that many feminist theologians fail to differentiate between voluntary and involuntary suffering and the role of suffering in the Christian life. Church teaching and practice have often failed to uphold the dignity and rights of women and have placed undue burdens on victims by the church's silence and disregard. Nevertheless, the cross of Christ need not be marginalized or plucked out of theology because of its emphasis on the centrality of Christ's suffering and death for salvation.

Many feminist theologies focus on women's experience of oppression as its basic framework for understanding. Subsequently, by promoting a "gospel" of ethics in order to establish equality and justice through human effort, they ultimately reject a theology of the cross. These feminist theologies do so by their consideration of the suffering Christ on the cross as an involuntary victim and model for humanity. This perspective fails to consider that Christ voluntarily laid down his life to reconcile God and humankind. Jesus is relegated to the victim role and is considered an example rather than Redeemer. The view of Christ as a model then places battered women in an untenable predicament. According to this way of thinking it would follow that women must also suffer as Christ suffered in order to be saved. The burden of proof is thrown upon the believer. Since feminist theologians reject this proposal (rightly so), then the salvific event must be expunged from theology. Luther's theology points out that the premise of Christ as only a model is faulty. The involuntary suffering battered women experience is not what Christ modeled on the cross. Salvation cannot be earned by this type of suffering. The work of salvation has been completed and, therefore, no amount of suffering at the hands of an oppressor can earn one salvation. Luther's theology of the cross does not eliminate the important role of suffering in the Christian life, but maintains that an understanding of this can only take place in the light of faith in Christ's completed work on the cross.

Additionally, many feminist concepts of revelation and salvation contrast sharply with Luther's theology. As discussed above, revelation defined as women's experience is fraught with problems. Defining women's experience in unidimensional terms is vague, simplistic, and generalized. Radical feminism identifies the revelation of the divine as being ontologically constitutive of women and existing through experience, and, therefore, revelation centers on subjective interpretation. The rational conclusion is that the source of divinity, in whatever form, emanates from the self. This belief system then begs the question, "Who determines which human experiences are authoritative and revelatory?" Salvation as described by many feminist theologians, as self-enlightenment leading to establishing justice on earth, is little more than a type of works righteousness. This conclusion is always problematic because it raises the perennial question: how much effort is enough to gain salvation?

Many feminist theologies do raise consciousness regarding women's experiences of oppression and abuse in our society. They also challenge church practices and theology that support and collude with the ongoing subjugation of women. But some feminists offer an alternative liberation theology that actually marginalizes the plight of women by rejecting church tradition and doctrine by claiming that ethics displaces theology. Some feminist theologies proclaim a gospel that centers on social and political liberation versus a theology of the cross that bases reconciliation work in Christ. The language of liberation and empowerment contrasts with the biblical language of reconciliation and the cross. These theologies offer a social gospel that focuses on human experiences as revelatory and ignores the centrality of Christ as the disclosure of God and hope for freedom. Most feminist theologies offer a valid and strong social analysis of the problem of domestic violence. Nevertheless, they are theologically weak. They tell us what to do but do not provide the power to do it. The focus is on law with no gospel. Therefore, many feminist theologies stand in sharp contrast to a theology of the cross which provides a strong foundation for effective practices in the work to end violence against women rooted in Christ as Savior, not victim.

A THEOLOGY OF THE CROSS

Therefore, what I propose as a theological foundation for this work of ending violence against women is a theology rooted in the cross of Christ. There are five characteristics of this theology that are relevant to examining the role of the prophetic call of the contemporary church:

First, a theology of the cross is confessional. That is, its central mission is to proclaim that salvation is found in Christ's death and resurrection. This undercuts theologies of idolatry that elevate others on the basis of race, gender, and class. Christ died that all may be free. When I hear abused women speak of needing to be "obedient" to abusive husbands because that's "what the Bible says" I know they have come under a theology of idolatry. This sin of idolatry maintains that power is gained as a result of one's gender and that suffering is somehow salvific. A theology of the cross defines the suffering of the crucified Christ *alone* as salvific. The sacrifice has already been given. Women do not need to "turn the other cheek" and "suffer in silence" to win their salvation. This is a form of works righteousness that is antithetical to the gospel. The theology of the cross addresses the themes of power, suffering, and freedom and lays them squarely at the foot of the cross. It is only faith in the Christ who frees that can overcome the lies of the abuser that perverts the Scriptures. It is faith in the Christ of power that can overcome church theologies of idolatry that would rather hold fast to "family values" than ensure the safety of women and children.

A theology of the cross means following the way of Christ. This is a journey of suffering and a walk of freedom. This suffering is not self-imposed but rather a result of following the One who suffered and calls us to come and take up our cross. It is also a way of hope because the Christian is assured of true freedom in Christ. Luther insisted that works not be self-imposed. In the same manner, he rejected self-chosen suffering as an avenue to salvation. Trials and affliction are consequences of living in the world.

> Therefore we do not say, 'Spare us the trial,' but, 'Do not lead us into it.' It is as if we were to say, 'We are surrounded on all sides by trials and cannot avoid them; however, dear Father, help us so that we do not fall prey to them and yield to them, and thus be overcome and vanquished.' He who gives way to them sins and becomes captive to sin, as St. Paul declares [Rom. 7:23]. (LW 42:71)

Luther's theology of the cross provides the lens in which to consider the role of suffering in the Christian life. His theology undercuts Christian theologies that accept the suffering endured by women victimized by violence as redemptive. This is a type of "works righteousness" that fails because it places the self in the role of Christ.

Second, a theology of the cross is relational. The beauty of the incarnation is that Christ became as we are, fully human. Jesus came not in splendor but in poverty and without any worldly recognition. At the foot of the cross we remember who we are and are humbled. True power is spiritual, Luther said. The power of the cross is hidden and cannot be grasped by those who claim power for themselves. Abused women can find their identity as daughters of God, and brides of Christ. Power does not lie with the batterer nor with churches that protect the batterer. Power resides with Christ alone. The cross reminds us that the abuser holds no real power before God. Human sin that brings division and oppression was overcome on the cross. Christ's healing love poured out to us through the cross leaves no room for the denigration of women. A confessing church is authentic, in that it is loyal to the gospel alone and no other ideology or person who would claim its loyalty.

Third, using a theology of the cross as a foundation for addressing violence against women moves the discussion from an ethical issue, that can easily be marginalized and then dismissed, to a problem that begs a response from the whole of the church. This happens as a result of the church proclaiming Christ. In other words, the work of ending violence is not salvific in itself, or it would be a form of works righteousness. Nevertheless, it does come indirectly out of the heart of the gospel. That is, oppression and violence against women violate the integrity of the gospel, and it is a stumbling block to the proclamation of the gospel. The dialectic of gospel and law is helpful in sorting out a theological response to this problem. It moves violence against women into the spotlight because it speaks to the very integrity of Christ's salvation message. God commands us to be "free for the other" and to "set free" those imprisoned. You cannot preach the authentic gospel and be detached from the situations that bind people. Nor, on the liberal theological side, maintain that salvation lies in earthly freedom. The freest among us may be the one hidden in a far corner in a prison in China. Nevertheless, because we are free in Christ we are also called to work for the freedom of others. A detached confessionalism is a life without discipleship and true authenticity.

Fourth, the theology of the cross uses the language of the cross. Luther described a theologian of the cross as one "who calls a thing what it is." In other words, we must be a confessing church that is prophetic, that speaks truth to power. Gerhard Forde emphasizes the importance of maintaining a theology of the cross that provides a precise language for a Christian perspective and application. He argues that our modern culture has been so over-sensitized and psychologized that we are afraid to call "a spade a spade."

> When we operate on the assumption that our language must constantly be trimmed so as not to give offense, to stroke the psyche rather than to place it under attack, it will of course gradually decline to the level of greeting-card sentimentality. The language of sin, law, accusation, repentance, judgment, wrath, punishment, perishing, death, devil, damnation and even the cross itself—virtually one-half of the vocabulary—simply disappears. It has lost its theological legitimacy and therefore its viability as communication. A theologian of the cross says what a thing is. In modern parlance: a theologian calls a spade a spade. One who 'looks on all things through suffering and the cross' is constrained to speak the truth. The theology of the cross, that is to say, provides the theological courage and the conceptual framework to hold the language in place.

The language of the *theologia crucis* provides the most relevant and useful foundation for creating language that accurately reflects the sin of violence by calling "a spade a spade." To refer to violence as a "problem" or to psychologize it for the church is to marginalize it as another "family issue." The reality is that not only is it a sin (using theological language) but an overwhelming criminal and global issue that affects most of humanity. We need to use accurate language that truly relates the nature of misogyny and violence. I no longer speak of domestic violence. That term has become so marginalized that it hardly registers a ripple in people's consciousness, let alone moves anyone to action. In legal language it is a human rights issue that continues to cause devastating suffering for women and girls in every nation.

Violence against women is also sin that is individual and communal when the church is silent. After giving a presentation on this issue I often hear from students and pastors the following statements: "I didn't know this was such a problem." "I had no idea this was so prevalent." "I never thought of this as a global issue." Why is there so much ignorance? Is it because the information isn't out there? No! It is because we marginalize and minimize the problem and don't use the language of the cross to put it front and center as a confessional issue. Moral issues beget educational and counseling programs; confessional issues move entire churches to act. The true Church of Christ *speaks* truth.

Fifth, whenever the gospel is hindered, a theology of the cross moves from confession to resistance in the context of community. It is here that Dietrich Bonhoeffer's interpretation of Luther's theology and the implication for the Christian church is most helpful. Community was a central theme for Bonhoeffer.[1] Eberhard Bethge argued that confession clarified the church's identity but that it was not enough to combat evil. Confession must accompany resistance in the Christian community.

Bonhoeffer introduced us in 1935 to the problem of what we today call political resistance. The levels of confession and of resistance could no longer be kept neatly apart. The escalating persecution of the Jews generated an increasingly intolerable situation, especially for Bonhoeffer himself. We now realized that mere confession, no matter how courageous, inescapably meant complicity with the murderers, even though there would always be new acts of refusing to be co-opted and even though we would preach "Christ alone" Sunday after Sunday. During the whole time, the Nazi state never considered it necessary to prohibit such preaching. Why should it?

Thus we were approaching the borderline between confession and resistance; and if we did not cross this border, our confession was going to be no better than cooperation with the criminals. And so it became clear where the problem lay for the Confessing Church: We were resisting by way of confession, but we were not confessing by way of resistance.[2]

Bethge argues that Bonhoeffer was a man for who confession became the foundation for action. He was a theologian and an activist. Indeed, his theology necessitated his resistance. Confession without resistance becomes an instrument of collusion with evil. Bonhoeffer did not lose his

---

1. Bonhoeffer closely aligns the church community with the Incarnate Christ. "The Body of Christ is identical with the new humanity which he has taken upon him. It is in fact the Church. Jesus Christ is at once himself and his Church (I Cor. 12.12)." See *The Cost of Discipleship*, Touchstone Books, 1995, 240–241.

2. Bethge, *Friendship and Resistance: Essays on Dietrich Bonhoeffer*, 1995, 24.

identity in Christ by his engagement in the world, nor did he refuse this involvement because of this identity.

> People today who confine themselves to confession and never cross the threshold often ask how a man like Bonhoeffer could theologically justify his identification with the conspirators. The question is frightful, because it is usually raised out of an isolated and isolating situation of detached confessionalism, unconscious of its own complicity with evil. My wife once gave the shortest answer: How can a confessing Christian theologically justify a lack of action?[3]

Community provides the context in which confession and resistance receive nurturance and direction. The role of confessions as statements of belief is central in the theology and ethic of Dietrich Bonhoeffer. There are many contributing factors that led to Bonhoeffer's decision to engage in acts of resistance. Nevertheless, for purposes of this study, Bonhoeffer reminds us of the role of confession in the task of ending violence against women. Proclamation of the gospel as the basis for social justice practice is clearly exemplified by Bonhoeffer's ethic and resistance activity.

Dietrich Bonhoeffer lived out his theology in his struggle and resistance to the evil that steadied and centered him in Christ. He was rooted in a confessional theology identity of the Christian church that did not allow him to be seduced into colluding with evil or withdrawing from the struggle into safety. Bonhoeffer's use of the language of the cross is instrumental in constructing a methodology for addressing institutional and social violence against women in any form. Repentance, forgiveness, and reconciliation are key themes that have meaning within the context of the proclamation of Christ as Savior.

Bethge expresses the language of the cross in the primary concepts of confession and resistance. Nevertheless, the paradigm provides a conceptual framework that connects theology and ethics. The church in Nazi Germany faced a dilemma when confronted with evil. Dietrich Bonhoeffer and many others were able to remember and clearly articulate their beliefs through confession. Rooted in confession and conversion they resisted evil and worked for love. There were those who forgot and denied their true identity as a people of God. They colluded with corrupt power. Some chose violence. Others withdrew and became silent. Bonhoeffer resisted the seduction of self-preservation and chose to con-

3. Bethge, 27.

fess the true gospel and, consequently, became the enemy of those who wielded crushing political power.

On the day of the church election in 1933 Bonhoeffer preached a sermon that outlined the church's struggle to find its identity and confess its faith. He based his sermon on Matt 16:13–14: "Who do you say that I am?"

> Peter's church—that means the church of rock, the church of the confession of Christ. Peter's church, that does not mean a church of opinions and views, but the church of the revelation; not a church in which what 'people say' is talked about but the church in which Peter's confession is made and spoken anew; the church which has no other purpose in song, prayer, preaching and action than ever to renew its confession of faith; the church which is always founded on rock as long as it remains within these limits, but which turns into a house built on sand, which is blown away by the wind, as soon as it is foolhardy enough to think that it may depart from or even for a moment neglect this purpose.[4]

Bonhoeffer notes that Peter and the church fail because of weakness, fear, seduction by the world. Therefore, confession is critical for the church to stay a church. "But it is not we who build. He builds the church. No man builds the church but Christ alone. . . . We must confess—He builds." Therefore, the confession of the cross of Christ identifies the church and is in itself an act of resistance.

Confession, which occurs in the context of community, takes a downward slide when community refuses to act in opposition to evil. Collusion is particularly insidious because it often presents itself as a self-righteous and pious Christianity. This is seductive to a church community. It offers the comfortable illusion for members that they are a faithful church. In fact, a church that confesses to follow Christ alone and yet allows for the destruction of others, including violence being perpetrated against women and children, is as responsible for the effects of evil acts as the instigators. A colluding church also participates in its own destruction.

Bonhoeffer could not envision a church that would oppose evil only in theory and not in practice. Discipleship included practical application of the gospel. Living out the faith meant acting *for* the *other*, *for* the *persecuted* and *opposing in deed* those who promulgated evil. In *The Cost of Discipleship*, Bonhoeffer writes of the necessity of the church to fulfill its

---

4. Bonhoeffer, "Church Election Sermons: 23rd July 1933," in *No Rusty Swords: Letters, Lectures and Notes 1928–1936.* 1965, 215, 217.

call as a "light" to others. This cannot be preached only from the pulpit, but rather it must be acted out in the world.[5]

> Again, it is not enough to teach the law of Christ, it must be *done*, otherwise it is no better than the old law. In what follows the disciples are told how to practice this righteousness of Christ. In a word, it means following him. It is the real and active faith in the righteousness of Christ. It is the new law, the law of Christ.[6]

In Bonhoeffer's teaching, writings, and activism, he echoes Luther's theology when he insists on the true meaning of freedom for the Christian. The Christian is free not for purposes of the self but rather, *for others*. Freedom can only be understood in relation to the other. Good works are a result of the grace of God setting followers free to act on behalf of others.

A Challenge to the Church

The central roles of confession and resistance in Bonhoeffer's theology and ethic are extremely vital issues for the contemporary church. The question Jesus posed to Peter, "Who do you say that I am?" was the critical question that Bonhoeffer put before the church in Nazi Germany. This is the same question we must put before the church today, who is Christ for us today? This is significant when considering the church's mandate to action in addressing the problem of violence against women. Confessing Christ without action can lead to a paralyzing institutionalization of the gospel. Who has the prophetic call? The answer is every Christian, because each is called to proclaim Christ. An integral work of that call is to feed the hungry, visit the sick, work for justice, and end the violence that destroys the lives of millions of victims worldwide everyday. The question of the prophetic call is the same perennial question the church dare not ignore.

Bonhoeffer's confessionalism was alive because he applied it to the crises of his situation. We are not battling national socialism. The challenge to the church is how can we apply the lessons learned from Luther and Bonhoeffer to our world today? Specifically, are there lessons to be learned from the work of Luther, Bonhoeffer, and the confessing church that can be applied to the issue of domestic violence in much the same way as many churches did in addressing racism and apartheid? Bonhoeffer maintained that there are three responses of the church when facing evil:

5. Bonhoeffer, *Cost of Discipleship*, 1995, 117.
6. Bonhoeffer, 125.

1. Speak in a prophetic voice: truth to power; 2. Give aid to victims; 3. Resist evil in action. These three responses of the church to a state that takes too much power or allows lawlessness (outlined above) are helpful in evaluating contemporary situations. When the state power impedes the work of the church or is self-destructive the church has a responsibility to act. Bonhoeffer suggests the first response as a direct response to the government (a call for justice) and the second as helping the victims of state action. These two can be easily applied to current situations of violence against women in parts of the world where laws protecting women are inconsistently and infrequently enforced or do not exist at all. The church must continue to cry out against injustice and aid those persecuted and oppressed. The third response involves direct political action against an evil system or state government. This may be straightforward in a situation that is *status confessionis* such as the policy of apartheid in South Africa (condemned as heretical). But at first glance the serious injustice of domestic violence would not appear to fit into a situation of crises and heresy. Overt support of gender violence by church denominations is sporadic. Nevertheless, I would argue that widespread covert support exists in areas where female genital mutilation, forced abortions and sterilizations, female infanticide, domestic violence, female slavery, forced prostitution, and mass rapes and sexual assaults as tools of war remain a part of the political and cultural fabric of life for women. There is little or no condemnation and resistance work done by churches in many parts of the world. As has been argued, when there is systemic violence perpetrated against women, as a consequence of their gender, then the gospel is distorted and undermined.

This is an area where Luther and Bonhoeffer's thoughts and writings should be struggled with in debate and discussion among community members. What should the church's response be to the widespread problem of violence against women? Many are responding. But so much more can be done. Bonhoeffer shines a bright light on an evil that continues to seduce a complacent church. His message is as relevant today as it was in the early twentieth century. The church need not abandon the language and theology of the cross in order to condemn violence against women and work to establish justice. It is because of the cross of Christ that the churches must resolve to condemn the destruction of women's lives and consider violence against women a matter of grave sin and heresy. Luther's theology of the cross provides the critical framework for a methodology that challenges the church to live out its mission of service and reconciliation.

The challenge to the church is to engage in a paradigm shift in addressing the evil of domestic violence. A language that includes the concepts and experience of confession, memory, suffering, obedience, and discipleship provides a working framework for addressing the church's prophetic role in ending violence against women. Luther's theology provides the methodology that ultimately raises the question of whether or not domestic violence is a confessional issue that requires prophetic church resistance. There should be a cohesive church response to the problem of violence against women as a confessional, not merely an ethical and moral, issue.

REFERENCES

Adams, Carol and Marie Fortune, eds. *Violence Against Women and Children: A Christian Theological Sourcebook*. New York: Continuum, 1995.

Bethge, Eberhard. *Dietrich Bonhoeffer*. Munich: Chr. Kaiser Verlag, 1967. Translation. London: Williams Collins Sons & Co., Ltd., 1970.

_____. *Friendship and Resistance: Essays on Dietrich Bonhoeffer*. Grand Rapids: William B. Eerdmans, 1995.

Bograd, Michelle. "Feminist Perspectives on Wife Abuse: An Introduction." In *Feminist Perspectives on Wife Abuse*, edited by Kersti Yllo and Michele Bograd. Newbury Park, California: Sage Publications, 1988.

Bonhoeffer, Dietrich. "Boundaries of Church and Church Union." In *Dietrich Bonhoeffer: Witness to Jesus Christ*. With an introduction by John de Gruchy. Minneapolis: Fortress Press, 1987.

_____. "The Church and the Jewish Question." In *Dietrich Bonhoeffer: Witness to Jesus Christ*. With an introduction by John de Gruchy. Minneapolis: Fortress Press, 1987.

_____. "Church Election Sermons: 23rd July 1933." In *No Rusty Swords: Letters, Lectures and Notes 1928–1936*. Translated by Edwin H. Robertson and John Bowdon. St. James Place, Lonson: Collins, Sons & Co., 1965.

_____. *Ethics*. New York: S.C.M. Press, 1955; (First Published *Ethik*, 1949); reprint, New York: Touchstone, 1995.

Brown, Joanne and Carole R. Bohn, eds. *Christianity, Patriarchy, and Abuse*. Cleveland: The Pilgrim Press, 1989.

de Gruchy, John, ed. *Bonhoeffer for a New Day: Theology in a Time of Transition*. Grand Rapids: Eerdmans, 1997.

_____. *Bonhoeffer and South Africa: Theology in Dialogue*. Grand Rapids: Wm. B. Eerdmans Co., 1984.

Elshtain, Jean Bethke. "Caesar, Sovereignty, and Bonhoeffer." *Lutheran Theological Seminary Bulletin* 76 (4) (Fall 1995): 5–39.

Forde, Gerhard. *On Being A Theologian Of The Cross: Reflections on Luther's Heidelberg Disputation, 1518*. Grand Rapids: William B. Eerdmanns, 1997.

_____. *Theology is for Proclamation*. Minneapolis: Fortress Press, 1990.

Forell, George Wolfgang. *Faith Active in Love: An Investigation of the Principles Underlying Luther's Social Ethics*. New York: The American Press, 1954.

_____. *The Proclamation of the Gospel in a Pluralistic World*. Philadelphia: Fortress Press, 1973.

_____. "The Rights of the Weak." In *Human Rights: Rhetoric or Reality*, George W. Forell and William H. Lazareth, 62–64. Philadelphia: Fortress Press, 1978.

Kelly, Geffrey B. and F. Burton Nelson, eds. *Dietrich Bonhoeffer: A Testament to Freedom*. San Francisco: Harper Collins, 1990, 1995.

Krusche, Gunter. "Human Rights in a Theological Perspective: A Contribution from the GDR." *Lutheran World* 24, no.1 59–65.

Lindberg, Carter. *Beyond Charity: Reformation Initiatives for the Poor*. Minneapolis: Fortress Press, 1993.

_____. "The Ministry and Vocation of the Baptized," *Lutheran Quarterly* 6 (Winter 1992): 385–401.

_____. "Theory and Practice: Reformation Models of Ministry as Resource for the Present," *Lutheran Quarterly* 27 (February 1975): 27–35.

Lull, Timothy F. ed. *Martin Luther's Basic Theological Writings*. Minneapolis: Fortress Press, 1989.

Luther, Martin. *Luther's Works*. Edited by Jaroslav Pelikan (Vol. 1–30) and Helmut T. Lehmann (Vol. 31–55). St. Louis: Concordia Publishing House, 1968.

Rasmussen, Larry and Renate Bethge. *Dietrich Bonhoeffer—His Significance for North Americans*. Minneapolis: Fortress Press, 1990.

14

Raising Our Voices

The Prophetic Call for Future Action

Joyce Holt

Praise be to the God and Father of our Lord Jesus Christ, the God of all comfort, who comforts us in all our troubles, so that we can comfort those in any trouble with the comfort we ourselves have received from God." (2 Cor. 1:3)

S HE SITS IN THE pew in her usual place, to the right of the pulpit, just behind the organ. It's Easter Sunday, and far more crowded than usual. Holding her head high she takes a deep breath and pretends that she is as 'normal' as any other woman in the sanctuary. She busies herself with the bulletin hoping to avoid the questions from well-meaning congregants who know her situation. Just the thought is a painful reminder that she is anything but normal. She quickly thinks of something else to fight back the tears, hoping they will not betray her by spilling down her cheeks. The music begins . . . she's safe.

The congregation stands and begins to sing, "Wonderful merciful Savior, precious Redeemer and Friend, who would have thought that a lamb could rescue the souls of men?" She has spent countless hours over the past several years pouring her heart out to God, and as the song ushers her into His presence, she forgets about the others with whom she is pressed shoulder to shoulder. Nothing distracts her from praising her wonderful, merciful Savior, Redeemer and Friend who rescued her soul—truly rescued her soul.

The music continues, "You are the One that we praise, You are the One we adore, You give us hope when our hearts have hopelessly lost the way." She lifts her voice and hands in praise—the familiar words have taken on an entirely new and deeper meaning. The tears, now streaming down her face, are a gift of praise to God for being there for her when no one else was, when others—yes, even her Christian "family"—turned their backs during her crisis.

Only months earlier she met with her pastor letting him know her dark secret—that verbal, emotional, and physical abuse had plagued her marriage. She described the fights that began over insignificant things like clogging the garbage disposal where she had peeled the potatoes for their evening meal—fights that were littered with degrading words . . . stupid . . . insane . . . b**** . . . —fights that preyed on her most intimate vulnerabilities, insecurities, hurts, and fears. She shared how her efforts to reason with him ended with bizarre twisting of the details that made every problem her fault. How, when the hurtful words that pierced her heart were not enough to reduce her to tears, a threatening fist would be raised to her face. She can still picture the tight-lipped angry grimace always present during fights. At times she would try to escape the hurtful words by running to a room and locking the door . . . only to have the lock picked and the verbal barrage continue. When the fights increased in frequency to a weekly and sometimes daily occurrence, she was driven into such despair and depression that she pleaded with God to end her life—even though she had two small children.

She disclosed to her pastor that she planned to file for divorce and a restraining order. She let him know of her concern for her safety and that her husband would publicly humiliate her in front of the congregation—one of his many manipulative tactics. She expected her pastor to be surprised—after all she and her husband were both active and well-liked members of the church—but she was the one who was surprised. Even as she shared the truth that was so shameful to her, the pastor glossed over the disclosure of abuse and pain and quickly focused the conversation on reconciliation with her husband. Why couldn't he understand that she had already endured years of deep pain in an attempt to save her marriage? Couldn't he see how this was devastating her—that she still loved her husband but could no longer tolerate the abuse—that it was unsafe for her and her children?

She disguised her shock at the pastor's reaction. She had learned to hide her reactions as a survival tactic to protect herself from her husband's unexplainable rages over seemingly minor issues. She pressed on, trying to help the pastor understand the truth of the situation by describing a couple of incidents of abuse in detail, including the night she called 911. She explained her attempts to save the marriage, including Christian marriage counseling that started within six months of their marriage, and the conversations she had seeking spiritual guidance from several highly respected women of faith in the church. Her explanation was to no avail. She left the meeting without having had the pastor express any understanding, compassion, concern for her own safety, or that of her children, or her spiritual well-being, and certainly no resolution. Instead she left with a feeling of emptiness and confusion and an even deeper sense of loneliness.

When the pastor called later that week she was delighted, thinking finally there would be love and support, and maybe an offer of help. Beyond all comprehension, the call bore none of the anticipated support—other than the offer for the church to pay for marriage counseling to bring them to reconciliation. Instead, the pastor requested that she step down from the ministry position in which she had served for over eight years. How could this happen? Her ministry provided her with deep connections to her church family. With her closest family a day's drive away, she needed to be surrounded physically and emotionally by being loved, hugged, validated, and affirmed. She needed someone to check to make sure she was safe—to give her a place to bring the children on the nights that she was not. She needed someone to help her find resources to assure her everyday needs for food and shelter were being met. She needed someone to help her negotiate the steps she needed to take to put her house on the market, repair the garbage disposal, find childcare, put together a budget, and look for a job. She needed someone to interact with her on a daily basis to help her wade through the tough spiritual issues she faced. She needed affirmation and validation that her husband's actions were abusive—and that abuse is never okay, and never God's will. Her entire life had been turned upside down, and now she had been separated from her church family.

Little did she know it was only the beginning of the issues she would face with her church. Although the forced sabbatical from ministry looked and felt like church discipline, she took advantage of the break and attended the church membership class on Sunday mornings. With only one final step required to achieve membership, she again received a phone call one day at her new job. This time the purpose of the call was to ask that she withdraw her application for membership "until a future time when a policy could be put in to place to deal with 'situations like hers.'" The shock and depth of hurt stripped her of her usual professional demeanor at work—she lowered her head to her desk and sobbed.

~

What feelings does this true account create in your heart? Are you filled with compassion? Do you have a knot in your stomach? Are you full of anger? I can hear the wheels turning—"MY church would NEVER do that!" But how can you be sure? The church in the account above is a well-respected, vibrant, Bible-teaching church that preaches the love of Christ and reaches out to the community to share God's love. How could such a church have handled this situation in a manner that caused an already devastating situation to become hurtful beyond imagination?

Like many churches, the church above did not set out to intentionally hurt the woman who disclosed her abuse—they were simply unprepared. In their seemingly small infraction of being unprepared, they didn't just miss the opportunity to represent the love of Christ to this woman; their actions represented an extreme opposite—the body of Christ rejected her, inflicting pain beyond imagination.

With domestic abuse impacting one out of three women in secular and faith communities alike, why are churches unprepared to handle this crisis when it arises? I would suggest that there are several reasons. First, most churches are unfamiliar with the characteristics of domestic violence and are therefore unable to identify a situation in their own congregation as a domestic violence issue rather than marital conflict. Domestic violence issues thus remain unaddressed.

Second, churches are either unaware of, or ignore, the prevalence of domestic violence. Accordingly, they take no action to prepare themselves and their congregation. They miss the opportunity to respond to believers, and at the same time miss the opportunity to reach non-believers who are facing the crisis of domestic violence.

Third, churches, already stretched beyond capacity handling the everyday needs of the congregation, believe that there are other resources that can handle this type of crisis. For these, and other reasons, many churches remain unaware of this "sleeping giant" and are, therefore, unprepared when a crisis arises.

Once a crisis occurs it is too late to prepare yourself and your church leadership to handle the situation correctly—like the church above, the situation careens out of control—leaving the physical and emotional safety, as well as the spiritual well-being of the survivor and her children, hanging in the balance. In many instances, it is at this point that the believer, rejected by the church, leaves the church vowing never to return, and walks away from God.

When a church acknowledges the prevalence of the problem of abuse and becomes educated it will be able to develop a God-honoring response that ministers to the needs of survivor and abuser, believer and non-believer. When a crisis arises, the church will become the fully functioning body of Christ, able to take appropriate, compassionate, immediate, and decisive action.

Will you be ready? Will your church be ready? Will the person—perhaps the pastor, a Bible study leader, small group leader, Sunday school teacher, or elder in your church, be ready when a domestic abuse crisis arises?

HOW ARE CHURCH LEADERS MISSING DOMESTIC VIOLENCE ISSUES IN THEIR OWN CHURCHES?

As stated above, being unfamiliar with the characteristics of domestic violence, most churches are unable to identify a situation in their own congregation as domestic violence. In many instances, especially those of verbal and emotional abuse, those experiencing abuse are also unable to "name" the issue as domestic abuse, adding to the difficulty for church leaders of correctly diagnosing the problem.

What is domestic violence? According to the National Domestic Violence Hotline, domestic violence can be defined as a pattern of behavior in any relationship that is used to gain or maintain power and control over an intimate partner. Abuse may be physical, sexual, emotional, economic, or psychological actions, or threats of actions, that influence another person. This includes any behaviors and tactics that frighten, intimidate, terrorize, manipulate, hurt, humiliate, blame, injure or wound someone. Such intentions are never God's plan for a healthy relationship, much less the relationship of marriage.

Domestic violence can happen to anyone of any race, age, sexual orientation, religion, or gender. It can happen to couples who are married, living together, or who are dating. Domestic violence affects people of all socioeconomic and educational levels.

It is also important to clearly understand what domestic violence is *not*. Domestic abuse is *not* about the couple's inability to resolve marital conflict, i.e., a husband or wife being mean to the other or not acting in a God-honoring manner to their spouse. Rather, it is about his desire to be in control.

Domestic abuse is *not* about the abuser's anger issues, but it is deeply rooted in the abuser's beliefs that he is superior; that he is central and his spouse is peripheral; that he is deserving of whatever will meet his needs; and that the spouse is there to meet those needs. Unless the abuser's belief system changes it is impossible to resolve this problem through marital counseling.

WHY SHOULD CHURCH LEADERS SPEND THEIR LIMITED TIME AND RESOURCES RESPONDING TO ABUSE?

Responding to the problem of abuse is going to take some of your church's resources that may already be spread too thin. Can't survivors look elsewhere? Don't they have family and friends, a counselor, or a secular support agency that can handle their issues? Why should you spend time developing a domestic violence response when there are others who can and do handle this group of "needy" people?

- Friends and families can be a tremendous support when they are local and emotionally healthy. However, many survivors have been alienated from friends and family by their abusers. Others live far from close family or have family who inflict further wounds. One friend told an abused woman she was too thin skinned and too tough on her husband even though there was emotional and verbal abuse, along with physical violence, resulting in a call to 911. A family member callously commented, "Don't think you're the only one . . . we've all been through it before." And "Get a divorce or get over it!"

- Counselors are not always trained to accurately identify the problem as abuse or be able to respond appropriately to the spiritual issues facing the survivor. One woman in counseling was asked by her Christian counselor why she didn't just give in and let her husband have his way all the time. At times counselors erroneously approach the problem as a marital issue and focus on reconciliation, to no avail.

- Community Support Groups provide excellent resources for understanding abuse and its characteristics, but they do not understand the spiritual issues faced by Christian survivors and are therefore often unable to respond to struggles surrounding headship, submission, forgiveness, and divorce.

So there are others who can respond to the needs of those impacted by domestic abuse, and bridges must indeed be built, but those who have suffered from abuse require not only their physical needs met, but also their spiritual needs. Believers will seek not only the compassion and love of Christ from their church family, but they will look for spiritual counsel that is crucial to their decision making process. Non-believers may also turn to God and the church in their time of crisis. Churches must prepare comprehensive, responsive solutions to offer a coordinated response with other professionals who understand the non-spiritual issues surrounding domestic violence.

Why should the church invest time dealing with this issue when other badly needed programs might have to be put aside? In all likelihood your congregation has already faced this problem. According to The Religion and Violence e-Learning (RAVE) Project, research shows that 83.2 percent of pastors have counseled at least one abused woman. If you have not been faced with this issue, statistics suggest that you will be very soon:

- One out of three women has been beaten, coerced into sex or otherwise abused during her lifetime;[1]

- Researchers within the field of family violence note that abuse crosses all religious boundaries and that the rates inside and outside the church are similar;[2]

- Twenty-eight percent of those surveyed in the Christian Reformed Church in 1989 had experienced at least one form of abuse.[3]

---

1. Silverman et al., Dating Violence. JAMA, 286(5), 2001.

2. Bureau of Justice Statistics Crime Data Brief, Intimate Partner Violence, 1993–2001. February 2003.

3. U.N. Study on the World's Women, 2000.

There are many more statistics that illuminate the magnitude of violence in Christian homes. For additional information please see www.theraveproject.org.

As founder of the Christian survivor support group, Hagar's Sisters, I have met with more than one hundred Christian women seeking help in the Boston metro area over the four-year period spanning 2003 through 2006. I have heard numerous stories of the hurt perpetrated by church leaders who just do not have the training to respond appropriately. Two additional accounts of survivors' interactions with the church appear in appendix A.

Surely the prevalence of abuse in the Christian community provides solid justification for church leaders to make this topic a priority. Yet disturbing statistics regarding clergy preparation, revealed by the research of Nancy Nason-Clark and the Religion and Violence Team at the University of New Brunswick, indicate that although domestic violence in the Christian community is as prevalent as in secular groups, only eight percent of pastors feel well prepared to respond to domestic violence.

Like Peter, as Christian leaders we are called to declare our love for Christ by obeying Jesus' directive, "Feed My sheep." Jesus sets the example as the Good Shepherd stating, "I lay down my life for my sheep." Responding to abuse requires that you consider your resources and develop an effective plan to respond to the needs of your sheep.

God has opened your eyes to the problem, even if only at this very moment, and has brought you to a point of decision: you can choose either to be part of the solution or part of the problem. There is no middle ground. Just as Saul stood by holding the cloaks of those who stoned Stephen to death, by doing nothing you become a passive advocate of abuse in Christian homes. God is responding to the cries of the abused and calling His people to action. The choice is yours—either disregard and deny the problem, or offer God's love by being a part of a comprehensive, international, biblically-based solution to the problem of abuse in Christian homes.

A DEMONSTRATION OF GOD'S RESPONSE
TO THE CRIES OF THE ABUSED

How is God moving on the topic of domestic abuse? My observation of God's hand is very noticeable as I stand amazed at God's calling, preparation, and continual blessing on Hagar's Sisters—a Christian Survivor Support group. Hagar's Sisters exists as a result of God's perfect plan in action. Time after time, when I shared my own story with another woman, astounding parallels in our situations were revealed, confirming God's perfect wisdom and timing had brought us together.

Joan: I met a couple at a family event at our church and by the end of the day I knew that I had found a new friend. This couple was new to the church and to the area so I invited Joan to attend Bible study with me. As our friendship grew, Joan and I shared our marital challenges and were astounded that there was such a similarity in our husbands' reactions and responses; we supported and encouraged each other as we struggled to find God's will for our marriages. As my prayers were answered, I saw God leading me toward divorce. Joan still struggled with what God would have her do. One night, I received an emergency message from Joan. When I called her she said that the FBI was at her house and had informed her that her husband had attempted to hire a hit man to kill her!

Two weeks later I filed for divorce and a restraining order. The similarities between our husbands and the ironic timing of both our circumstances having reached a breaking point at the same time resulted in a tight bond between us that no one else could understand. In retrospect we were able to see God's hand in bringing us together as friends. God was at work.

Jodi: Following on the heels of Joan's and my common events, I attended a new Sunday school class. My heart sank as they opened the lesson and I realized that the topic was, "Wives submit to your husbands." I fought back the tears. I watched for an appropriate time to politely exit the class. Before I knew it the teacher asked us to team up with another person at the table to answer questions. There was only one other person at the table with me, thankfully a woman. I made a weak joke about not being the best person to be partnered with for this discussion. She replied that she might not be the best person either. In a moment of vulnerability, I shared with her that I was going through a divorce. Her eyes grew as she admitted the same—but that her situation was not a normal divorce.

We quickly found that we both were in abusive relationships and had restraining orders against our husbands! I told her about my friend Joan, and recommended that we get together. God was beginning to build a group.

Susan: Before Joan, Jodi, and I got together I again attended a women's event. Sitting next to a woman I had met only once before, the speaker asked participants to get together with another person to discuss the presentation topic. Although the topic has long since escaped me, it was appropriate for me to share what was going on in my life, and again we discovered the unfortunate commonality. Susan was in a verbally abusive relationship and, after 18 years, was contemplating divorce.

I could continue at length about how God pulled this group of women together to form Hagar's Sisters. In each case you would see God's hand at work. By the time the group got together for the first time, there were five women from one church who desperately needed Him and each other. Four years later there are over one hundred stories of how God has brought his injured sheep to Hagar's Sisters—a place offering God's love, affirmation, safety and emotional healing.

In light of the ease with which the group was formed, you can imagine my surprise when I learned from Dr. Catherine Clark Kroeger, President of Peace and Safety in the Christian Home (PASCH), that it was rare for Christian women to come together in a group setting to talk about such a deep secret. It was obviously the hand of our almighty God.

As time progressed and the group grew, God continued to bless our efforts even though we had no staff and no funding. Through the volunteer efforts of a team of survivors (mostly single mothers with very little discretionary time) women in need were reached. God opened doors and provided opportunities to reach other Christian women by presenting at conferences. As well, opportunities to reach non-believers came through participation in television tapings such as Radio Bible Class Day of Discovery, Dateline NBC, and local cable television shows. Opportunities for spiritual renewal have also been available through annual retreats at a donated location with guest speakers from across the world who donated their time. In addition, we received our first funding after three and a half years of operating with no budget, along with an offering from Grace Chapel in Lexington, Massachusetts. Additionally, attorneys Graham & Harsip and Hamilton, Brook, Smith and Reynolds volunteered their legal services *pro bono*. God continues to bring Hagar's Sisters resources and to open doors to other Christian organizations working to end abuse in the family context.

WHAT CAN MY CHURCH DO?

If you have chosen to be a part of the solution—congratulations! Expect amazing things as the Holy Spirit empowers your actions, just as He has Hagar's Sisters! You have actually already taken several steps toward becoming a part of the solution without even knowing it. By reading the opening story and two journal entries, you have increased your "heart knowledge." In *A Many Colored Kingdom, a*uthor Elizabeth Conde-Frazier concludes heart knowledge is necessary for learning and working compassionately. By developing heart knowledge, you build your capacity to empathize and understand the issues the survivor faces. One "Sister" commented that the reason the support group was valuable to her was, "Those who understand will say, 'I *believe* you.' Those who do not will say, 'I understand,' but they don't. You can see it in their eyes."

Further development of heart knowledge is necessary and can be gained by listening to or reading survivor stories. As you become more knowledgeable, you will grow in your ability to respond in an appropriate, loving manner. In making the decision to be a part of the solution you have acknowledged the problem of abuse, as well as the opportunity to be proactive in working toward a solution. Your actions in this area will impact positively those currently struggling with abuse. As a forerunner in this newly recognized area of ministry, your actions will also impact positively future generations as you become an example to other Christians, prompting their action as well.

WHAT ARE THE NEXT STEPS?

Abuse is complex. So how do we begin to tackle such a pervasive social issue? It may not be as difficult as you think. Before we get started though, let's take a look at what survivors need.

The first time I was asked to speak on developing a survivor support group, I was stuck. I could not tell anyone how to start a group because God had done all the work. I decided to survey Hagar's Sisters, and through that process gleaned a number of items crucial to each woman's healing. Survivors want to share the journey of pain and healing with people who understand, and although they are in pain, they want to help others who are hurting. Survivors continue to return for meetings because the experience becomes richer as bonds deepen. Meetings provide women with:

- *Validation* of each other based on common experiences, and spiritual validation through the power of God's word;

- *An emotionally safe place to share their experience.* Survivors have been deeply hurt by their abuser, by friends and family, and by people in the church, Survivors can be vulnerable at meetings to freely share their hurts, anger, and issues with each other and with God;

- *No pressure or expectation to share.* An atmosphere of love, not judgment, makes even silence comfortable;

- *A place to learn, challenge and grow.* Women learn the definition of abuse as well as a biblical perspective on abuse. They also learn how to handle practical issues like managing finances and how to negotiate the legal system. They discuss tough situations and challenge each other to honor God in their decisions;

- *Spiritual and emotional support* through topical Bible study and prayer.

DARE TO DREAM

Now is the fun part—dare to dream of what our almighty and loving God, who gives us immeasurably more than we could ever ask or imagine, can do to address domestic violence in the Christian home! What if there were no limits on time, funding, helpers, or facilities? What would the church's response to survivors be—lavish love, compassion, understanding, empathy, assurance of safety, as well as physical, emotional, and spiritual needs being met.

WHAT STEPS CAN THE CHURCH TAKE TO MAKE THIS DREAM A REALITY?

Christian survivors are often torn between their commitment to God and their desire to be free from abuse, so they will frequently approach church leaders with questions about the spiritual implications of experiencing domestic violence. Church leaders must be prepared in advance by undertaking in-depth Bible study of topics relevant to domestic abuse, including gender roles, headship, submission, forgiveness, and divorce.

It is important that church policy clearly speaks out against abuse and in support of survivors. The creation of a church response protocol would serve to inform and guide leaders about appropriate, consistent support for those impacted by abuse. The protocol should cover a number of subjects—theological issues; policies and procedures to protect and support survivors and their children; and responses to abusers that ensure accountability and a recovery path. Legal considerations, including restraining orders, custody arrangements, and spousal support also should be addressed.

Education of the survivor reveals to her options for change in her life. She may gain hope through learning her options, and hope can strengthen her motivation to act on her own behalf.

Education in support of the church's response protocol is needed for Pastors and anyone else who might be viewed as a leader in the church—including Sunday school teachers, elders, deacons, Bible study leaders, small group leaders, and childcare workers. Those in leadership positions are perceived by the community and by the congregation to be representatives of the church. Are you willing to risk a survivor and her children being unwittingly placed in danger by one of your representatives?

Educational resources for church leaders, survivors, and abusers are available through Peace and Safety in the Christian Home (www.peace andsafety.com), the RAVE (religion and violence e-learning) Project (www.theraveproject.org), and from Hagar's Sisters.

MEETING THE NEEDS OF SURVIVORS

Survivors experience a myriad of crises brought on by separation from their spouse. Their immediate needs may include one or all of the following: shelter, food, medical care, child care, Christian counseling from those who understand abuse, emergency financial assistance, legal assistance, assistance from a community-based victim advocate, and literature designed specifically for the survivor. On a longer-term basis, survivors who separate from their spouse may need assistance with the children, help with household projects, and fellowship with Christian families who can offer strong male role models for their children.

Survivor support groups can direct survivors to resources available in the community. However, emergency financial assistance is often non-existent. As a powerful agent for change, the church can step in and provide emergency financial support for victims, and also fund Christian survivor support groups who can identify and help prioritize need.

If there is no local survivor support group, the church should take the opportunity to build bridges with secular organizations and to direct survivors appropriately. Connecting with secular organizations also will allow your church to show God's love outside your faith community and further its reach as a resource to Christians utilizing secular-based services, such as a shelter.

Due to the extreme nature of domestic violence crises, many times survivors become the sole focus of our attention, to the exclusion of the abuser. Although the success rate for abuser intervention programs has been very low, recent research has demonstrated that when abusers are accountable to, and supported by, their faith leader and their church, program completion rates soar—completion being one indicator of a desire to change. Men who have acted abusively can change given the proper education, motivation, resources, and support.

Each of us has the opportunity to become a new creation through Christ—abusers included. Change for an abuser is not a quick or easy process, however. It requires authentic repentance, a willingness to change (thinking and behavior), accountability, and long-term education.

Do not be deceived by the silence of those experiencing abuse. Domestic violence is a problem within the Christian community generally and in your church specifically. It is the dark secret kept by women who sit next to you in church, in your small group, and at the church picnic. God is calling the church to respond. Show the love of Christ to those deeply in need by being ready to act when women in your church disclose abuse exists within their Christian home.

APPENDIX A

Linda: "I am totally alone with you, God, in my despair and black pit. I see no way out except to end my life in this world. This new abuse I cannot bear. It is the worst of all. I have come forward for help and protection from the man who is stalking me. I am totally humiliated. Any human dignity I had is now gone. I am full of shame and despair. All You have put in authority turn away from me. God, why did You save me and give me hope and a new life, a church, and a community of faith, only to have me suffer an abuse that far outweighs any blow from a fist, any terror brought by a drunken man in an abusive rage? To have the church turn its back on me is the deepest and fiercest blow I have ever known. All hope is gone; nothing is left that is true. I want to die now. Please end my agony."

Tami: "I was ashamed of what had I been going on in our marriage and I kept it a secret. When we started to attend (the church), I didn't dare let anyone know that my home life was a wreck and that my husband and I led separate lives even though we sat together in church. I wanted everyone to think we were a healthy couple so that I would be welcomed in the church. Because there was no love or affection at home, and I have no close family, I desperately needed church fellowship, but I was afraid that if you knew of the domination, control, abuse, and oppression that you would reject me, and then where would I turn for the love I needed? (Some days it feels like my worst dream has come true.) I managed to convince you of this false portrayal of our marriage for a few years until the Lord charged in and broke down my protective walls, and said, 'The Truth will set you free. Trust me. Follow me.'"

NOTES FROM THE DIARY OF A SURVIVOR:

You were not there when I asked my husband to work on the marriage and was told I was selfish and unsubmissive, when I expressed my hesitation at going into debt and was told I didn't know how to think and that I should do as I'm told. You were not in the car when he banged on the steering wheel, nearly drove us to our death, shouting obscenities at me, told me he'd give me a knot in my stomach, that he was going to leave me, dropped me off in the driveway and took off.

You were not in my home any of the days when he banged on the furniture, slammed his fist right in front of me, lunged at me with accusations, used foul language, and threatened to walk out. You were not there when I could not take a shower because there was no lock on the bathroom door and I was terrified of what he might do.

You were not there for the sessions of marriage counseling that I begged for, and when my husband dropped out I pleaded with him to continue, regardless of the lack of progress. Nor were you there when he saw two counselors (one time each) and said, "I know this is what I need but I don't want to do it," and, "I don't like the way I treat you but I can't control myself. I don't want to change." You were not there the nights when I lay awake, not feeling safe in my own home.

You were not there when I was doubled up in pain from the physical manifestations of anxiety and fear. My counselor was there and remembers the weeks of violence and rejection—the excruciating misery of my marriage being torn apart—when I called her desperately in tears in between our weekly appointments. You did not see me when my health failed—and my counselor quickly arranged medical care for me.

When my husband retreated from me and from the family, I knew our marriage had ended. You did not walk with me week after week as I clung to the Lord for healing, when I sought out support groups, and read books, and attended retreats where I was washed with the Word and cleansed and released from chains that kept me in bondage—nor did you rejoice with me when He began to strengthen me, set me free, and bring me to wholeness and restoration. I am not going back to a place of bondage. The Lord has freed me and I am moving forward, with the Lord as my husband, my head, my strength, and my provision.

. . . Just the thought that membership would be withheld for any reason other than not being a Christ follower is confirmation of my worst fear of being judged/discriminated against based on my marital status.

. . . By postponing membership I am being told that I am (an) unacceptable part of the body. God accepted me into His family—I am a child of God.

Why is that not good enough for church membership?

15

The Rebuke of Peace

Catherine Clark Kroeger

FREQUENTLY WE OF THE faith community have ignored, denied, silenced, and minimized when it comes to matters of domestic violence; and frequently our lack of attention has made matters worse. All too often we have failed to look honestly at the issues, but the scriptures call us unequivocally to bold confrontation of the uncomfortable realities. We must reexamine both our attitudes and our actions in light of the biblical mandates. The Bible says that a bold rebuke can bring peace,

> Whoever winks the eye causes trouble, but the one who rebukes boldly makes peace. The mouth of the righteous is a fountain of life, but the mouth of the wicked conceals violence. (Prov. 10:10–11, NRSV following Septuagint text)

No one gives a better rebuke than the prophet Ezekiel,

> The Word of the Lord came to me; O mortal, prophesy against the shepherds of Israel. Prophesy and say to them:

> To the shepherds: thus says the Lord God. Ah, you shepherds of Israel, who have been tending yourselves! Is it not the flock that the shepherds ought to tend? You partake of the fat, you clothe yourselves with the wool, and you slaughter the fatlings; but you do not tend the flock. You have not sustained the weak, healed the sick, or bandaged the injured. (Ezek. 34:1–4)

Sadly this is all too true in many contemporary churches—to be quite truthful, it is true of you and me. We know quite well that our churches silence, minimize, ignore, and deny the abuse that is present in one-quarter of the families that fill our pews. We know that we have not sustained the weak, healed the sick, or bandaged the injured. All too often we have gnashed our teeth and wrung our hands in despair. Even those of us involved in helping ministries must confess that we have not called our faith community to accountability.

It was not so in the early days of the church, when people cried "Behold how these Christians love one another." The Emperor Julian the Apostate, a bitter foe of the church, was intent on returning the Roman Empire to paganism. He complained that Christianity was growing because the Christians gave loving care to everyone in ways that the heathen did not.

> Why do we not observe that it is their [the Christians'] benevolence to strangers . . . and the . . . holiness of their lives that have done the most to increase their religion? . . . When . . . the impious Galileans support not only their own poor, but ours as well, all men see that our people lack aid from us.[1]

That was in 363 AD. What a reproach that the situation should be reversed in large segments of the church in 2005! The reproach of Ezekiel declared:

> You have not brought back the strayed, or looked for the lost; but you have driven them with hash rigor, and they have been scattered for want to anyone to tend them; scattered, they have become prey for every wild beast. (34:4–5)

We know full well that the place where God's children should most expect aid and support has been the most cruelly judgmental. Sometimes even the most basic needs—such as a listening ear, transportation, food, financial assistance, help in developing a safety plan, and prayer support—have not been forthcoming. Worse yet, some of us have seen desperate women driven from the very doors of the church. They are lectured, rebuked, shamed, and rejected. They are asked to resign positions of leadership while their abusers continue to play an active part in the life of the church. Some are ordered to return home immediately even if it is to a life-threatening situation. How often we have stood by in shock as we see these victims revictimized by their own faith communities. Churches famed for their generosity in other circumstances withhold help from their own flock if the issue is one of domestic abuse.

---

1. Julian the Apostate, *Letter to Arsarcius.* 69.71 trans. by Wright., *The Works of the Emperor Julian*, 1923.

Many an endangered Christian woman finds it necessary to turn to secular community resources to obtain food for her children, and counseling on how to keep them safe. There they are given information about food stamps and restraining orders and shelters and rebuilding their lives. What we have failed to give the secular community has provided.

Ezekiel 34 continues:

> My sheep stray through all the mountains and over every lofty hill;
> My flock is scattered all over the face of the earth, with none to
> take thought of them and none to seek them. (34:6)

Many a victim is no longer in the church. At the time of their most desperate need, they were most oppressed and rejected. They suffer terrible disillusionment and cynicism. Embittered and disenfranchised, they seek to find their way in a world that shows less hostility than they have found in the church. A disenchanted member of an outstanding evangelical church confided to me that although her church was famed for its practical generosity, she had had to turn to secular sources for guidance just to survive and to provide for her children.

And yet the scriptures tell us,

> He who withholds what is due to the poor affronts his Maker; He
> who shows pity for the needy honors God. (Prov. 14:31–Tanakh)

The church stands in need not only of those who will minister to people in abusive family situations, but it also stands in need of those who will assume a prophetic role, who will call the church to accountability, who will sound the trumpet and call God's people to re-examine their ways. Many have been involved in good deeds, but now there must be words as well. We are reminded of St. Francis' dictate, "Preach the Gospel in every way. If necessary, use words!"

Sometimes help is not forthcoming because there are those who maintain that the prevalence of abuse is greatly exaggerated and a concern for victims quite unnecessary. I am reminded of C.S. Lewis' observation that one of the devil's cleverest tricks is convincing folk that he does not exist. If the problem does not exist, then we do not have to do anything about it. If you are worried about the accuracy of the statistics about domestic violence, just consult Nancy Nason-Clark; or the figures released by hospitals, morgues, and police stations; or the pronouncement of the surgeon general that domestic abuse is the number one public health problem of women. What are we to do with the body count of fifteen hundred women a year in America? "Whoever winks the eye causes trouble, but the one who rebukes boldly makes peace."

Many times we do not move forward because we are so conflicted about the biblical mandates. Is it right to help someone in need, or wrong to assist any disruption of the marital bond? Is it right to send a church member to a shelter for abused women? Sometimes we have even set saving a marriage above saving a life. But if one partner is killed, there is no marriage left. A community shelter is not established to promote divorce, but to provide safety to endangered women and children.

Sometimes we have so cherished the lovely ideal of Christian marriage that we cannot bear to look at the terrible travesty that may be present in an individual circumstance. The Bible does not say that such a marriage is a picture of Christ's love for the church, but rather that Christ's love for the church should be a model in Christian marriage. A husband who abuses his wife cannot possibly be a picture of Christ's love for the church.

Another obstacle is our reticence to intervene when we do not know whether or not to believe a disclosure about abuse in a church family. How can we decide who is telling the truth? It is better to err on the side of keeping a family safe before we try to sort everything out. Diane DeHaan has done signal service in developing a protocol that can the used by churches in such situations. In advance of a disclosure, a responsible plan can be put in place that will be fair, safe, and effective.

Perhaps our biggest challenge is in dealing appropriately with what the Bible says about the husband as head of the wife. If we are committed to the scriptures as our only infallible rule of faith and practice, then we must examine this concept carefully.

All of us realize the "head" in the first instance refers to a body part that sits on top of the rest of our body. It is the most visible member, so that we can have a head count when we want to know how many people are present. This was true as well among the ancient Greeks, and just like us they could use the word to mean the entire person, or even the entire sum of the total parts. Each language uses words in different ways, and a meaning in one language does not necessarily transfer to another. In Hebrew, the word for "head" could mean boss or chief, but this was far less frequent in first century Greek, the language of the New Testament.

Sometimes the word for "head" implied point of beginning or source, and this has been a topic of much scholarly debate.

But the ancients viewed the head as the organ that provided life and promoted growth in the rest of the body. Thus St. Augustine described love as the head that produced all the other Christian virtues. It was the fertile soil from which the rest of the Christian graces sprang up.

In commenting on Galatians 5:22–23, he wrote:

> The Apostle Paul, when he wishes to commend the fruit of the spirit against the works of the flesh, put this at the head: "The fruit of the spirit is love," he said; and then the rest, as springing up from this head, are twined together. These are joy, peace, patience, kindness, goodness, faith, perseverance, self control and chastity.[2]

Perhaps we can illustrate this concept of the head as supplying growth and support from ancient art. At the source or beginning of a river, the head of a god was often placed. Here in the Isthmus of Corinth, we see the head of Achelous the river god, as the stream flows forth from this starting point. Around him are the gods of the pantheon in full figure, but we see only his head because the river itself is his body. Another depiction of Achelous again shows only his head while the other gods are shown in full figure.

Among the ancient Orphics there was a belief that the dead sank beneath the bosom of Persephone, goddess of death. After nine years, they emerged and took on a new bodily form. Here we see a group of funerary offerings that depict the moment of re-entry into the upper world. Note that the tiny new heads are sprouting up from the head of Persephone. They are shown as buds, surrounded by emerging leaves as they push up into the world of the living.

These last figurines predate the New Testament era, but let us pay a visit near Pompeii, to a splendid country villa that was buried by the eruption of Mount Vesuvius in 79 AD. The excavations have only recently been completed. The colors painted on the walls are still vibrant, and in this particular chamber fronting out on a garden, we have a series of fountains portrayed. The frescoes make a lovely vista for the garden, and it was indeed arresting to discover that one of these painted fountains actually

---

2. Translation from *McInerny Let's Read Latin: Introduction to the Language of the Church*, 1995. p. 99

arises from a male head! The head is producing a lovely fountain that gushes forth water.

But more than this, there was an understanding in the ancient world that the head was the organ that produced growth. Like many physicians of his day, Philo, a contemporary of Paul and Jesus, declared that limbs of the body drew life from the forces in the head.[3] This is very close to the description that the Apostle Paul gives us of the function of the head in relationship to the body. In the only two Pauline passages that delineate the action of the head we read,

> From the head the entire body *grows* with the *growth* of
> God as it is supplied by the head and held together by every
> ligament and sinew. (Col. 2:19)

Paul gives very nearly the same concept when he turns to the relationship of head and body in Ephesians chapter 4, certainly a passage to take very seriously when we are considering Ephesians chapter 5. The Apostle wrote:

> Let us grow up in all things unto Him who is Christ, the Head. He
> causes the body to *build itself up* in love as the head *provides empow-*
> *erment* according to the proportion appropriate for each member as
> they are bound and supported by every sinew. (Eph. 4:15–16)

The head does not cause any part of the body to wither or shrivel up. The head does not demean, humiliate, intimidate, or abuse the body. No, the head supports the body and causes it to build itself up in love, to develop all its potential, bound in loving relationship to those around it. Just so Christ the heavenly bridegroom works to present to himself a glorious church, not having spot or wrinkle, matured by his love.

If we are to be faithful to the scriptures, these are the passages to which we must refer when we speak of Christian marriage and the appropriate relationship between husband and wife. How joyful a picture this presents.

But we are not finished with all that Ezekiel has to say. He continues:

> Hear then, O shepherds, the word of the Lord! As I live—declares
> the Lord God: Because My flock has been a spoil—My flock has
> been a prey for all the wild beasts, for want of anyone to tend them,
> since My shepherds have not taken thought of My flock, for the

---

3. Philo, On Rewards and Punishments, 125.

shepherds tended themselves instead of tending the flock—hear indeed, O shepherds, the word of the Lord: Thus said the Lord God: I am going to deal with the shepherds! I will demand a reckoning of them for My flock. (34:7–9)

Yes, it is we who perceive the problem that must demand a reckoning. God calls a lot of unlikely and unwilling people to be prophets. It is the role of a prophet first to perceive evil among God's people, then to bring God's Word to bear upon it, and then to demand appropriate action. We need to stop wringing our hands and start opening our Bibles.

The calling of a prophet is often unpopular, and many of the biblical prophets offered their objections. Jonah tried to escape by going to sea but got on with the task after three days and three nights in the whale's belly. Moses complained that he was a rotten public speaker, and Jeremiah said that he was but a child. As God's Word burned within him, he found that he could no longer refrain from his mission of proclamation.

> His Word was like a raging fire in my heart
> Shut up in my bones; I could not hold it in,
> I was helpless. (Jer. 20:9)

Let's face it—the prophets who are called to bring the message to our contemporary faith communities sit right here in this room.

We are people of the book. Not only do we believe that the Bible is our only infallible rule for faith and practice—we also believe that the scriptures themselves are tremendously powerful in reaching human hearts and consciences. We may not be effective preachers, but the Scriptures are. That is our weapon in the hostility and complacency that we find all too often within our churches. We have the Word of God, what the Apostle Paul called the sword of the spirit. The writer of the Epistle to the Hebrews noted:

> The Word of God is alive, more energizing and incisive than any two-edged sword, penetrating definitively between soul and spirit, joints and marrow, critically examining the lusts and motives of the heart. (Heb. 4:12)

We have a dynamic that we have not even recognized. Confronting people with the power of the Scriptures will make a difference. We must speak with conviction even if we lack eloquence. The power lies in the

Word of God rather than in our own abilities. We can break through the rigidity of legalism with the might of truth.

We do not need to have a theological education to lay hold of a few significant portions of scripture and insist that they be applied in relevant situations. Again and again people say to me "Oh, I never thought of that passage as applying to domestic violence!" Well, the Holy Spirit who inspired the composition of the scriptures in the first place, can open people's eyes.

Again and again the Bible tells us that we need to teach one another. The inspired Word of God becomes effective as we lay its claims and commands upon one another's hearts. We are told to teach and admonish one another (Col. 3:16; cf., Jer. 31:34; Heb. 8:11), to spur one another to love and good works (Heb. 10:24) and to straighten one another out when we wander off the right path. We do this most powerfully by applying relevant scripture.

This is not a matter of mere proof-texting, of putting together isolated bits and pieces. It is voicing our conviction that the whole Bible speaks of righteousness and justice, of concern for the marginalized and oppressed, of calling God's people to account for their sinful conduct. Within that we may apply relevant passages that speak to a particular situation. We may cite particular texts that are indicative of the whole. And we must speak with the knowledge that we have scriptural authority behind us.

To return to our Ezekiel text:

> Thus says the Lord God: Here am I! I am going to take thought for My flock, and I will seek them out. As a shepherd seeks out his flock when some animals in his flock have gotten separated, so I will seek out My flock, I will rescue them from all the places to which they were scattered on a day of cloud and gloom. . . . I will look for the lost, and I will bring back the strayed; I will bandage the injured, and I will sustain the weak. . . . And as for you, My flock, thus said the Lord God: I am going to judge between one animal and another. To the rams and the bucks: Is it not enough to you to graze on choice grazing ground, but you must also trample with your feet what is left from your grazing? And is it not enough for you to drink clear water, but you must also muddy with your feet what is left? And My flock graze on what your feet have trampled and drink what feet have muddied. Assuredly, thus said the Lord God to them: Here am I, I am going to decide between the stout animals and the lean. Because you pushed with flank and

shoulder against the feeble ones and butted them with your horns until you scattered them abroad, I will rescue My flock and they shall no longer be a spoil. I will decide between one animal and another.... (34:11–22)

Yes, we have often been blind to the members of the flock who abuse those weaker than themselves. Some of the ewes and lambs have been pushed away from the healing waters that the church can give. Victims have been butted and battered when they should have been assisted. Although their need demands our response, we haven't gotten our message across.

Over a hundred times, the Bible says that abuse—whether physical, verbal, emotional, or sexual—is wrong, and within our church we must have zero tolerance for such conduct. This must be proclaimed from the pulpit, expounded in Bible studies, and discussed in small groups. Study materials must be made available in both written and audio-visual form. It should be made clear that the scriptures forbid leadership positions to those who mistreat their own families (1 Tim. 3:3; Titus 1:7). It may not win us a popularity prize, but much can be accomplished in the fellowship hour and the parking lot!

While prayer is a mighty weapon, and usually the most effective method, "just praying about it" is not enough. After we have asked God for wisdom, we must voice our concerns to the offender.

Many offenders are confused and frightened by their own behavior. Consistent, caring, Christian guidance can be an invaluable help. If Christian leaders fail to confront the perpetrator, the individual may feel that his or her behavior is really not much of a problem after all.

Many scriptural texts call us to intervene rather than to ignore wrongdoing (Gal. 6:1; Matt. 18:15; 1 Thess. 5:11–14; Jas. 5:20). This is not a pleasant task and may draw some very unpleasant consequences—but then the role of prophet has always carried with it an element of risk. The confrontation must be made with love and with the promise of support as the offender seeks to change his ways.

The most effective way of treating the abuser appears to be in a group situation rather than in an individual arrangement. Programs usually run from forty to fifty-two weeks, with two hour sessions once a week. Couples counseling is contraindicated and the groups need to be conducted by well-trained individuals.

Not all of the complex problems surrounding domestic violence can be adequately addressed by the church, and there are other resources available in the community that may appropriately be used. Nevertheless the role of the faith community is essential.

Recent research reveals that abusers are more likely to complete a batterer intervention program if the client has been referred by the pastor or spouse. Early involvement brings a significantly better hope of altered behavior. Higher completion rates are found among clients who are still married. In short, the sooner the better.

Much can be gained by prayer support and demonstrations of care for the perpetrator, as well as the victim. The Bible tells us that when one suffers, all of the body of Christ suffers. All of us are frail and sinful human beings who have been both victims and perpetrators, and we can stand with all who embark on a healing journey. Our aim is not condemnation but transformation!

Ed Shei, doctoral candidate at Asbury Theological Seminary, wrote his dissertation about changing Christians' attitudes toward domestic violence, using "No Place for Abuse" as the instrument to effect change. The book was far more effective in challenging the readers to come to the aid of victims and not very good at inspiring them to confront the perpetrators. Shei wrote "Churches are in the belief business, and changing beliefs is critical to changing men's treatment of women." Based on the work of Mary Nomme Russell, he offered three relationship beliefs that need to be transformed in order to stop abuse:

(1) self as central and separate needs to be transformed to self as connected;

(2) self as superior needs to be transformed to self as equal; and,

(3) self as deserving needs to be transformed to self as mutually engaged.

There's an old jingle that says:

> For every evil under the sun
> There's a remedy or there's none.
> If there is one, try and find it
> If there is none, never mind it.

Most Christian approaches have taken the "never mind it" approach to the abuser because there seems to be so little that really can be done to intervene. But there are some faith-based approaches that appear effective. I believe that we could give information about such programs. All too often neither therapists, nor pastors, nor concerned Christians are aware of the potential for healing abusers. We could try to bring clinical know-how, biblical guidance, and moral suasion to those seeking to deal with the root of the problem.

Ezekiel's prophecy calls for transformation, but in the end it promises peace and safety:

> I the Lord will be their God . . . And I will grant them a covenant of friendship. I will banish vicious beasts from their land, and they shall live secure in the wasteland, they shall even sleep in the woodland. (34:24–25)

Yes, our rebuke, like that of Ezekiel, may result in peace and safety. You may say that I have been preaching to the choir. Well, who else is there that will listen? It is the duty of choir members to lift up their voices! Let us get on with the task of calling our faith communities to better patterns of faith and practice.

16

Conclusion

PASCH BEGAN AS A small group of therapists, sociologists, domestic violence experts, clergy, biblical scholars, survivors, and dedicated Christians. Our first conference elicited the remark "I can't believe we're actually having a *Christian* conference on abuse."

Increasingly we have found many of God's people working in their own corners, and here we seek to join our voices. In fact, our collection celebrates the diversity of voices amongst us. We do not profess to have all the answers—just that we are committed to finding them, to building up the churches to take on their God-given responsibility to minister when there is need.

In the Christian community, our strengths and weaknesses are curiously interwoven. On the one hand, there is the zeal to do good—and this is a great strength. Yet, on the other hand, the refusal to acknowledge the presence of abuse in church families detracts from our strength. Sometimes, the church is better at concealment than at transparency. Sometimes we push for hasty reconciliation in problematic relationships. Sometimes we demand instant forgiveness that may only serve to perpetuate the problem.

In our troubled world, Christian people should have the decided advantage of being able to differentiate between right and wrong. Sometimes victims think they are to blame. Sometimes offenders shirk responsibility for the abuse they have inflicted upon another. Sometimes our knowledge of right and wrong causes us to be inappropriately judgmental. But really our mission is to bring healing and hope.

Another strength of the Christian church across the world is the willingness to help those in need. We can respond promptly with food, funds, transportation, clothing, toys, care for the children, and other necessities required by violated women and their families. We can be a supportive presence at the police station or court room, in the hospital or shelter. Sometimes though this strength of reaching out becomes a liability—when we think that the church can handle this task alone.

As Nancy Nason-Clark's research reveals, many pastors try to do it alone. Thus, clergy often fail to refer those who come to them for help to domestic violence experts in the community. Amongst those pastors who are most poorly equipped to respond, referrals are the lowest. Julie Owens' dramatic story reveals the danger of inappropriate advice—offered in isolation—from a religious leader. And Reverend Al Miles discusses the propensity of denominations to look for a "quick fix," especially in cases involving those in church leadership positions. Catherine Clark Kroeger's chapter also highlights the need for the shepherds to safeguard the lives of the sheep—*exactly who is guarding the flock?*

We must always remember the power of our words and our actions. Hagar's Sisters, the support group described by Joyce Holt, attempts to provide what many faith communities have failed to offer. *Just a cup of cold water* offered in the name of Christ gives the message that God cares about the temporal needs of those who suffer. Yet, clearly more than cold water must be provided. Sometimes, therapeutic resources are necessary. As Marjorie Kroeger reveals, those involved in relationships that are impacted by sexual addiction require ongoing professional intervention. Psychologist Dan Schaefer calls the men to accountability—to reform their thinking as well as their behaviour. And these journeys toward change and hope require not only the compassion of the Christian community but the wisdom borne from years of professional training and experience. A stunning example of an integrated response to violence occurs in the story told by Bruce and Karen McAndless-Davis.

But community agencies alone cannot meet the many and varied practical and spiritual needs of those who seek their help. That is why building bridges between communities of faith and local community-based resources should be a top priority. The language of hope, outlined by Barbara Fisher-Townsend, is a central ingredient interweaving what churches have to offer and the best practices of helping professions. Alternatively, the language of regret surfaces in Lanette Ruff's research with evangelical Protestant mothers. Dialogue between the church and helping professions augments the journey toward wholeness in family life. That is why FaithLink, the Calgary organization described by Irene Sevcik and Marlette Reed, believes that religious/spiritual leaders and communities need to be—and can be—engaged with the broader community in addressing issues of family and sexual violence.

Wisdom dictates that we use our resources to rescue the victim from volatile scenes, to provide safety and strategic planning. Our essential task as communities of faith is to remind survivors and offenders alike that God is always there and always cares. The loving fellowship of believers can envelop survivors with support and reassurance and prayer. We are a community of prayer. We are also a worshipping community. In this way, women who suffer can be led into the healing power of worship—challenging false guilt and offering spiritual grace. Martha Thorson provides a gentle rebuke for those believers who suggest forgiveness in the absence of repentance. In her explication of the theology of the cross, Elizabeth Gerhardt asks us to remember that it was Christ's suffering, not human suffering, that brings salvation. In this way, she calls the church to engage in a paradigm shift and in so doing to begin to address the evil of violence in and beyond our midst. Dan Allender also talks about the importance of mercy in facing the evil of abuse. Facing our fallenness means we need to address under what circumstances the raping of Eve and the fury of Adam invades marital relationships.

The church can be a faithful witness to the terror and degradation of violence in the family context. In the web-based resource to assist churches and their leaders in responding to domestic violence, The RAVE Project www.theraveproject.org tells the story of domestic violence using stained glass. In this way, the pain of the past is interwoven with the power of healing and hope.

THE BEGINNING

Like a created work of stained glass, no two families look alike.

The individual pieces of glass reflect diversity—*family members are different from one another.*

The stained glass window represents connection—*the web of relationships we call family bring women, men and children into contact with each other.*

In the beginning, there is peace.

THE CHAOS

When violence strikes within the home, peace and harmony evaporate.
Chaos is created.

The glass is shattered into many pieces.
Life will never be the same again.

THE AFTERMATH

Pain and brokenness abound. There is disconnection and isolation. Shame and secrecy rule. The impact is felt by young and old alike.

REBUILDING

New portraits can be created from broken shards of glass.
    Jagged pieces, rough to the touch, and piercing to the skin, can be:
    reshaped;
    reconfigured;
    reset.

RENEWAL

Beauty can be borne out of brokenness. There is the dawn of a new day.

The white dove, with wings outstretched, represents spiritual strength to overcome even the greatest of challenges.

The language of the spirit brings hope.

NEW BEGINNINGS

Another family portrait of stained glass emerges, sometimes bearing a resemblance to the one before, sometimes not.

The individual pieces of glass reflect diversity.

The stained glass window represents connection.

Celebrate the beauty of new beginnings!